W9-AZL-820

WE SHALL SEE GOD

WE SHALL SEE
GOD

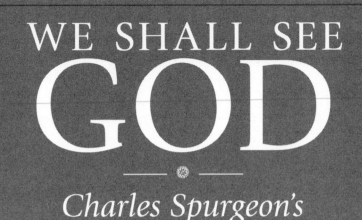

Charles Spurgeon's
classic devotional thoughts on Heaven

RANDY
ALCORN

TYNDALE HOUSE PUBLISHERS, INC.
CAROL STREAM, ILLINOIS

Visit Tyndale's exciting website at www.tyndale.com.

Visit Eternal Perspective Ministries at http://www.epm.org.

TYNDALE and Tyndale's quill logo are registered trademarks of Tyndale House Publishers, Inc.

We Shall See God: Charles Spurgeon's Classic Devotional Thoughts on Heaven

Designed by Jennifer Ghionzoli

Edited by Stephanie Voiland

Library of Congress Cataloging-in-Publication Data

Alcorn, Randy C.
  We shall see God : Charles Spurgeon's classic devotional thoughts on heaven / Randy Alcorn.
    p. cm.
  Includes bibliographical references (p.   ).
  ISBN 978-1-4143-4554-3 (hc)
  1. Heaven—Christianity—Prayers and devotions. I. Spurgeon, C. H. (Charles Haddon), 1834-1892. II. Title.
  BT846.3.S68 2011
  236′.24—dc22   2010054407

Printed in the United States of America

17   16   15   14   13   12   11
7   6   5   4   3   2   1

To my sons-in-law, Dan Franklin and Dan Stump

*What a joy and privilege to have entrusted, ten years ago,
our precious daughters, Karina and Angela, to the lifelong care
of two godly men who seek to honor our Lord Jesus. Nanci and
I couldn't be happier with the fathers of our treasured grandsons,
Jake, Matthew, Tyler, and Jack! As lovers of the deep things of God,
I hope you both will profit from the insights of Charles Spurgeon
I've enjoyed assembling for this book. I look forward to our friendship
and fellowship in the days ahead, and eternal Christ-centered
adventures on God's New Earth. I anticipate that someday we will
sit down together at dinner with King Jesus and Spurgeon and
many others and have some incredible conversations!*

CONTENTS

ACKNOWLEDGMENTS

Thanks to Spurgeon-lover Diane Meyer for long ago helping me compile some of Spurgeon's sermons on Heaven. Thanks to Steve Tucker, Doreen Button, Stephanie Anderson, Nanci Alcorn, and Kathy Norquist for their keen editorial input. Thanks to Bob Schilling for his welcome research assistance and Bonnie Hiestand for help typing and reformatting portions of the book. Thanks to Scott Lindsey and Logos Bible Software for their wonderful complete collection of Spurgeon sermons! Thanks to Ron Beers and Carol Traver and the whole team at Tyndale—what a joy to work with you. And special thanks to Stephanie Voiland at Tyndale House for her thoughtful and outstanding editing of the submitted manuscript.

INTRODUCTION
Who Was Charles Spurgeon?

C harles Haddon Spurgeon was born in Essex, England, on June 19, 1834, and after forty-one years as a preacher in London, died January 31, 1892. Spurgeon's early preaching ministry took place while the American Civil War was being fought "across the pond." He was born a year before Samuel Clemens (Mark Twain) and died a year before Henry Ford completed the first automobile.[1]

Spurgeon came to faith in Christ at age fifteen, when a snowstorm forced him to take shelter in a Methodist chapel where a service was in progress. There his heart was opened to salvation in Christ. The text that moved him was Isaiah 45:22 (NKJV): "Look to Me, and be saved, all you ends of the earth! For I am God, and there is no other."

He preached his first sermon at sixteen and began his work as a full-time pastor at seventeen. Then, starting at age nineteen, he became pastor of London's New Park Street Chapel. By age twenty he was preaching to crowds of up to two thousand. The biblical depth and theological insight of the messages Spurgeon wrote and preached at that age seem almost unbelievable, yet for one and a half centuries, his words have stood the test of time.* Later, upon completion of the much larger Metropolitan Tabernacle, he preached to crowds of six thousand.

No matter where Spurgeon spoke, nearly every seat was filled. When the Metropolitan Tabernacle was being repaired, the church rented the immense Agricultural Hall in another part of London. The hall was filled to capacity each week, with twenty thousand people in attendance to hear him preach. When he spoke at the Crystal Palace, the exact size of the crowd was counted by turnstile: 23,654. And all this was happening at a time when there were no microphones and no public address systems! Imagine the toll it took upon Spurgeon to project his voice so the crowds could hear him, especially later in life when he was frequently very ill.

Four times a year he asked his church members to stay away on a Sunday evening so unbelievers could fill the seats and hear God's Word.

To say Spurgeon's church was ministry minded is an understatement. The Metropolitan Tabernacle stayed open from 7 a.m. to 11 p.m. seven days a week, offering not only spiritual training but also many social programs to assist the needy. Additionally, a thousand church members regularly conducted ministry meetings outside the Tabernacle.

Spurgeon's impact is inseparable from the faithful laborers of his church. Once, when asked for the secret of his success, Spurgeon replied, "My people pray for me."[2]

---

* See his sermon "The Immutability of God," which he preached at age twenty, and you'll see what I mean (http://www.spurgeon.org/sermons/0001.htm).

Though he wasn't college educated, Spurgeon eventually founded, gave direction to, and taught at a two-year pastors' college. His book *Lectures to My Students* reveals that many of his lessons were full of spiritual insights as well as practical ways for students to develop their voices so their congregations could hear them. By 1866 Spurgeon's trainees had begun eighteen new churches in London alone. He modeled hard work for his student-pastors and said to them, "Ours is more than mental work—it is heart work, the labor of our inmost soul."

During his lifetime, Spurgeon founded and maintained sixty-five different institutions, including orphanages, social welfare services, mission groups, and homes for unwed mothers. He also established organizations for distributing literature. He sent people door-to-door to distribute Bibles, Christian books, magazines, and tracts—mostly ones he'd written. His tracts were widely circulated at Oxford and Cambridge, as well as to individual homes. In 1878 alone, ninety-four of these literature distributors made a total of 926,290 home visits. They didn't simply sell books; they talked about spiritual questions and shared the gospel with the people of London.

Charles was twenty-one when he married Susannah Thompson. (She was at first unimpressed when she heard him preach, but she learned and grew under his teaching before they began a courtship.) They had twin sons, Thomas and Charles, who also became preachers. Susannah was a great support to Charles, praying for and encouraging him. After a serious illness she became a semi-invalid and was rarely able to attend church. But she remained active in ministry, collecting funds to supply free resources—her husband's books and those of Puritan writers—for poor pastors. She recorded that she sent books to missionaries around the world, including places such as Ceylon, China,

Jamaica, India, Trinidad, Russia, the Congo, Canada, Argentina, the Cayman Islands, Spain, Damascus, Nigeria, Timbuktu . . . and even my home state, Oregon.

Spurgeon preached to perhaps 10 million people in his lifetime, often speaking ten times a week at various locations, including congregations his own church had planted. He wrote out his sermons fully before preaching but brought into the pulpit only a note card with an outline. As he spoke, stenographers would take down the sermon as it was delivered. Spurgeon then had one day to revise the transcripts before they were sent off for publication. In those times of telegraph, his messages became available across the Atlantic, in America, within two days and around the world within a week. Hundreds of thousands of copies were sold weekly, for a penny each.

Spurgeon's 3,561 sermons are bound in sixty-three volumes. They are contained on thirty-eight thousand pages of small print and total about 20 million words. In addition to his sermons, he wrote many books, including a four-part autobiography; a massive, seven-volume series on Psalms called *The Treasury of David*; books on prayer and other single topics; and the classic devotionals *Morning by Morning* and *Evening by Evening* (best known in their combined form, *Morning and Evening*).

For his book *Commenting and Commentaries*, Spurgeon read three to four thousand volumes of reference works, then chose a mere 1,437 of them to critique for the benefit of pastors and Bible students. (Wondering if he ever slept, I was relieved to discover he had research assistants!)

Spurgeon's book *John Ploughman's Talk* uses homespun, somewhat humorous language about virtues and vices. He addresses practical issues such as hard work and idleness, gossiping, and spending. He also produced a magazine called *The Sword and the Trowel*.

Starting when Spurgeon was twenty-one, his sermons were published in annual volumes. These volumes went to press for sixty-three years, the last of them put into print twenty-six years after his death. In the span of six years alone, from the time Spurgeon was twenty-one until he was twenty-seven, his books sold over 6 million copies. It's possible that even today no author, Christian or otherwise, has as much material in print as Charles Haddon Spurgeon.

His preaching and writing affected his world far and wide while he lived and continue to do so even today. His sermons have been printed in Chinese, Japanese, Russian, Arabic, and many other languages. Today, some 120 years after his death, Spurgeon's works are still read and studied and preached on by Christians of various backgrounds and denominations.

Why Spurgeon's Sermons about Heaven?

I quoted from Spurgeon here and there in my book *Heaven*, but I have since found a wealth of additional material about the subject in his sermons. Spurgeon preached dozens of sermons primarily about Heaven and many others in which Heaven plays a prominent role. Spurgeon never wrote a book on Heaven, but what he said about it could fill several books. Compiling his writings on the topic has been my happy task. When placed side by side, Spurgeon's teachings about Heaven are some of the most poignant, moving, and biblically insightful I have ever read on the subject (and I've read over 150 books about Heaven).

Though there have been a few compilations of his sermons on Heaven, they are not easily accessible for readers. *Twelve Sermons on Heaven*, published in 1899; *C. H. Spurgeon's Sermons on Heaven and Hell*, published in 1962; and *The Father's House: 25 Spurgeon Sermons on the Subject of Heaven* are all out of print, and many of Spurgeon's most powerful words about Heaven don't appear in them.

Even if these sermon compilations were still in print, they wouldn't gain the audience they deserve. Why? First, Spurgeon's sermons are often around seven thousand words, a third the size of a small book. Second, they are difficult to navigate, partly due to extraordinarily long paragraphs and sentences. Third, changes in the English language from Spurgeon's time until now make understanding him a challenge. And fourth, Spurgeon's messages sometimes deal with issues that relate to London in his day and to his own church. He names people, places, and events unfamiliar to the modern reader.

I've found that many people who say "I love Spurgeon" haven't read any of his sermons. Most of his readers are familiar only with *Morning and Evening*, by far his most popular work. Yet most of Spurgeon's richest words can be found in his sermons. This book is my attempt to help readers access wonderful Spurgeon insights into Heaven they might otherwise never know.

Why an Abridged Form?

My desire for this book is to give to readers Spurgeon's words in a form they are likely to read. To do so, I've sought to select the most relevant content out of even obscure passages and pare it down to a more accessible size.*

In the published versions of his sermons, Spurgeon's paragraphs are usually more than three hundred words and sometimes more than six hundred. That means about one paragraph break per page

---

* Readers who wish to can look up the complete sermons in printed volumes or find them online in various places, including the marvelous Spurgeon archive at www.spurgeon.org. (A complete collection of Spurgeon's sermons is available at www.logos.com/epm.)

and sometimes two whole pages without a single paragraph break. That practice, acceptable in the 1800s, is a serious obstacle for today's reader. For this reason I have divided the average Spurgeon paragraph into five. This allows some of his more powerful statements to stand out rather than disappear in a sea of words.

Similarly, I have shortened sentences to clarify them. (I did not, however, shorten one particular 161-word sentence, because I thought it was both beautiful and clear.)

I've sometimes substituted words to more plainly communicate Spurgeon's thoughts to a contemporary audience. These changes amount to less than 3 percent of the overall material. My intent is to restore Spurgeon's meaning for today's reader who might otherwise miss it because of the unfamiliar language.

My original goal was to alter not a single word of Spurgeon's. Yet as a writer of thirty years and of thirty-some books, I learned long ago that others' edits can and nearly always do help my writing considerably. If this is true when my editor, my audience, and I share the same dialect, how much more is it true when the English language has changed so significantly in the past 150 years? With his desire for as many people as possible to hear the truth, Spurgeon would not, I believe, object to having his more antiquated words updated for a new audience. I hope Spurgeon lovers are consoled by my respect for his word choices and my reluctance to change them except when necessary.

What Kinds of Changes Have Been Made?

In cases where Spurgeon's phrases could be confusing for contemporary readers, explanatory information is offered in brackets. For instance, when Spurgeon's text says covenant seal, I have added [circumcision] to clarify the meaning. There are some expressions Spurgeon uses often for which repeated brackets would be distracting—for example, Sabbath, by which he means not Saturday but Sunday, when his three score years and ten has been changed to seventy years, kith and kin is now friends and family, ere is before, calumny is denigration, habiliments is clothing, and methinks is I think.

Some of the punctuation practices of nineteenth century England, such as dashes preceded by commas, are not followed today. In order to prevent readers from being distracted, these marks have been standardized. I've changed Mount Sion to Mount Zion; Elias to Elijah; builded to built; cometh to comes; and thee, thou, and thine to their modern equivalents.

In some cases I have replaced unfamiliar words or phrases with more understandable ones. For example, the cockatrice den is now the serpent's den. Spurgeon said the New Earth will be clothed with verdure; I've changed this to clothed with lushness. Hastening amain becomes hurrying full speed; works of supererogation is now works of moral superiority. The Lord God Omnipotent Reigneth is now the Lord God Almighty reigns. In a strait betwixt becomes torn between the two, conflagration becomes fiery destruction, and chiliasm becomes a thousand years.

Though the word is lowercase in Spurgeon's original, I have taken the liberty of capitalizing Heaven, as I have done in my other books, because it is the proper name of a real place, just as Saturn or Portland or New England. We need this reminder because Heaven has become so vague and ethereal in the modern mind that many don't think of it as a real place at all.

Occasionally I italicize a word or a phrase when it appears to me that Spurgeon would have emphasized it as he spoke.

The typical excerpt in this book is approximately one-seventh the size of the sermon from which it's been taken. The biblical text Spurgeon used for each sermon is included at the beginning of the first excerpt from that sermon. Other excerpts from the same sermon begin with a different biblical passage, chosen to correlate with the content.

Instead of the King James Version (kjv) that Spurgeon used, I cite the English Standard Version (esv) for clarity. The King James Version was an excellent translation for its day, but now, four hundred years later, many of the words are obscure and unfamiliar to modern readers. Plus, important ancient manuscripts have been discovered since then that give us a more precise understanding of what the original inspired biblical manuscripts said.

I have selected from Spurgeon's sermons what I consider the best material related to Heaven. I have omitted paragraphs and sometimes whole pages of surrounding material, but I have sought to be contextually sensitive in this process, and I believe what has been left out does not differ from the meaning of the included material. For the sake of flow, I decided not to include ellipses to indicate missing text.

Trust me when I say I have no illusion that Spurgeon needed my help to be more eloquent! The only advantage I have on him is that I share a common vernacular with the readers of today, and I understand that they might disconnect from a wonderful message if they were to come across words such as habiliments, trysting, calumny, kith and kin, and even speaketh and saith and persevereth. Without these minor edits, methinks many modern readers would not stay with Spurgeon long enough to fall in love with his Christ-exalting passion and his unparalleled insights into Heaven.

Why Spurgeon?

Spurgeon's reputation and influence centered on his unapologetic declaration of Scripture. This made him the subject of continuous conversation by those who loved him and by those who despised him. Sometimes called "the last of the Puritans," Spurgeon preached about God's greatness and sovereign grace and spoke openly about Hell and the need for repentance, making himself unpopular with many newspaper writers who took every opportunity to portray him in the worst light. He reluctantly yet boldly pointed out the doctrinal errors in the Church of England and among his fellow Baptists.

God's words, as Spurgeon well knew, are far more valuable than anything people have to say. God promises that his Word "shall not return to [him] empty, but it shall accomplish that which [he purposes], and shall succeed in the thing for which [he] sent it" (Isaiah 55:11). God does not make that promise about your words or my words or Charles Spurgeon's words, but only his Word. However, Spurgeon took great pains to conform his preaching to God's Word, and he did so in the face of severe criticism. We need to hear Spurgeon's voice because he was faithful to speak God's Word, and today there aren't nearly enough voices like his.

One of the highest compliments was paid to Spurgeon by a public enemy who spoke of Spurgeon's faithfulness in standing up for God's Word: "Here is a man who has not moved an inch forward in all his ministry, and at the close of the nineteenth century is teaching the theology of the first century, and . . . is proclaiming the doctrines of Nazareth and Jerusalem current eighteen hundred years ago." Spurgeon's response was to smile and say, "Those words did please me!"

Why the Additional Content?

The final aspect of this book that requires comment is one that makes me squirm a little. Originally I handed in to the publisher a book that was, aside from this introduction, 100 percent Spurgeon. My publisher asked me to supplement Spurgeon's meditations with some of my own thoughts about Heaven, a number of them drawn from my multiple books on the subject. I resisted this, primarily because I thought it presumptuous to coauthor a book with a man who not only towers over me but could not be reached for permission!

But in the end I was won over by the thought that readers familiar with my writing may be introduced to Spurgeon for the first time, and perhaps I could offer those who already love Spurgeon some additional insights they might appreciate. (I also think he would like the fact that 100 percent of the royalties from my books, including this one, go to further Christ-centered, Kingdom causes; hence, I am not making money off Spurgeon's efforts.)

In each of my portions, I refer back to something Spurgeon has said in his sermon. Sometimes I integrate stories from Spurgeon's life that help give context and personal meaning to his words. I also quote other authors whose books Spurgeon read and loved, including Augustine, Martin Luther, John Calvin, Richard Baxter, and Jonathan Edwards.

To say that I am the junior contributor in any venture involving Spurgeon is a vast understatement. Nevertheless, I trust that Spurgeon would approve of this work and would welcome giving more people the opportunity to read and understand his uncommonly insightful words.

Whether you know Spurgeon's works or not, you are in for a treat. Learn about Heaven at the feet of one who was called the prince of preachers and whose knowledge of God was equaled only by his passion for God.

Randy Alcorn

DYING IS BUT GOING HOME

Excerpted from "Why They Leave Us"
Sermon #1892

Suggested by the death of Charles Stanford, D.D.,
minister of Denmark Place Chapel, Camberwell
Delivered on Lord's Day morning, March 21, 1886,
at the Metropolitan Tabernacle, Newington

Charles Spurgeon delivered this sermon just three days after the death
of his friend and fellow pastor Charles Stanford. In it, he encourages
his congregation to view death as a home-going, as the gateway to full
union with Christ.

*Father, I desire that they also, whom you have given me, may
be with me where I am, to see my glory that you have given
me because you loved me before the foundation of the world.*

JOHN 17:24

SPURGEON Breathe the home air. Jesus tells us that the
air of his home is *love*: "You loved me before the foundation of
the world."

Brothers and sisters, can you follow me in a great flight? Can
you stretch broader wings than the condor ever knew and fly
back into the unbeginning eternity? There was a day before all

days when there was no day but the Ancient of Days. There was a time before all time when God only was, the uncreated, the only existent One. The Divine Three—Father, Son, and Spirit—lived in blessed camaraderie with each other, delighting in each other.

Oh, the intensity of the divine love of the Father to the Son! There was no world, no sun, no moon, no stars, no universe, but God alone. And the whole of God's omnipotence flowed forth in a stream of love to the Son, while the Son's whole being remained eternally one with the Father by a mysterious essential union.

How did all this which we now see and hear happen? Why this creation? this fall of Adam? this redemption? this church? this Heaven? How did it all come about? It didn't need to have been. But the Father's love made him resolve to show forth the glory of his Son. The mysterious story which has been gradually unfolded before us has only this one design—the Father would make known his love to the Son and make the Son's glories to appear before the eyes of those whom the Father gave him.

This Fall and this redemption, and the story as a whole, so far as the divine purpose is concerned, are the fruit of the Father's love to the Son and his delight in glorifying the Son.

That [the Son] might be glorified forever, [the Father] permitted that he should take on a human body and should suffer, bleed, and die. Why? So that there might come out of him, as a harvest comes from a dying and buried grain of wheat, all the countless hosts of elect souls, ordained forever to a joy exceeding bounds. These are the bride of the Lamb, the body of Christ, the fullness of him who fills all in all. Their destiny is so high that no language can fully describe it. God only knows the love of God and all that it has prepared for those who are the objects of it.

Beloved, I am lost in the subject now. I breathe that heavenly air. Love surrounds all and conquers grief. I will not cause the temperature to fall by uttering any other words but this—hold your friends lovingly but be ready to yield them to Jesus. Don't hold them back from the One to whom they belong.

When they are sick, fast and pray. But when they are departed, do much as David did, who washed his face and ate and drank. You will go to them; they cannot return to you. Comfort yourselves with the double thought of their joy in Christ and Christ's joy in them. Add the triple thought of the Father's joy in Christ and in them.

Let us watch the Master's call. Let us not dread the question—who next, and who next? Let none of us start back as though we hoped to linger longer than others. Let us even desire to see our names in the celestial roll call. Let us be willing to be dealt with just as our Lord pleases.

Let no doubt intervene; let no gloom encompass us. Dying is but going home. Indeed, there is no dying for the saints. Charles Stanford is gone! Thus was his death told to me: "He drew up his feet and smiled." Likewise you and I will depart. He had borne his testimony in the light, even when blind. He had cheered us all, though he was the greatest sufferer of us all. And now the film has gone from the eyes, the anguish is gone from the heart, and he is with Jesus. He smiled. What a sight was that which caused that smile!

I have seen many faces of dear departed ones lit up with splendor. Of many I could feel sure that they had seen a vision of angels. Traces of a reflected glory hung about their countenances.

Oh, brothers and sisters, we shall soon know more of Heaven than all the Christian scholars can tell us! Let us go home now to our own dwellings, but let us pledge ourselves that we will meet again. We will meet with Jesus, where he is, where we shall behold his glory.

———— ✺ ————

ALCORN ☞ Charles Spurgeon, always God centered rather than man centered, starts this message on Heaven with an emphasis on the triune God, whose eternal fellowship among Father, Son, and Spirit is the basis for all our relational capacities and longings and joy.

Spurgeon, speaking this message at age fifty-one, passionately anticipated Heaven. He speaks with a warm fondness for his colleague Charles Stanford, who lived and preached in south London, not far from Spurgeon. Stanford had been blinded by glaucoma five years before his death, but he continued to write with the aid of a typewriter until his life ended, just before Spurgeon's message.

Notice Spurgeon's confidence that Heaven is the place of great union with Christ and reunion with redeemed loved ones. As a caring pastor, Spurgeon desires his people to understand that embracing the gospel should change their view of death. He says, "Let no doubt intervene; let no gloom encompass us. Dying is but going home." Only six years later, at age fifty-seven, Spurgeon himself would go home to Jesus, joining his friend Charles Stanford.

Jesus came to deliver us from the fear of death, "so that by his death he might break the power of him who holds the power of death—that is, the devil—and free those who all their lives were held in slavery by their fear of death" (Hebrews 2:14-15, NIV). In light of the coming resurrection of the dead, the apostle Paul asks, "Where, O death, is your victory? Where, O death, is your sting?" (1 Corinthians 15:55, NIV).

We should not romanticize death. But those who know Jesus should realize that death is the gateway to never-ending joy.

Grasping what the Bible teaches about Heaven shifts our center of gravity and radically alters our perspective on life. This is why we should always seek to keep Heaven in our line of sight.

In 1952, Florence Chadwick stepped off Catalina Island, California, into the waters of the Pacific Ocean, determined to swim to the mainland. An experienced swimmer, she had already made history as the first woman to swim the English Channel both ways.

The weather that day was foggy and chilly; Florence could hardly see the boats accompanying her. Still, she swam steadily for fifteen hours. When she begged to be taken out of the water, her mother, in a boat alongside her, told her that she was close and that she could make it. But Florence, physically and emotionally exhausted, stopped swimming and was pulled into the boat. It wasn't until she was on board that she discovered the shore was less than half a mile away. At a news conference the next day, she said, "All I could see was the fog. . . . I think if I could have seen the shore, I would have made it."[3]

When you face discouragement, difficulty, or fatigue, or when you feel surrounded by the fog of uncertain circumstances, are you thinking, *If only I could see the shore, I could make it?*

Set your sights on Jesus Christ, the Rock of salvation. He is the One who has promised to prepare a place for those who put their hope in him, a place where they will live with him forever. If we can learn to fix our eyes on Jesus, to see through the fog and picture our eternal home in our mind's eye, it will comfort and energize us, giving us a clear look at the finish line.

When the apostle Paul faced hardship, beatings, and imprisonment, he said, "One thing I do: Forgetting what is behind and straining toward what is ahead, I press on toward the goal to win the prize for which God has called me heavenward in Christ

Jesus" (Philippians 3:13-14, NIV). What gave Paul the strength and perspective to "press on toward the goal"? A clear view of Heaven.

Ask your Savior for his grace and empowerment, and keep your eyes on the shore. By his sustaining grace, you'll make it.

IN THE FATHER'S HOUSE

✳

Excerpted from "Why They Leave Us"
Sermon #1892, March 21, 1886

Spurgeon continues the sermon he delivered on the heels of the death of two of his friends and fellow pastors. Note the tangible terms he uses to describe Heaven as his Father's home.

> *Let not your hearts be troubled. Believe in God; believe also in me. In my Father's house are many rooms. If it were not so, would I have told you that I go to prepare a place for you? And if I go and prepare a place for you, I will come again and will take you to myself, that where I am you may be also. And you know the way to where I am going.* JOHN 14:1-4

✳

SPURGEON ☜ Where was Jesus when he uttered the words of our text? If I follow the language I might conclude that our Lord was already in Heaven. He says, "Father, I desire that they also, whom you have given me, may be with me where I am, to see my glory" (John 17:24).

Does he not mean that they should be in Heaven with him? Of course he does. Yet he was not in Heaven. He was still in the midst of his apostles in the body upon Earth, and he had yet Gethsemane and Golgotha facing him before he could enter his glory. He had prayed himself into such an exaltation of feeling that his prayer was in Heaven, and he himself was there in spirit.

What a hint this gives to us! How readily may we quit the field of battle and the place of agony, and rise into such fellowship with God that we may think and speak and act as if we were already in possession of our eternal joy! By the passion of prayer and the confidence of faith we may be caught up into Paradise.

I have taken this text because it has taken hold on me. Our beloved brother Charles Stanford has just been taken from us. I seem to be standing as one of a company of disciples, and my brethren are melting away. My brothers, my comrades, my delights are leaving me for the better land.

We have enjoyed holy and happy fellowship in days of peace, and we have stood shoulder to shoulder in the battle of the Lord. But we are melting away. Before we look round, another will have departed. We see them for a moment, and they vanish from our gaze. It is true they do not rise into the air like the Divine Master from the Mount of Olives, yet do they rise, I am persuaded of that. Only the poor body descends, and that descent is for a very little while. They rise to be forever with the Lord.

The grief is to us who are left behind. What a gap is left where Hugh Stowell Brown* stood! Who is to fill it? What a gap is left where Charles Stanford stood! Who is to fill it? Who among us will go next?

We stand like men amazed. Why this constant thinning of our ranks while the warfare is so stern? Why this removal of the very best when we so much need the noblest examples?

I am bowed down and could best express myself in a flood of

---

* Hugh Stowell Brown was a well-known preacher and social reformer in Liverpool. He died in February 1886, about a month before Spurgeon preached this sermon.

tears as I survey the line of graves so newly dug. The Master is gathering the ripest of his fruit, and well does he deserve them. His own dear hand is putting his apples of gold into his baskets of silver, and as we see that it is the Lord, we are bewildered no longer.

His word, as it comes before us in the text, calms and quiets our spirits. It dries our tears and calls us to rejoicing as we hear our heavenly Bridegroom praying, "Father, I desire that they also, whom you have given me, may be with me where I am, to see my glory." We understand why the dearest and best are going. We see in whose hand is held the magnet which attracts them to the skies. One by one they must depart from this lowland country to dwell above, in the palace of the King, for Jesus is drawing them to himself.

Our dear babes go home because "he will gather the lambs in his arms; he will carry them in his bosom" (Isaiah 40:11). And our ripe saints go home because the Beloved comes into his garden to gather lilies. These words of our Lord Jesus explain the continual home-going. They are the answer to the riddle which we call death.

The first thought about the continual gathering to the house above will be the home word, the rallying word: *Father.* If there is to be a family gathering and reunion, where should it be but in the father's house? Who is at the head of the table but the father? All the interests of the children unite in the parent, and he feels for them all.

What can be more right than that children should go home to their father? From him they came; to him they owe their life. Should they not always tend toward him, and should not this be the goal of their being, that they should at last dwell in his presence?

Because Jesus comes from the Father and leads us back to the

Father, therefore there is a Heaven for us. Whenever we think of Heaven, let us chiefly think of the Father. For in our Father's house are many mansions, and it is to the Father that our Lord has gone that he may prepare a place for us.

ALCORN  Spurgeon thinks of Heaven as a tangible place where our Savior desires to be with us. He names another friend among many who had recently died: Hugh Stowell Brown. Spurgeon speaks of real people living in that real place called Heaven.

He refers to the present Heaven, where the spirits of God's people go upon dying, and to the future Heaven, where our bodies will be raised in eternal reunion with our spirits, so we will be whole and perfect people, united in giving God praise. Spurgeon says, "Only the poor body descends, and that descent is for a very little while. They rise to be forever with the Lord."

Many people can't resist spiritualizing what the Bible teaches about Heaven. Some people assume that Heaven is not so much an actual place as a state of being or a spiritual condition. But that's not what Jesus said about it. He spoke of a house with many rooms in which he would prepare a place for us (John 14:2). Jesus told the disciples, "I will come back and take you to be with me that you also may be where I am" (John 14:3, NIV). He used tangible, earthly, spatial terms to describe Heaven. The phrase "come back and take you" indicates movement and a physical destination.

If we reduce Heaven to something less than or other than a place, we strip Christ's words of their meaning.

The Bible promises us that one day, after the Resurrection,

Heaven will be centered on the New Earth—the place where God's people will live forever. What are the implications of living forever on a transformed Earth? It means that we don't need to look up at the clouds to imagine Heaven; we simply need to look around us and imagine what all we see would be like without sin and death and suffering and corruption.

When I anticipate my first glimpse of Heaven, I remember the first time I went snorkeling. I saw countless fish of every shape, size, and color. And just when I thought I'd seen the most beautiful fish, along came another that was even more striking. Etched in my memory is a certain sound—the sound of a gasp going through my rubber snorkel as my eyes were opened to that breathtaking underwater world.

I imagine our first glimpse of Heaven will cause us to similarly gasp in amazement and delight. That first gasp will likely be followed by many more as we continually encounter new sights in that endlessly wonderful place.

Imagine Earth—all of it—in its original condition. The happy dog with the wagging tail, not the snarling beast, beaten and starved. The flowers unwilted, the grass undying, the blue sky unpolluted. People smiling and joyful, not angry, depressed, and empty. If you're not in a particularly beautiful place, close your eyes and envision the most breathtaking place you've ever been, complete with swaying palm trees, sparkling rivers, jagged mountains, crystal waterfalls, or powdery snowdrifts. Spurgeon—on days when he was accosted by the back alleys, crime, disease, and stench in parts of London—might have imagined the British coast he enjoyed visiting.

Think of friends or family members who loved Jesus and are with him now. Picture them with you, walking together in this place. All of you have powerful bodies, stronger than those of an Olympic decathlete. You are laughing, playing, talking, and reminiscing. Now you see someone coming toward you. It's Jesus, with a big smile on his face. You fall to your knees in worship. He pulls you up and embraces you.

At last, you're with the person you were made for, in the place you were made for. Everywhere you go, there will be new people to meet, including Charles Spurgeon and his friends Charles Stanford and Hugh Stowell Brown. There will be new places to enjoy, new things to discover. What's that you smell? A feast? A party's ahead. And you're invited.

GROANING FOR PERFECTION

Excerpted from "Creation's Groans and the Saints' Sighs"
Sermon #788

Delivered on Lord's Day morning,
January 5, 1868, at the Metropolitan Tabernacle, Newington

There is no getting around it: groaning will always be part of our story here on this fallen Earth. But Spurgeon encourages us to wait and hope for the day when God will make all creation new, the day Heaven will literally come to Earth.

> *We know that the whole creation has been groaning together*
> *in the pains of childbirth until now. And not only the creation,*
> *but we ourselves, who have the firstfruits of the Spirit,*
> *groan inwardly as we wait eagerly for adoption as sons, the*
> *redemption of our bodies.* ROMANS 8:22-23

SPURGEON ☞ I wish you to observe that we are linked with the creation. Adam in this world was in perfect liberty. Nothing confined him. Paradise was exactly fitted to be his home. There were no wild beasts to devour him, no rough winds to cause him injury, no blighting heats to bring him harm. But in this present world, everything is against us.

Ungodly men prosper well enough in this world. They root

themselves and spread themselves like green bay trees: this world is their native soil; but the Christian needs the greenhouse of grace to keep himself alive at all. Out in the world he is like some strange foreign bird, native of a warm and sultry climate, that being let loose here under our wintry skies is ready to perish.

God will one day change our bodies and make them fit for our souls, and then he will change this world itself. It is no speculation to say that we look for new heavens and a New Earth where righteousness dwells, and that there will come a time when "the lion shall eat straw like the ox" and "the leopard shall lie down with the young goat" (Isaiah 11:6-7).

We expect to see this world that is now so full of sin to be turned into a paradise, a garden of God. We believe that the Tabernacle of God will be among men, that he will dwell among them and they shall see his face, and his name shall be on their foreheads. We expect to see the New Jerusalem descend out of Heaven from God.

In this very place, where sin has triumphed, we expect that grace will much more abound.

If such be the bright hope that cheers us, we may well groan for its realization, crying out,

> *"O long-expected day, begin;*
> *Dawn on these realms of woe and sin."**

Brothers and sisters, we are like warriors fighting for the victory; we don't as yet share in the shout of triumph. Even up in Heaven [the saints] have not yet received their full reward.

When a Roman general came home from the wars, he entered Rome secretly and slept at night and tarried by day, perhaps for

---

* From the hymn "Lord of the Sabbath, Hear Us Pray," by Philip Doddridge, 1737.

a week or two, among his friends. He went through the streets, and people whispered, "That is the general, the valiant one," but he was not publicly acknowledged. But, on a certain set day, the gates were thrown wide open, and the general, victorious from the wars in Africa or Asia, with his snow-white horses bearing the trophies of his many battles, rode through the streets, which were strewn with roses, while the music sounded, and the multitudes, with glad acclaim, accompanied him to the Capitol. That was his triumphant entry.

Those in Heaven are blessed, but they have not had their public entrance. They are waiting till their Lord shall descend from Heaven with a shout, with the trump of the archangel and the voice of God. Then their bodies shall rise; then the world shall be judged; then the righteous shall be divided from the wicked. And then, the Prince at their head, the whole of the blood-washed host, wearing their white robes, and bearing their palms of victory, shall march up to their crowns and to their thrones to reign forever and ever!

For this fulfillment the believing heart is panting, groaning, and sighing.

A Christian's experience is like a rainbow, made up of drops of the griefs of Earth and beams of the happiness of Heaven. It is a checkered scene, a garment of many colors. He is sometimes in the light and sometimes in the dark.

The text says, "We groan." It is not the hypocrite's groan, when he goes mourning everywhere, wanting to make people believe that he is a saint because he is wretched. We groan *within ourselves*. Our sighs are sacred things; these griefs and sighs are too hallowed for us to tell abroad in the streets. We keep our longings to our Lord, and to our Lord alone.

It appears from the text that this groaning is universal among the saints: there are no exceptions. To a greater or lesser extent we all feel it. He that is most endowed with worldly goods and he who has the fewest, he that is blessed in health and he who is racked with sickness—we all have, in our measure, an earnest, inward groaning toward the redemption of our body.

The apostle says we are waiting, by which I understand that we are not to be irritable, like Jonah or Elijah, when they said, "Let me die." Nor are we to sit still and look for the end of the day because we are tired of work. Nor are we to become impatient and wish to escape from our present pains and sufferings till the will of the Lord is done.

We are to groan after perfection, but we are to wait patiently for it, knowing that what the Lord appoints is best. Waiting implies being ready. We are to stand at the door expecting the Beloved to open it and take us away to himself.

I do not know a more beautiful sight to be seen on Earth than a man who has served his Lord many years and who, having grown gray in service, feels that he must soon be called home. He is rejoicing in the firstfruits of the Spirit which he has obtained, but he is panting after the full harvest of the Spirit which is guaranteed to him. It is a pleasant and precious thing to so wait and to so hope.

Oh, before those days fully come, quit the service of the false master who never can reward you except with death! Cast your arms around the Cross of Christ, and give up your heart to God. Then, come what may, "neither death nor life, nor angels nor rulers, nor things present nor things to come, nor powers, nor height nor depth, nor anything else in all creation, will be able to separate us from the love of God in Christ Jesus our Lord" (Romans 8:38-39).

While you shall for a while sigh for more of Heaven, you will soon come to the dwelling places of happiness where sighing and sorrow shall flee away.

———————— ✿ ————————

ALCORN ☞ Spurgeon says of those now in Heaven, "They are waiting till their Lord shall descend from Heaven. . . . Then their bodies shall rise; then the world shall be judged; then . . . [they] shall march up to their crowns and to their thrones to reign forever and ever!" When Scripture speaks about the coming New Earth, much of what it says may *not* apply to the Heaven we go to when we die. For instance, Scripture makes it clear that we will eat and drink in our resurrection bodies on the New Earth (Isaiah 25:6; Matthew 8:11; Luke 22:18, 29-30; Revelation 19:9). But that doesn't mean we will eat and drink in the *present* Heaven— the place where God's people who have departed from Earth now live.

Remember, those now in Heaven do not yet have resurrection bodies. (Theologians debate whether the saints have temporary physical forms there, but certainly our current bodies will remain in the grave until the resurrection of the dead.) Likewise, when we describe the present Heaven, it will not necessarily correspond with what the eternal Heaven—the New Earth—will be like.

Does this sound confusing? I understand. But once you abandon the assumption that Heaven cannot change, it all makes perfect sense. *God* does not change, but God says that Heaven will change. For one thing, he will eventually relocate Heaven to the New Earth (Revelation 21:1-2).

The present Heaven and the future Heaven can both be called Heaven because they are God's dwelling place. Yet they are not synonymous. The present Heaven is in the angelic realm, distinctly separate from Earth. By contrast, the future Heaven will be in the human realm, on Earth, in a resurrected universe. The dwelling place of God will be the dwelling place of humanity:

"I saw a new heaven and a new earth. . . . I saw the holy city, new Jerusalem, coming down out of heaven from God. . . . And I heard a loud voice from the throne saying, 'Behold, the dwelling place of God is with man. He will dwell with them, and they will be his people, and God himself will be with them as their God'" (Revelation 21:1-3).

When the New Jerusalem comes down out of Heaven from God, where will it go? To the New Earth. From that time on, God's dwelling place—Heaven—will be with his redeemed people, on Earth.

God, who is omnipresent, may dwell centrally wherever he wishes. Wherever he chooses to put his throne *is* Heaven. When he puts his Kingdom throne on the New Earth, it will transform the New Earth into Heaven.

Jesus says of anyone who would be his disciple, "My Father will love him, and we will come to him and make our home with him" (John 14:23). This is a picture of God's ultimate plan—not to take us up to live in a realm made for him, but to come down and live with us in the realm he made for us.

When Jesus Christ came to Earth, one of the names given to him was Immanuel, which means "God with us." The Incarnation means that God came down to live with us. And when Jesus ascended to Heaven in his resurrected body, he demonstrated that the Incarnation wasn't temporary. The New Earth will be Heaven incarnate, just as Jesus Christ is God incarnate.

Though utopian idealists are wrong to believe that humans can achieve "Heaven on Earth," the fact is, there *will* be Heaven on Earth. That's God's dream. It's God's plan. And he—not we— will certainly accomplish it.

SEEING WHAT WE'VE ALWAYS LONGED TO SEE

Excerpted from "Creation's Groans and the Saints' Sighs"
Sermon #788, January 5, 1868

We can't yet see things clearly because we can't yet see God clearly. However, in the midst of our squinting and straining, we can anticipate the day we will see him as he truly is—when our joy will be complete.

> *As it is written, "What no eye has seen, nor ear heard, nor the heart of man imagined, what God has prepared for those who love him"—these things God has revealed to us through the Spirit. For the Spirit searches everything, even the depths of God. For who knows a person's thoughts except the spirit of that person, which is in him? So also no one comprehends the thoughts of God except the Spirit of God. Now we have received not the spirit of the world, but the Spirit who is from God, that we might understand the things freely given us by God.* 1 CORINTHIANS 2:9-12

SPURGEON ☞ The whole creation is fair and beautiful even in its present condition. I have no sort of sympathy with those who cannot enjoy the beauties of nature.

Climbing the lofty Alps, wandering through the charming valley, skimming the blue sea, or traversing the lush green forest, we have felt that this world, however desecrated by sin, was evidently built to be a temple of God, and the grandeur and the glory of it plainly declare that "the earth is the Lord's and the fullness thereof" (Psalm 24:1).

The Earth in ruins reveals a magnificence which shows the sign of a royal founder and an extraordinary purpose. Creation glows with a thousand beauties even in its present fallen condition, yet clearly enough it is not as when it came from the Maker's hand—the slime of the serpent is on it all—this is not the world which God pronounced to be "very good."

We hear of tornadoes, of earthquakes, of tempests, of volcanoes, of avalanches, and of the sea which devours its thousands. There is sorrow on the sea, and there is misery on the land, and into the highest palaces as well as the poorest cottages, death, the insatiable, is shooting his arrows while his quiver is still full to bursting with future woes.

It is a sad, sad world. Thorns and thistles it brings forth, not from its soil alone, but from all that comes of it. Earth wears upon her brow, like the mark of Cain, the brand of transgression.

If there were no future to this world as well as to ourselves, we might be glad to escape from it, counting it to be nothing better than a huge penal colony, from which it would be a thousand mercies for both body and soul to be liberated.

At this present time, the groaning and anguish which are general throughout creation are deeply felt among the sons of men. There is a general wail among nations and peoples. You can hear it in the streets of the city. May God in mercy put his hand to the helm of the ship and steer her safely.

The apostle Paul tells us that not only is there a groan from Creation but this is shared in by God's people (Romans 8:22-23).

We were once simply a part of the Creation, subject to the same curse as the rest of the world, "children of wrath, like the rest of mankind" (Ephesians 2:3). But distinguishing grace has made a difference where no difference naturally was. We are now no longer treated as criminals condemned but as children and heirs of God. We have received a divine life by which we are made partakers of the divine nature, having "escaped from the corruption that is in the world because of sinful desire" (2 Peter 1:4).

The Spirit of God has come unto us so that our bodies are the temples of the Holy Spirit (1 Corinthians 6:19). God dwells in us, and we are one with Christ. We have at this present moment in us certain priceless things which distinguish us as believers in Christ from all the rest of God's creatures. "We *have*," says the text (1 Corinthians 2:12), not "we hope and trust sometimes we have," nor "possibly we may have," but "we have, we know we have, we are sure we have."

Believing in Jesus, we speak confidently—we have unspeakable blessings given to us by the Father. True, many things are yet in the future, but even at this present moment, we have obtained an inheritance. Brethren, we have repentance, that gem of the first water [baptism]. We have faith, that priceless, precious jewel. We have hope, which sparkles—a hope most sure and steadfast. We have love, which sweetens all the rest.

We have that work of the Spirit within our souls which always comes before admittance into glory. We are already made new creations in Christ Jesus (2 Corinthians 5:17) by the fully adequate working of the mighty power of God the Holy Spirit.

So, brothers and sisters, when God gives us "faith, hope,

and love . . . these three" (1 Corinthians 13:13), when he gives us "whatever is true, whatever is honorable, whatever is just" (Philippians 4:8), as the work of the Holy Spirit, these are to us the promises of the coming glory. If you have the Spirit of God in your soul, you may rejoice over it as the pledge and token of the fullness of bliss and perfection that "God has prepared for those who love him."

———————— ❊ ————————

ALCORN ☞ In Heaven the barriers between redeemed human beings and God will be gone forever. "The groaning and anguish which are general throughout creation" that Spurgeon speaks of will be replaced by the joy of seeing things clearly for the first time. Why? Because not only will we see God, he will be the lens through which we see everything else—people, ourselves, and the events of this life.

To look into God's eyes will be to see what we've always longed to see: the One who made us for his own good pleasure.

What is the essence of eternal life? "That they know you, the only true God, and Jesus Christ, whom you have sent" (John 17:3, NIV). Our primary joy in Heaven will be seeing and knowing God. All other joy will be derivative, flowing from the fountain of our relationship with God.

Jonathan Edwards, who lived a century before Spurgeon and whose theology Spurgeon shared, describes in one of his sermons the delight we can anticipate in Heaven: "God himself is the great good which [the redeemed] are brought to the possession and enjoyment of by redemption. He is the highest good, and the sum of all that good which Christ purchased. . . . The redeemed will indeed enjoy other things . . . but that which they shall enjoy in the angels, or each other, or in anything else whatsoever, that will yield them delight and happiness, will be what will be seen of God in them."[4]

The psalmist Asaph says, "Whom have I in heaven but you? And earth has nothing I desire besides you" (Psalm 73:25, NIV). This may seem an overstatement—is there *nothing* on Earth this man desires but God? Yes, we desire many other things—but in desiring them, it is really *God* we desire. Augustine called God "the end of our desires." He prayed, "You have made us for yourself, O Lord, and our hearts are restless until they rest in you."[5]

In Heaven we'll at last be freed of self-righteousness and self-deceit. We'll no longer question God's goodness; we'll see it, savor it, enjoy it, and declare it to our companions. Surely we will wonder how we ever could have doubted his goodness. One look at the scarred hands of our Savior will suffice, for then our faith will be sight—we shall see God.

Jonathan Edwards, with Spurgeonesque eloquence, said in a 1733 sermon, "God is the highest good of the reasonable creature, and the enjoyment of him is the only happiness with which our souls can be satisfied. To go to heaven fully to enjoy God, is infinitely better than the most pleasant accommodations here. Fathers and mothers, husbands, wives, children, or the company of earthly friends, are but shadows. But the enjoyment of God is the substance. These are but scattered beams, but God is the sun. These are but streams, but God is the fountain. These are but drops, but God is the ocean."[6]

LONGING FOR OUR RESURRECTION BODIES

Excerpted from "Creation's Groans and the Saints' Sighs" Sermon #788, January 5, 1868

For anyone who has ever felt dragged down by illness or depression or just the general malaise that comes from having an imperfect body, this message offers hope about our resurrection bodies.

> *You, who once were alienated and hostile in mind, doing evil deeds, he has now reconciled in his body of flesh by his death, in order to present you holy and blameless and above reproach before him, if indeed you continue in the faith, stable and steadfast, not shifting from the hope of the gospel that you heard, which has been proclaimed in all creation under heaven, and of which I, Paul, became a minister.* COLOSSIANS 1:21-23

SPURGEON ⟐⟐⟐ Brothers and sisters, as soon as a man believes in Christ, he is no longer under the curse of the law. As to his spirit, sin has no more dominion over him, and the law has no further claims against him. His soul is transformed from death to life, but the body, this poor flesh and blood, does it not remain as before?

Not in one sense, for the members of our body, which were instruments of unrighteousness, become—by sanctification—the instruments of righteousness unto the glory of God, and the body which was once a workshop for Satan becomes a temple for the Holy Spirit, wherein he dwells. But we are all perfectly aware that the grace of God makes no change in the body in other respects. It is just as subject to sickness as before, pain's intensity is felt quite as sharply through the heart of the saint as the sinner, and he who lives near to God is no more likely to enjoy bodily health than he who lives at a distance from him.

The greatest piety cannot preserve a man from growing old, and although in grace he may be "like a cedar . . . full of sap and green" (Psalm 92:12, 14), yet the body will have its gray hairs, and the strong man will be brought to totter. The body is still subject to the evils which Paul mentions when he says of it that it is subject to decay, to dishonor, to weakness, and is still a natural body.

Nor is this a small thing, for the body has a depressing effect upon the soul. A man may be full of faith and joy spiritually, but I will defy him under some forms of disease to feel as he would. The soul is like an eagle, to which the body acts as a chain, which prevents it from soaring.

Moreover, the appetites of the body have a natural attraction to that which is sinful. The natural desires of the human frame are not in themselves sinful, but through the degeneracy of our nature, they very readily lead us into sin, and through the corruption which is in us, even the natural desires of the body become a very great source of temptation.

The body is redeemed with the precious blood of Christ. It is redeemed by a price, but it has not as yet been redeemed by power. It still lingers in the realm of bondage and is not yet brought into the glorious liberty of the children of God. Now this is the cause of our groaning and mourning, for the soul is so married to the body that when it is itself delivered from condemnation, it sighs to think that its poor friend, the body, should still be under the yoke.

Will it ever be set free? Oh my beloved, do not ask the question. This is the Christian's brightest hope. Many believers make a mistake when they long to die and long for Heaven. Those things may be desirable, but they are not the ultimate for the saints. The saints in Heaven are perfectly free from sin and, so far as they are capable of it, are perfectly happy. But a disembodied spirit never can be perfect until it is reunited to its body.

God made man not pure spirit but body and spirit, and the spirit alone will never be content until it sees its physical frame raised to its own condition of holiness and glory.

Think not that our longings here below are not shared in by the saints in Heaven. They do not groan so far as any pain can be, but they long with greater intensity than you and I for the "adoption . . . the redemption of our bodies" (Romans 8:23).

People have said there is no faith in Heaven, and no hope. They know not what they say—in Heaven faith and hope have their fullest swing and their brightest sphere, for glorified saints believe in God's promise and hope for the resurrection of the body.

The apostle Paul tells us that "apart from us they [those who died in faith] should not be made perfect" (Hebrews 11:40)—that is, until our bodies are raised, theirs cannot be raised; until we get our adoption day, neither can they get theirs.

The Spirit says come, and the bride says come—not the bride on Earth only, but the bride in Heaven says the same, bidding the happy day speed on when the trumpet shall sound and the dead shall be raised incorruptible, and we shall be changed.

For it is true, beloved: the bodies that have turned into dust will rise again, the fabric which has been destroyed by the worm shall become a nobler being, and you and I, though the worm devour this body, shall in our flesh behold our God.

> *These eyes shall see him in that day,*
> *The God that died for me;*
> *And all my rising bones shall say,*
> *"Lord, who is like to you?"*

Thus we are sighing that our entire self, in its trinity of spirit, soul, and body, may be set free from the last trace of the Fall. We long to put off corruption, weakness, and dishonor, and to wrap ourselves in incorruption, in immortality, in glory, in the spiritual body which the Lord Jesus Christ will bestow upon all his people.

❊

ALCORN ☞ When Spurgeon speaks about the challenges of disease and physical ailments, he knows what he is talking about. Not only did he suffer from gout, arthritis, and a liver disease, but three years before he preached this message his wife, Susannah, became a semi-invalid at age thirty-three. For the rest of her life she was seldom able to hear her husband preach.

Earlier in his ministry Spurgeon proved himself courageous in the face of disease. All London knew his reputation of visiting the sick during the dreaded cholera epidemic of the 1850s, at a time when that disease was untreatable and its cause was unknown.

Spurgeon also mentions illness as having "a depressing effect upon the soul." He says, "A man may be full of faith and joy spiritually, but I will defy him under some forms of disease to feel as he would." Spurgeon knew about this effect firsthand, as he also suffered from chronic depression. He writes, "Depression comes over me whenever the Lord is preparing a larger blessing for my ministry; the cloud is black before it breaks, and overshadows before it yields its deluge of mercy. Depression has now become to me as a prophet in rough clothing, a John the Baptist, heralding the nearer coming of my Lord's richer benison [blessing]." [7]

Spurgeon asks in this sermon, "Will [the soul] ever be set free? Oh my beloved, do not ask the question. This is the Christian's brightest hope." Being with Christ in Heaven is wonderful, but it is not the Christian's ultimate hope. He says, "The saints in Heaven are perfectly free from sin and, so far as they are capable of it, are perfectly happy. But a disembodied spirit never can be perfect until it is reunited to its body."

Of Americans who believe in a resurrection of the dead, two-thirds believe they will not have bodies after the Resurrection.[8] But this is self-contradictory. A nonphysical resurrection is like a sunless sunrise. There's no such thing. Resurrection by its very definition means that we will have bodies. If we didn't have bodies, we wouldn't be resurrected! R. A. Torrey, an American evangelist and pastor from the early 1900s, writes, "We will not be disembodied spirits in the world to come, but redeemed spirits, in redeemed bodies, in a redeemed universe."[9] If we don't get the resurrection of the body right, we'll get nothing else right concerning our eternal future.

Our bodies don't merely house the real us—they are as much a part of who we are as our spirits. When God sent Jesus to die, it was for our bodies as well as our spirits. He came to redeem not just the breath of life (our spirits) but also the dust of the ground (our bodies). When we die, it isn't that our real selves go to the present Heaven and our fake selves go to the grave. Rather, part of us goes to the grave to await our bodily resurrection and part goes to the present Heaven, where we'll await Christ's return to Earth, our bodily resurrection, the final judgment, and the creation of the new heavens and the New Earth. If we fail to grasp this truth, we will fail to understand the biblical doctrine of Heaven.

Theologian Anthony Hoekema says it well: "Resurrected bodies are not intended just to float in space, or to flit from cloud to cloud. They call for a new earth on which to live and to work, glorifying God. The doctrine of the resurrection of the body, in fact, makes no sense whatever apart from the doctrine of the new earth."[10]

We will never be all God intended for us to be until body and spirit are again joined in resurrection.

The empty tomb is the ultimate proof that Christ's resurrection body was the same body that died on the cross. If resurrection means the creation of a new body, Christ's original body would have remained in the tomb. When Jesus said to his disciples after his resurrection, "It is I myself" (Luke 24:39), he was emphasizing to them that he was the same person—in spirit and body—who had gone to the cross. His disciples saw the marks of his crucifixion, unmistakable evidence that this was the same body.

At age twenty-one, Spurgeon wrote a catechism for the families of his church to serve as "a great safeguard against the increasing errors of the times."[11] He drew heavily from the Westminster catechisms, written two hundred years earlier. In its historic crystallization of orthodox doctrine, the Westminster Larger Catechism (1647) states, "The self-same bodies of the dead which were laid in the grave, being then again united to their souls forever, shall be raised up by the power of Christ." The Westminster Confession says, "All the dead shall be raised up, with the self-same bodies, and none other." "Self-same bodies" affirms the doctrine of continuity through resurrection.

The only bodies we've ever known are weak and diseased remnants of the original bodies God made for humans. But the bodies we'll have on the New Earth, in our resurrection, will be even more glorious than those of Adam and Eve.

Inside your body, even if it is failing, is the blueprint for your resurrection body. You may not be satisfied with your current body or mind—but you'll be thrilled with your resurrection upgrades. With them you'll be better able to serve and glorify God and enjoy the eternity of wonders he has prepared for you.

WILL I BE MYSELF IN HEAVEN?

✦

Excerpted from "Departed Saints Yet Living"
Sermon #1863

Suggested by the decease of the earl of Shaftesbury
Delivered on Lord's Day morning,
October 4, 1885, at the Metropolitan Tabernacle, Newington

Will I be myself in Heaven? Will you be yourself? Will we recognize other people? In this sermon Spurgeon emphasizes the personal nature of Heaven—that we will be more ourselves, not less, in Heaven.

> *That the dead are raised, even Moses showed, in the passage about the bush, where he calls the Lord the God of Abraham and the God of Isaac and the God of Jacob. Now he is not God of the dead, but of the living, for all live to him.* LUKE 20:37-38

———— ✦ ————

SPURGEON ☞ God is not the God of the dead—that cannot be! If Abraham, and Isaac, and Jacob are reduced to a handful of ashes, God cannot be at this moment their God.

We cannot take a dead object to be our God; neither can Jehovah be a God of lifeless clay. God is not the God of rotting flesh and utter destruction. God is not the God of that which has ceased to be. We only have to put the idea into words to make it dissolve before the glance of reason. A living God is the God of living men; and Abraham, Isaac, and Jacob are still alive.

God is not only the God of Abraham's soul but of Abraham as a whole—his body, soul, and spirit. God is the God of Abraham's body. We are sure of that because the covenant seal [circumcision] was set upon the flesh of Abraham. Where the doubt might be, there is the confirming seal, namely, in his mortal body. There was no seal set upon his soul, for the soul had life and could not see death. But it was set upon his body, which would die, to make sure that even it would live.

The Lord intends that the material nature of man and of creation shall be uplifted and that the body shall be raised incorruptible, and therefore he has given seals which touch the outward and material. The water in which the body is washed [baptism] and the bread and wine with which the body is nourished [communion] are tokens that not only spiritual and invisible blessings are coming to us but that our mortal bodies will be redeemed and purified.

The grave cannot hold any portion of those God has chosen: eternal life is the portion of the whole man. God is the God of our entire being—spirit, soul, and body—and all live unto him in their entirety. The whole of the covenant shall be fulfilled to the whole of those with whom that covenant was made.

It is clear that they live *personally*. It is not said, "I am the God of the whole body of the saints in one mass." But "I am the God of Abraham, Isaac, and Jacob." God will make his people to live individually. My mother, my father, my child—each will personally exist.

Abraham is Abraham, Isaac is Isaac, Jacob is Jacob. The three patriarchs were not all melted into one common Abraham, nor Isaac into one imaginary Isaac. Neither was any altered so as to cease to be himself. Abraham, Isaac, and Jacob are all literally living as actual men—and the same men as they used to be. Jacob is Jacob, and not an echo of Abraham; Isaac is Isaac, and not a rehearsal of Jacob. All the saints exist in their personalities, identities, distinctions, and idiosyncrasies.

What is more, the patriarchs are mentioned by their names; and so it is clear they are known: they are not three anonymous bodies but Abraham, Isaac, and Jacob.

Many inquire, "Shall we know our friends in Heaven?" Why should we not? The saints in Heaven are never spoken of in Scripture as moving about anonymously, but their names are spoken of as written in the Book of Life. Why is this?

The apostles knew Moses and Elijah on the Mount though they had never seen them before. I cannot forget old John Ryland's* answer to his wife:

"John," she said, "will you know me in Heaven?"

"Betty," he replied, "I have known you well here, and I shall not be a bigger fool in Heaven than I am now; therefore I shall certainly know you there." That seems to be clear enough.

We read in the New Testament, "Many will come from east and west and recline at table with Abraham, Isaac, and Jacob in the kingdom of heaven" (Matthew 8:11)—not sit down with three unknown individuals in iron masks nor three spirits who make a part of the great pantheistic cosmos nor three spirits who are as exactly alike as pins made in a factory, but Abraham, Isaac, and Jacob.

Within a very short space you and I shall be among the shining ones. Some of us may spend our next Sunday with the angels. Let us rejoice and be glad at the bare thought of it. Some of us are not

---

* John Ryland (1753–1825) was an English pastor, a theologian, and the director of a Baptist seminary at Enfield. He is also the author of various works, including the three-volume *Contemplations on the Beauties of Creation*.

doomed to live here through another winter. We shall pass beyond these autumn fogs into the golden light of the eternal summer before another Christmas Day has come. Oh, the joy which ought to thrill through our souls at the thought of such amazing bliss!

Concerning those that have gone before us, we gather from this whole text that they are not lost. We know where they are. Neither have they lost anything, for they are what they were and more. Abraham has about him still everything that is Abrahamic; he is Abraham still. And Isaac has everything about him that properly belongs to Isaac. And Jacob has all about him that makes him God's Israel.

These good men have lost nothing that really pertained to their individuality, nothing that made them precious in the sight of the Lord. They have gained infinitely. They are Abraham and Isaac and Jacob now at their best, or rather they are waiting till the trumpet of the Resurrection shall sound when their bodies also shall be united to their spirits, and then Abraham, and Isaac, and Jacob will be completely Abraham, and Isaac, and Jacob, world without end.

As Abraham is not lost to Isaac nor to Jacob nor to God nor to himself, so are our beloved ones by no means lost to us. We are by no means deprived of our dear ones by their death. They *are*; they are themselves; and they are ours still.

ALCORN ✐ Charles Dickens lived in London much of the time Charles Spurgeon did, and he wrote *A Christmas Carol* in 1843, when Spurgeon was nine years old. Most likely Spurgeon read it or had it read to him while growing up. In the story, Ebenezer Scrooge is terrified when he sees a phantom.

"Who are you?" Scrooge asks.

"Ask me who I *was*," the ghost replies.

"Who were you then?" says Scrooge.

"In life I was your partner, Jacob Marley."

Contrast Jacob Marley's ghost with Job, who said, "After my skin has been destroyed, yet in my flesh I will see God; I myself will see him with my own eyes—I, and not another" (Job 19:26-27, NIV).

Jesus called people by name in Heaven, including Lazarus in the present Heaven (Luke 16:25) and Abraham, Isaac, and Jacob in the future Heaven (Matthew 8:11). A name denotes a distinct identity. As Spurgeon insists, the fact that people in Heaven can be called by their earthly names demonstrates that they remain the same people—without the bad parts—forever.

Spurgeon says of believers who have died, "They are what they were and more. Abraham has about him still everything that is Abrahamic; he is Abraham still." He rightly points out that Isaac and Jacob haven't been melted into Abraham. Rather, Abraham is with his son Isaac and his grandson Jacob. And so we will forever be with our parents and children and siblings and friends who love Jesus. You will be yourself in Heaven. Not someone who never before existed, but someone who has been transformed into a better person than you've ever been.

Spurgeon says the patriarchs are not "three spirits who make a part of the great pantheistic cosmos." That notion of spiritual anonymity has gained increased traction in our era. In Buddhism, Hinduism, and New Age mysticism, individuality is obliterated or assimilated into nirvana. Biblically, however, even though we may feel lost in God's immensity, we ultimately find our identity when we are found in him. "Whoever loses their life for me will find it" (Matthew 16:25, NIV).

Just as each of us has a unique genetic code and fingerprints here on Earth, we should expect the same in our new bodies. God is the creator of individual identities and personalities. He makes no two snowflakes alike, much less two people. Not even "identical twins" are completely identical. Individuality preceded sin and the Curse. It's God's plan, and he receives greater glory through our differences than he would if we were all alike. I love what Spurgeon says about how our uniqueness will manifest itself in Heaven: "All the saints exist in their personalities, identities, distinctions, and idiosyncrasies." It is not sin that sets us apart from one another but God, our Creator. Yes, even many of our idiosyncrasies are not the result of the Curse but of God's playful creativity!

Heaven's inhabitants don't simply rejoice over nameless multitudes coming to God. They rejoice over each and every person (Luke 15:4-7, 10). That's a powerful affirmation of Heaven's view of each person as an individual, someone whose life is observed and cared for.

When Jesus was resurrected, he didn't become someone else; he remained who he had been before his resurrection: "It is I myself" (Luke 24:39). In John's Gospel, Jesus deals with Mary, Thomas, and Peter in very personal ways, drawing on his previous knowledge of them (John 20–21). When Thomas said, "My Lord and my God!" (John 20:28, NIV), he knew he was speaking to the same Jesus he'd followed. When John said, "It is the Lord!" (John 21:7, NIV), he meant, "It's really him—the Jesus we have known."

"'As the new heavens and the new earth that I make will endure before me,' declares the LORD, 'so will your name and descendants endure'" (Isaiah 66:22, NIV). Our personal histories and identities will continue from one Earth to the next. Jesus said that he would drink the fruit of the vine again, *with* his disciples, *in* his Father's Kingdom (Matthew 26:29).

When the Bible says that the names of God's children are written in the Lamb's Book of Life (Revelation 20:15; 21:27), I believe those are our earthly names. For instance, God calls people in Heaven by their earthly names—Abraham, Isaac, and Jacob. To have the same name written in Heaven that was ours on Earth speaks of the continuity between this life and the next.

In addition to our earthly names, we'll receive new names in Heaven (Isaiah 62:2; 65:15; Revelation 2:17; 3:12). But new names don't invalidate the old ones.

A man wrote to me expressing his fear of losing his identity in Heaven: "Will being like Jesus mean the obliteration of self?" He was afraid that we'd all be alike, that he and his treasured friends would lose the distinguishing traits and eccentricities that make them special. But he needn't worry. We can all be like Jesus in character yet remain very different from one another in personality.

Distinctiveness is God's creation, not merely a fleeting whim. What makes us unique will survive. In fact, much of our uniqueness may be uncovered for the first time in Heaven. We'll be real people with real desires, but holy ones. We'll have real feelings, but feelings redeemed from pride and insecurity and wrong thinking. We'll be ourselves—with all the good and none of the bad. And we will consider it, in just the right sense, a privilege to be who God has made us to be.

THE JOY OF ETERNAL LIFE

✳

Excerpted from "Departed Saints Yet Living"
Sermon #1863, October 4, 1885

When we think about eternal life, does it spark in us feelings of joy or of fear? This sermon speaks to the never-ending happiness that awaits us.

> *These all died in faith, not having received the things promised, but having seen them and greeted them from afar, and having acknowledged that they were strangers and exiles on the earth. For people who speak thus make it clear that they are seeking a homeland. If they had been thinking of that land from which they had gone out, they would have had opportunity to return. But as it is, they desire a better country, that is, a heavenly one. Therefore God is not ashamed to be called their God, for he has prepared for them a city.*
>
> HEBREWS 11:13-16

———— ✳ ————

SPURGEON ☞ Here eternal life is implied: God is not the God of the dead, but of the living (Luke 20:38).

Does the eternal God covenant with creatures that shall live only seventy years, then go out like a candle snuff?

When David said in dying, "He has made with me an everlasting covenant" (2 Samuel 23:5), his comfort lay in his belief that he should live in the everlasting age to enjoy the fruit of that covenant. How could there be an everlasting covenant with a creature who would cease to exist?

In very deed the covenant that God made with Abraham was not altogether, or even mainly, concerning temporary things. It was not the land of Canaan alone of which the Lord spoke to Abraham, but the patriarchs declared plainly that they desired "a better country, that is, a heavenly one" (Hebrews 11:16).

Even when they were in Canaan, they were still looking for a country, and the city promised to them was not Jerusalem, for according to Paul in the eleventh chapter of Hebrews, they still were looking for a "city that has foundations, whose designer and builder is God" (verse 10).

They did not find in their earthly lives the complete fulfillment of the covenant, for they received not the promises but saw them from afar and were persuaded of them. The temporary blessings which God gave to them were not their expected inheritance, but they took hold upon invisible realities and lived in expectation of them. The covenant blessings were of an order and a class that could not be contained within the space of this present mortal life.

Now if the Lord made with them a covenant concerning eternal blessings, these saints must live to enjoy those blessings. God did not promise endless blessings to the creatures of a day.

More especially, beloved, it is to be remembered that for the sake of these eternal things the patriarchs had given up passing or temporary enjoyments. Abraham might have been a quiet prince in his own country living in comfort, but for the sake of the spiritual blessing, he left Chaldea and came to wander in the pastures of Canaan, in the midst of enemies, and to dwell in tents in the midst of discomforts.

[The patriarchs] left friends and family and all the advantages of settled civilized life to be rangers of the desert, exiles from their fatherland. They were the very types and models of those who have no abiding city here. Therefore, for certain, though they died in hope, not having received the promise, we cannot believe that God deceived them. Their God was no mocker of them, and therefore they must live after death.

They had lived in this poor life for something not seen as yet, and if there be no such thing and no future life, they had been duped and deceived into a mistaken self-denial. If there be no life to come, the best philosophy is that which says, "Let us eat and drink, for tomorrow we die" (Isaiah 22:13; 1 Corinthians 15:32).

Do you not see the force of our Savior's reasoning? God, who has led his people to abandon the present for the future, must justify their choice.

Besides, the Lord had staked his honor and his reputation upon these men's lives. "If you want to know how I deal with my servants, go and look at the lives of Abraham and Isaac and Jacob."

Does the Lord intend us to judge his goodness to his servants from the written life of Jacob? Or from the career of any one of his servants? The judgment must include the ages of endless happiness. This present life is but the brief introduction to the volume of our history. It is but the rough border. These rippling streams of life come not to an end but flow into the endless, shoreless ocean of bliss.

Abraham, Isaac, and Jacob have long been enjoying happiness and shall enjoy it throughout eternity. He [God] would not have spoken as he did if the visible were all and there were no future to counterbalance the tribulations of this mortal life. God is not the God of the short lived, who are so speedily dead, but he is the living God of an immortal race, whose present is but a dark passage into a bright future which can never end.

———————— ❈ ————————

ALCORN ☞ Spurgeon's happiness about Heaven—his joyful anticipation about being with God and his followers in that place— stands in stark contrast to most people's view of the afterlife.

Many believe this life is all there is. Their philosophy? "You go around only once, so grab for whatever you can."

If you're a child of God, you do *not* just go around once on Earth. This one earthly life is not all there is. You get another— one far better and without end. You'll inhabit the New Earth! You'll live with the God you cherish and the people you love as an undying person on an undying Earth. Those who go to Hell are the ones who go around only once here.

We use the term *eternal life* without thinking what it means. *Life* is an earthly existence in which we work, rest, play, and relate to one another in ways that include using our creative gifts to enrich culture and then enjoy it. Yet we have redefined *eternal life* to mean an off-Earth existence stripped of the defining properties of what we know life to be. Eternal life means enjoying forever the finest moments of life on Earth the way they were intended. Since in Heaven we'll finally experience life at its best, it would be more accurate to call our present existence the *beforelife* rather than to call what follows the *afterlife*.

After reading my novel *Deadline*, which portrays Heaven as a real and exciting place, a woman wrote me, "I've been a Christian since I was five. I'm married to a youth pastor. When I was seven, a teacher at my Christian school told me that when I got to Heaven I wouldn't know anyone or anything from Earth. I was terrified of dying. I was never told any different by anyone. . . . It's been really hard for me to advance in my Christian walk because of this fear of Heaven and eternal life."

Let those words sink in: "this *fear* of Heaven and eternal life." Referring to her recently transformed perspective, she said, "You don't know the weight that has been lifted off of me. . . . Now I can't wait to get to Heaven."

When an English vicar was asked by a colleague what he expected after death, he replied, "Well, if it comes to that, I suppose I shall enter into eternal bliss, but I really wish you wouldn't bring up such depressing subjects."

I believe there's one central explanation why so many of God's children have such a vague, negative, and uninspired view of Heaven: the work of Satan.

Some of Satan's favorite lies are about Heaven. Revelation 13:6 (NIV) tells us the satanic beast "opened its mouth to blaspheme God, and to slander his name and his dwelling place and those who live in heaven." Our enemy chooses three main targets to slander: God's person, God's people, and God's place—namely, Heaven.

Satan need not convince us that Heaven doesn't exist. He need convince us only that Heaven is a boring, unearthlike place. If we believe that lie, we'll be robbed of our joy and anticipation, we'll set our minds on this life and not the next, and we won't be motivated to share our faith. Why should we share the "Good News" that people can spend eternity in a boring, ghostly place that we are not looking forward to ourselves?

Satan hates the New Heaven and the New Earth as much as a deposed dictator hates the new nation and the new government that replace his. Satan cannot keep Christ from defeating him, but he can persuade us that Christ's victory is only partial, that God will abandon his original plan for mankind and for the Earth.

Because Satan hates us, he's determined to rob us of the joy we'd have if we believed what God tells us about the magnificent world to come.

FALLING ASLEEP

Excerpted from "Fallen Asleep"
Sermon #2659

Intended for reading on Lord's Day,
January 28, 1900 (C. H. Spurgeon Memorial Sabbath)
Delivered by Spurgeon on Lord's Day evening,
January 29, 1882, at the Metropolitan Tabernacle, Newington

When someone we love dies or when we look ahead to our final breath, it feels like death is the crushing blow. But for the believer, death no longer has the final say. For all who are in Christ, death is just the moment before we truly wake up.

> *I delivered to you as of first importance what I also received: that Christ died for our sins in accordance with the Scriptures, that he was buried, that he was raised on the third day in accordance with the Scriptures, and that he appeared to Cephas, then to the twelve. Then he appeared to more than five hundred brothers at one time, most of whom are still alive, though some have fallen asleep.* 1 CORINTHIANS 15:3-6

SPURGEON ☞ Witnesses of Christ's resurrection died as other men did. They had no immunity from death and no extreme old age was granted to them, for the apostle [Paul] said, "Some have fallen asleep" (1 Corinthians 15:6).

From this fact, I gather that earthly lives, which appear to us to be extremely necessary, may not be so regarded by God. The Lord sometimes takes away from us those whom we can least spare. This should teach us—if we are wise enough to learn the lesson—to regard the most invaluable person in our own Israel as being only lent to us by the Lord, for a season, and liable to be summoned to higher service at any moment.

I never expect now to come to this place, on two succeeding Sundays, without hearing that some one or other of our friends has departed. Almost every day this truth is impressed upon me: "Some have fallen asleep."

In the heathen part of the catacombs of Rome, the inscriptions over the place where their dead were buried are full of grief and despair. Indeed, the writers of those inscriptions do not appear to have been able to find words in which they could express their great distress, their agony of heart, at the loss of child or husband or friend. They pile the mournful words together, trying to describe their grief. Sometimes they declare that the light has gone from their sky now that their dear ones are taken from them.

"Alas! Alas!" says the record. "Dear Caius has gone, and with him all joy is quenched forever, for I shall see him no more." Paganism is hopeless to comfort the bereaved. But when you come into that part of the catacombs which was devoted to Christian burial vaults, everything is different. There you may constantly read these consoling words: "He sleeps in peace." There is nothing dreadful or despairing in the inscriptions there; they are submissive, they are cheerful, they are even thankful. Frequently they are victorious, and the most common emblem is not the quenched torch, as it is on the heathen side, where the light is supposed to have gone out forever, but the palm branch, to signify that the victory remains eternally with the departed one. It is the glory of the Christian religion to have let light into the grave, to have taken away the sting from death, and in fact, to have made it *no more death to die.*

The saints in Heaven have a better rest than sleep can give, but sleep is the nearest word we can find to describe the state of the blessed. They have no poverty, no toil, no anguish of spirit, no remorse, no struggling with indwelling sin, no battling with foes without and fears within. "They may rest from their labors, for their deeds follow them!" (Revelation 14:13).

Oh, what a sweet thing to fall asleep—to enjoy perfect calmness and to be beyond the reach of all influences which make life here to be so sorrowful!

Do not regard your departure out of the world as a thing to be surrounded with horror. Do not conjure up hobgoblins, evil spirits, darkness, and terror. "The valley of the shadow of death," of which David spoke, I do not think was ever meant to be applied to dying. For it is a valley that he walks through, and he comes out again at the other side. It is not the valley of death, but only of the shadow of death.

I have walked through that valley many times—right through from one end of it to the other—and yet I have not died. The grim shadow of something worse than death has fallen over my spirit, but God has been with me, as he was with David, and his rod and his staff have comforted me. Many here can say the same.

I believe that, often, those who feel great gloom in going through "the valley of the shadow of death" feel no gloom at all when they come to the valley of death itself. There has generally been brightness there for the most sorrowful spirits. And those who, before coming there, have groveled in the dust, have been empowered to mount as on eagles' wings when they have actually come to the place of their departure into the future state.

———— ❋ ————

ALCORN ☞ The Bible confirms what Spurgeon says—that unbelievers are right to dread death and believers are right to joyfully anticipate where death will bring them. "The dust returns to the ground it came from, and the spirit returns to God who gave it" (Ecclesiastes 12:7, NIV). At death, the human spirit goes either to Heaven or to Hell. There is no third alternative.

Christ depicted Lazarus and the rich man as conscious in Heaven and in Hell, respectively, immediately after they died (Luke 16:22-31). Jesus told the dying thief on the cross, "Today you will be with me in paradise" (Luke 23:43, NIV). The apostle Paul says that to die is to be with Christ (Philippians 1:23) and to be absent from the body is to be present with the Lord (2 Corinthians 5:8).

These passages make clear that there is no "soul sleep," a long period of unconsciousness between life on Earth and life in Heaven. Though Spurgeon uses the phrase "fallen asleep," which is found in 1 Corinthians 15:6 and other passages, sleep is a euphemism for death and describes the body's outward peaceful appearance. The physical part of us "sleeps" until the Resurrection, while the spiritual part of us immediately relocates to a conscious existence in Heaven (Daniel 12:2-3; 2 Corinthians 5:8).

The book of Revelation describes human beings talking and worshiping in Heaven prior to the resurrection of the dead (Revelation 4:10-11; 5:8; 7:9-11). These examples demonstrate that our spiritual beings are conscious, not sleeping, after death. (Nearly everyone who believes in soul sleep argues that souls are disembodied at death. But it's not clear how disembodied beings *could* sleep, because sleeping involves a physical body.)

I've read at memorial services the following depiction of a

believer's death. It captures the sense of tranquility Spurgeon sees
in the biblical view of death as a sort of sleep:

> I'm standing on the seashore. A ship at my side spreads
> her white sails to the morning breeze and starts for the
> blue ocean. She's an object of beauty and strength, and
> I stand and watch her until, at length, she hangs like
> a speck of white cloud just where the sea and the sky
> come down to mingle with each other. And then I hear
> someone at my side saying, "There, she's gone."
>
> Gone where? Gone from my sight, that is all. She is
> just as large in mast and hull and spar as she was when
> she left my side. And just as able to bear her load of living
> freight to the place of destination. Her diminished size is
> in *me*, not in her.
>
> And just at the moment when someone at my side says,
> "There, she's gone," there are other eyes watching her
> coming, and there are other voices ready to take up the
> glad shout, "Here she comes!"
>
> And that is dying.[12]

SEEING OUR LOVED ONES IN THE MORNING

❀

Excerpted from "Fallen Asleep"
Sermon #2659, January 29, 1882

When death comes to take away someone we love, we grieve—and rightly so. But for the believer, that grief is infused with hope. Our loved ones are not truly lost—after all, we know where they are, and we will see them again.

> *Even though I walk through the valley*
> *of the shadow of death,*
> *I will fear no evil,*
> *for you are with me;*
> *your rod and your staff,*
> *they comfort me.*
> *You prepare a table before me*
> *in the presence of my enemies;*
> *you anoint my head with oil;*
> *my cup overflows.*
> *Surely goodness and mercy shall follow me*
> *all the days of my life,*
> *and I shall dwell in the house of the LORD forever.*

PSALM 23:4-6

SPURGEON There is a dear old friend of mine, now in Heaven. When he came to this church one Sunday, I said to him, "Our old friend so-and-so has gone home." The one to whom I spoke was an old man himself, one of our most gracious elders, and he looked at me in a most significant way, and his eyes twinkled as he said, "He could not do better, dear Pastor. He could not do better. And you and I will do the same thing one of these days. We also shall go home!"

Our aged friend has himself gone home since that time, and now I say of him, "He could not have done better." Why, that is where good children always go at night—home.

Oh! Let us not live in this world as if we thought of staying here forever, but let us try to be like a pious Scotch minister who was very ill and, being asked by a friend whether he thought himself dying, answered, "Really, friend, I care not whether I am or not, for if I die, I shall be with God. And if I live, he will be with me."

But as for those who have fallen asleep in Jesus, we need not fret or trouble ourselves about them. When children go upstairs to bed, do their elder brothers and sisters, who sit up later, gather together and cry because the other children have fallen asleep? Ah, no! They feel that they have not lost them, and they expect to meet again in the morning; and so do we!

Therefore, let us not weep and lament to excess concerning the dear ones who have fallen asleep in Christ, for all is well with them. They are at rest; shall we weep about that? They are enjoying their eternal triumph; shall we weep about that? They are as full of bliss as they can possibly be; shall we weep about that? If any of your sons and daughters were taken away from you to be made into kings and queens in a foreign land, you might shed a tear or two at parting, but you would say, "It is for their good; let them go."

And do you begrudge your well-beloved their crown of glory and all the bliss which God has bestowed upon them? If the departed could speak to us, they would say, "Bless God for us. Do not sit down and mourn because we have entered into his glory, but rather rejoice because we are with him where he is."

Therefore, let us comfort one another with these words.

Did you ever notice, concerning Job's children, that when God gave him twice as much substance as he had before, he gave him only the same number of children as he formerly had? The Lord gave him twice as much gold and twice as much of all sorts of property, but he only gave him the exact number of children he had before. Why did he not give the patriarch double the number of children as well as twice the number of cattle? Why, because God regarded his children who had died as being Job's still.

They were dead to Job's eye, but they were visible to Job's faith. God numbered them still as part of Job's family, and if you carefully count up how many children Job had, you will find that he had twice as many in the end as he had in the beginning. In the same way, consider your friends who are asleep in Christ as still yours—not a single one lost.

ALCORN ⟫ Spurgeon performed countless funerals, but he wasn't the sort of pastor who didn't get to know his people until they were dying. In fact, he had a weekly time set aside to meet individually with people who had trusted Christ and wanted to become church members. It appears he came to know by name at least six thousand church members by this one method alone. He heard each of them tell how he or she had come into a relationship with Jesus. So in his sermons, when he speaks of church people who have died, in many cases he knew them well. And he looked forward to a great reunion in which people of the Metropolitan Tabernacle would one day see each other again in the presence of Christ.

Death is painful, and it's an enemy. But for those who know Jesus, death is the *final* pain and the *last* enemy. "[Christ] must reign until he has put all his enemies under his feet. The last enemy to be destroyed is death" (1 Corinthians 15:25-26). We on this dying Earth can relax and rejoice for our loved ones who are in the presence of Christ.

As the apostle Paul tells us, though we naturally grieve at losing loved ones, we are not to "grieve like the rest of mankind, who have no hope" (1 Thessalonians 4:13, NIV). Our parting is not the end of our relationship, only an interruption. We have not lost them, because we know where they are. Don't you love Spurgeon's point about children going upstairs to bed? Of course brothers and sisters don't weep over their sleeping siblings, because "they expect to meet again in the morning; and so do we!"

When they die, those covered by Christ's blood are experiencing the joy of Christ's presence in a place so wonderful that Christ called it Paradise. And one day, we're told, there will be a magnificent reunion. They and we "will be with the Lord forever. Therefore encourage one another with these words" (1 Thessalonians 4:17-18, NIV).

Jonathan Edwards, whose theology of sovereign grace Spurgeon loved, saw no conflict between anticipating our relationships with God and anticipating our relationships with our loved ones in Heaven:

Every Christian friend that goes before us from this world is a ransomed spirit waiting to welcome us in heaven. There will be the infant of days that we have lost below, through grace to be found above. There the Christian father, and mother, and wife, and child, and friend, with whom we shall renew the holy fellowship of the saints, which was interrupted by death here, but shall be commenced again in the upper sanctuary, and then shall never end. There we shall have companionship with the patriarchs and fathers and saints of the Old and New Testaments, and those of whom the world was not worthy. . . . And there, above all, we shall enjoy and dwell with God the Father, whom we have loved with all our hearts on earth; and with Jesus Christ, our beloved Savior, who has always been to us the chief among ten thousands, and altogether lovely; and with the Holy Spirit, our Sanctifier, and Guide, and Comforter; and shall be filled with all the fullness of the Godhead forever![13]

What a world that will be—to live in rich eternal fellowship with the triune God and the great family of his redeemed. I'm overwhelmed just thinking of it. What a great God we'll enjoy and serve forever! What a great time we'll have together there! I look forward to meeting every reader of my books who knows Jesus and being reunited with those I've known here on Earth. I can't wait for the great adventures we'll have with Christ and one another, with Edwards and Spurgeon, with Mary and Joseph, with our ancestors and children who have fallen asleep before us. Deep and joyful human relationships will be among God's greatest gifts in Heaven—relationships that by God's grace will never end.

SEEING THE FACE OF JESUS

✸

Excerpted from "The Heaven of Heaven"
Sermon #824

Delivered on Lord's Day morning,
August 9, 1868, at the Metropolitan Tabernacle, Newington

The most astonishing sight we can anticipate in Heaven is not streets of gold or pearly gates or loved ones who have died before us. It will be coming face-to-face with our Savior.

They will see his face, and his name will be on their foreheads.
REVELATION 22:4

─────── ✸ ───────

SPURGEON ☞ The text says they shall "see his face," by which I understand two things. First, that they shall literally and physically, with their risen bodies, actually look into the face of Jesus. Second, that spiritually their mental faculties shall be enlarged so that they shall be enabled to look into the very heart and soul and character of Christ, so as to understand him, his work, his love, his all in all, as they never understood him before.

They shall literally, I say, see his face, for Christ is no phantom. In Heaven, though divine, he is still a man, and therefore material like ourselves. The very flesh and blood that suffered upon Calvary is in Heaven. The hand that was pierced with the nail now at this moment grasps the scepter of all worlds. That very head which was bowed down with anguish is now crowned with a royal crown. And the face that was so marred is the very face which beams brilliantly amid the thrones of Heaven. Into that selfsame face we shall be permitted to gaze. Oh, what a sight!

We shall see and know even as we are known, and among the great things that we shall know will be this greatest of all, that we shall know Christ. We shall know the heights and depths and lengths and breadths of the love of Christ that *exceeds* knowledge.

In the blessed vision the saints see Jesus, and they see him clearly. We may also remark that they see him always, for when the text says they shall "see his face," it implies that they never at any time are without the sight. Never for a moment do they unlock their arm from the arm of their Beloved. They are not as we are—sometimes near the throne, sometimes far away; sometimes hot with love, sometimes cold with indifference, sometimes bright as angels, sometimes dull as clods. Rather, forever and ever they are in closest association with the Master, for they shall "see his face."

They surely see his face the more clearly because all the clouds of care are gone from them. Some of you while sitting here today have been trying to lift up your minds to heavenly contemplation, but you cannot. The business has gone so wrong this week; the children have annoyed you so much; sickness has been in the house so severely. You feel in your body quite out of order for devotion—these enemies break your peace.

God's people are bothered by none of these things in Heaven, and therefore they can see their Master's face. They are not burdened with Martha's cares; they still occupy Mary's place at his feet (Luke 10:38-42). When you and I have laid aside the farm and the merchandise and the marrying and the burying, which come so fast upon each other's heels, and when we will be forever with the Lord, then

> *Far from a world of grief and sin,*
> *With God eternally shut in.**

Furthermore, the glorified see God's face more clearly because there are no idols to stand between him and them. Our idolatrous love of worldly things is a chief cause of our knowing so little of spiritual things. One cannot fill his life cup from the pools of Earth and yet have room in it for the crystal streams of Heaven. But they have no idols there in Heaven—nothing to occupy the heart, no rival for the Lord Jesus. He reigns supreme within their spirits, and therefore they see his face.

The sight of Christ's face will be, to the *ungodly*, eternal destruction, separation from the presence of the Lord. But if there are some men who shall see his face, who shall sit down and delight themselves in gazing upon the face of the great Judge upon the throne, then those persons are certainly saved.

Here it is our joy of joys to have the Lord smiling upon us, for if he be with us, who can be against us? In Heaven, then, they have this to be their choice privilege. They are attendants who stand always in the monarch's palace, secure in the monarch's smile. They are children who live unbrokenly in their Father's love. They know it and rejoice to know it evermore.

All the saints shall see their Master's face. The thief dying on the cross was with Christ in Paradise. Whether dying young or old, whether departing after long service of Christ or dying immediately after conversion as with the thief, of all the saints shall it be

---

* From the hymn "Ye Waiting Souls, Arise," by Charles Wesley, 1749.

said in the words of the text, they shall "see his face." What more can apostles and martyrs enjoy?

Do you regret that your friends have departed? Do you lament that your wife or husband and child and father and grandparent have all entered into their rest? Don't be so unkind to yourself, so cruel to them. Rather, soldier of the Cross, be thankful that another has won the crown before you. May you press forward to win it too.

Life is but a moment: how short it will appear in eternity. And though impatience considers it a long wait, yet faith corrects her and reminds her that one hour with God will make the longest life to seem but a point of time.

———— ❈ ————

ALCORN ⟿ In the Old Testament we're told that Moses saw God but not God's face: "You cannot see my face," God said, "for no one may see me and live. . . . You will see my back; but my face must not be seen" (Exodus 33:20, 23, NIV).

The New Testament says that God "lives in unapproachable light, whom no one has seen or can see" (1 Timothy 6:16, NIV). To see God's face has been utterly unthinkable.

That's why, when we're told in Revelation 22:4 that we'll see God's face, it should astound us. For this to happen, it will require that we undergo radical change between now and then. "Without holiness no one will see the Lord" (Hebrews 12:14, NIV). It's only because we'll be fully righteous in Christ, deemed completely sinless, that we'll be able to see God and live.

This is the wonder of our redemption, which Spurgeon celebrated and we should also—to be welcomed into the very presence of our Lord and to see him face-to-face! What will we see in his eyes? Though we cannot experience redemption's fullness yet, we can gain a foretaste now: "We have confidence to enter the Most Holy Place by the blood of Jesus" (Hebrews 10:19, NIV). "Let us then with confidence draw near to the throne of grace" (Hebrews 4:16).

These verses tell us something wonderful beyond comprehension: the blood of Jesus has bought us full access to God's throne room and his Most Holy Place. Even now, he welcomes us to come there in prayer. In eternity, when we're resurrected beings, not only will he permit us to enter his presence in prayer, but he will welcome us to *live* in his presence as resurrected beings.

David says, "One thing I ask from the LORD, this only do I seek: that I may dwell in the house of the LORD all the days of my life, to gaze on the beauty of the LORD and to seek him in his temple" (Psalm 27:4, NIV). David was preoccupied with God's person, and also with God's place. He longed to be where God was and to gaze on his beauty. God, who is transcendent, became immanent—manifested among us—in Jesus Christ, who is Immanuel, "God with us" (Matthew 1:23, NIV). So whenever we see Jesus in Heaven, we will see God. Because Jesus Christ is God, and a permanent manifestation of God, he could say to Philip, "Anyone who has seen me has seen the Father" (John 14:9, NIV). Along with Spurgeon, we can anticipate literally looking into Christ's face and exclaiming, "Oh, what a sight!"

Shut your eyes and imagine seeing Jesus. What a wondrous thought! More than that, what a wondrous promise!

GOD DRIES OUR TEARS

Excerpted from "No Tears in Heaven"
Sermon #643

Delivered on Sunday morning,
August 6, 1865, at the Metropolitan Tabernacle, Newington

For anyone who knows what it is to weep over sin or loss or pain, Heaven offers a beautiful promise: one day God himself will wipe the tears from our eyes. And even better, one day he will transform those tears into laughter.

> *The Lamb in the midst of the throne will be their shepherd, and he will guide them to springs of living water, and God will wipe away every tear from their eyes.* REVELATION 7:17

SPURGEON ✎ The night is dark, but the morning comes. Over the hills of darkness, the day breaks forth. True, the grave is still before you, but your Lord has snatched the sting from death and the victory from the grave.

Do not, you burdened brother or sister, limit yourself to the confining miseries of the present hour. Rather, gaze with fondness on the enjoyment of the past, and view with equal love the infinite blessings of eternity past, when you did not exist, but when God chose you for himself and wrote your name in his

Book of Life. Then let your glance flash forward to eternity future to see the mercies which will be yours even here on Earth and the glories which are stored up for you beyond the skies.

I will be greatly rewarded if I can minister comfort to one person whose spirit is heavily burdened by leading that person to remember the glory which is yet to be revealed.

You cannot, dear friends, pass through the wilderness of this world without discovering that thorns and thistles grow abundantly in it. And that, step as you may, your feet must sometimes feel the sudden and unexpected wound. The sea of life is salt to all men. We may forget to laugh, but we will always know how to weep. As the saturated clouds must drip, so must the human race, cursed by the Fall, weep out its frequent griefs.

I see before me a bottle: it is dark and foul, for it contains tears distilled by the force of the fires of sin. Sin is more frequently the mother of sorrow than all the other pains of life put together. Dear brothers and sisters, I am convinced that we endure more sorrow from our sins than from God's darkest providence.

I want you to think with me of fountains of tears which would exist even in Heaven, tears that the glorified saints would inevitably weep if God did not, by a perpetual miracle, take away those tears. It strikes me that if God himself did not interfere by a perpetual outflow of abundant comfort, the glorified would have many good reasons for weeping.

You say, "How is this?" In the first place, if it were not for God's gracious intervention, what tremendous regret they would have for their past sins. The more holy a person is, the more he hates sin. It is a proof of growth in sanctification, not that repentance becomes less acute, but that it becomes more and more deep.

Surely, dear friends, when we are made perfectly holy, we will have a greater hatred of sin. If on Earth we could be perfectly holy, I think we would do nothing else but mourn. To think that so foul and dirty and poisonous a thing as sin had ever stained us! To think that we would have offended such a good and gracious and tender and richly loving God. The very sight of Christ, "the Lamb in the midst of the throne" (Revelation 7:17), would make [the redeemed ones in Heaven] remember the sin from which he purified them. The sight of their heavenly Father's perfection would be blinding to them if it were not that by some sacred means which we know nothing about, God wipes away all these tears from their eyes.

Though they can't help but regret that they have sinned, perhaps they know that sin has been made to glorify God by the overcoming power of almighty grace; that sin has been made to be a dark background, a sort of setting for the sparkling jewel of eternal, sovereign grace.

They sing, "To him who loves us and has freed us from our sins by his blood" (Revelation 1:5). But they sing that heavenly song without a tear in their eyes. I cannot understand how this can be, for I know I could not do it in my present condition. Let this be the best reason: that God has wiped away every tear from their eyes.

If God would take me to Heaven this morning, and if he did not intervene by a special act of his omnipotence and dry up that fountain of tears, I would almost forget the glories of Paradise in the midst of my own shame that I have not preached more earnestly and have not prayed more fervently and have not labored more abundantly for Christ.

The apostle Paul tells the Christians, "For three years I did not cease night or day to admonish everyone with tears" (Acts 20:31). This text is one that none of us can read without shame and tears. And in Heaven, I think, if I saw the apostle Paul, I would burst into tears, if it were not for this text, which says that "God will wipe away every tear."

Who but the almighty God could do this?

———————— ❋ ————————

ALCORN ☞ Revelation 21:4 also speaks of God dealing with his people's tears: "He will wipe away every tear from their eyes; and there will no longer be *any* death; there will no longer be *any* mourning, or crying, or pain" (NASB, emphasis added).

This includes the tears of suffering over sin and death; the tears of oppressed people; the cries of the poor, the widow, the orphaned, the unborn, and the persecuted. God will wipe away the tears of racial injustice. Such crying shall be no more.

Spurgeon says, "I am convinced that we endure more sorrow from our sins than from God's darkest providence." So true. God will indeed wipe away our tears, but he could not do so without first wiping away our sins.

But what about tears of *joy* in Heaven? Can you imagine joy flooding your eyes as you meet Christ and as you're reunited with loved ones? Have you ever laughed so hard it brought tears to your eyes? I think Christ will laugh with us, and his wit and fun-loving nature will be our greatest source of endless laughter. Spurgeon writes, "I do believe, in my heart, that there may be as much holiness in a laugh as in a cry; and that sometimes, to laugh is the better of the two."

Spurgeon speaks of life under the Curse: "We may forget to laugh, but we will always know how to weep." But when God stops the weeping, surely he will replace it with laughter. Jesus said, "Blessed are you who hunger now, for you will be satisfied. Blessed are you who weep now, for you will laugh. Blessed are you when people hate you, when they exclude you and insult you. . . .

Rejoice in that day and leap for joy, because great is your reward in heaven" (Luke 6:21-23, NIV).

That we will laugh in Heaven, then, is not a speculation; it is Christ's explicit promise. Laughter is a reward for our present weeping. Anticipating the laughter to come, Jesus says we should "leap for joy" *now*. Can you imagine someone leaping for joy in utter silence, without laughter? Our present laughter serves as a foretaste of the great laughter that awaits us.

My wife, Nanci, loves pro football. She opens our home to family and friends for Sunday night games. If you were to come to our house, you'd hear cheers and groans, but the dominant sound in the room, week after week, is laughter. It's the same with any group of rejoicing people. There may be hugging, backslapping, playful wrestling, singing, and storytelling. But always there is laughing. Laughter is God's gift to humanity, a gift that will be raised to new levels after our bodily resurrection.

Spurgeon used his wit to provoke laughter in private and in public. He said in one of his sermons, "If by a laugh I can make men see the folly of an error better than in any other way, they shall laugh."

Where did humor originate? Not with people, angels, or Satan. God created all good things, including good humor. If God didn't have a sense of humor, we as his image bearers wouldn't either. That he has a sense of humor is evident in his creation. Consider aardvarks and baboons. Take a good look at a giraffe. You have to smile, don't you? God made us to laugh and to love to laugh. It's therapeutic. The new universe will ring with laughter.

The only laughter that won't have a place in Heaven is the sort that late-night comedians often engage in—laughter that mocks troubled people, makes light of human suffering, or glorifies immorality. Jesus makes a sobering comment in Luke

6:25 (NIV), in which he addresses not only Heaven but also Hell: "Woe to you who are well fed now, for you will go hungry. Woe to you who laugh now, for you will mourn and weep." When will those who laugh now mourn and weep? In the afterlife.

All those who have not surrendered their lives to God, who exploit and ignore the needy, who ridicule the unfortunate, and who flout God's standards of purity will have all eternity to mourn and weep. They will never laugh again.

One of Satan's great lies is that God—and everything good— is joyless and humorless, while Satan—and evil—brings pleasure and satisfaction. In fact, it's Satan who is humorless. Sin didn't bring him joy; it forever stripped him of joy. In contrast, envision Jesus with his disciples. If we cannot picture him teasing them and laughing with them, we need to reevaluate our understanding of the Incarnation. We need a biblical theology of humor that prepares us for an eternity of celebration and spontaneous laughter.

As Spurgeon says, we may sometimes forget to laugh here, but there will be no end to the laughter when we find our fulfillment in the presence and the promises of our God. Cling to that blood-bought promise concerning our future in Heaven: *we will laugh.*

HELL CAN'T QUENCH HEAVEN'S JOY

❁

Excerpted from "No Tears in Heaven"
Sermon #643, August 6, 1865

Not one to shy away from difficult topics, Spurgeon tackles two troubling realities in this sermon: first, that some people we don't much care for will be in Heaven and, second, that some people we love will be in Hell.

[The rich man called to Abraham], "Father Abraham, have mercy on me, and send Lazarus to dip the end of his finger in water and cool my tongue, for I am in anguish in this flame." But Abraham said, "Child, remember that you in your lifetime received your good things." . . . And [the rich man] said, "Then I beg you, father, to send him to my father's house—for I have five brothers—so that he may warn them, lest they also come into this place of torment." But Abraham said, "They have Moses and the Prophets; let them hear them." And [the rich man] said, "No, father Abraham, but if someone goes to them from the dead, they will repent." [Abraham] said to [the rich man], "If they do not hear Moses and the Prophets, neither will they be convinced if someone should rise from the dead."

LUKE 16:24-25, 27-31

———— ❁ ————

SPURGEON ☞ Perhaps another source of tears may suggest itself to you, namely sorrow in Heaven for our mistakes, misrepresentations, and unkindness toward other Christian brothers and sisters.

How surprised we will be to meet some saints in Heaven whom we did not love on Earth! We would not fellowship with them at the Lord's Table. We would not acknowledge that they were Christians. We looked at them suspiciously if we saw them in the street. We suspected their zeal as being nothing better than a show and an exaggeration, and we looked on their best efforts as having sinister motives at the heart. We said many unkind things and felt a great many more than we said.

When we see these unknown and unrecognized brothers and sisters in Heaven, won't their very presence naturally remind us of our offenses against Christian love and spiritual unity? I can't imagine a perfect man looking at another perfect man without regretting that he ever treated him in an unkind manner.

I am sure as I walk among the saints in Heaven, I cannot (in the natural order of things) help feeling, *I did not assist you as I ought to have done. I did not sympathize with you as I ought to have done. I spoke a harsh word to you. I was alienated from you.* And I think you would all have to feel the same; inevitably you must. If it were not that by some heavenly means, and I don't know how, the eternal God will so overshadow believers with the abundant bliss of his own self that even that cause of tears will be wiped away.

Has it never struck you, dear friends, that if you go to Heaven and see your dear children left behind unconverted, it would naturally be a cause of sorrow?

My mother told me that if I perished in Hell, she would have to say "Amen" to my condemnation. I knew it was true and it sounded awful, and it had a good effect on my mind.

It really is a very terrible spectacle—the thought of a perfect being looking down in Hell, for instance, as Abraham did, and yet feeling no sorrow. For you will remember that, in the tenor in which Abraham addresses the rich man, there is nothing of pity; there is not a single syllable which indicates any sympathy with him in his dreadful woes. And one does not quite comprehend that perfect beings, God-like beings, beings full of love and everything that constitutes the glory of God's complete nature, would still be unable to weep, even over Hell itself. They cannot weep over their own children lost and ruined!

Now, how is this? If you will tell me, I will be glad, for I cannot tell you. I do not believe that there will be one bit less tenderness, that there will be one fraction less of friendliness, love, and sympathy—I believe there will be more—but that they will be in some way so refined and purified that while compassion for suffering is there, hatred of sin will be there to balance it, and a state of complete equilibrium will be attained.

Perfect acceptance of the divine will is probably the secret of it, but it is not my business to guess. I don't know what handkerchief the Lord will use, but I do know that he will wipe away every tear from their eyes.

————— ❀ —————

ALCORN ✎ How could we enjoy Heaven knowing that a loved one is in Hell? Spurgeon isn't the only one to puzzle over this question.

Although it may sound harsh, I offer this thought: in a sense, none of our loved ones will be in Hell—only some whom we *once* loved. Our love for our companions in Heaven will be directly linked to God, the central object of our love. We will see him in them. We will not love those in Hell because when we see Jesus as he is, we will love only—and will *want* to love only—whoever and whatever pleases and glorifies and reflects him. What we loved in those who died without Christ was God's beauty we once saw in them. When God forever withdraws from them, I think they'll no longer bear his image and no longer reflect his beauty. Therefore, paradoxically, in a sense they will *not* be the people we loved.

I cannot prove biblically what I've just stated, but I think it rings true, disturbing as it is. The reality of Hell should break our hearts and take us to our knees—and to the doors of those without Christ. Today, however, Hell has become "the *H* word," seldom named, rarely talked about, even among those who believe the Bible. It doesn't even appear in many evangelistic booklets. To our modern sensibilities, Hell seems disproportionate, a divine overreaction.

Many people imagine that it is civilized, humane, and compassionate to deny the existence of an eternal Hell. But in fact, it is arrogant that we, as creatures, would dare to make such an assumption in opposition to what God the Creator has clearly revealed. Perhaps we don't want to believe that others deserve eternal punishment, because if they do, so do we. But by denying the endlessness of Hell, we minimize Christ's work on the cross. Why? Because we lower the stakes of redemption.

If we truly understood God's nature and ours, we would be shocked not that some people could go to Hell (where else would sinners go?) but that any would be permitted into Heaven. If Christ's crucifixion and resurrection don't deliver us from an eternal Hell, his work on the cross is less heroic, less potent, less consequential, and thus less deserving of our worship and praise. As theologian William G. T. Shedd puts it, "The doctrine of Christ's vicarious atonement logically stands or falls with that of eternal punishment."[14]

What Spurgeon's mother told him—that she would have to say "Amen" to his condemnation if he did not repent—is remarkably similar to J. I. Packer's difficult but biblical perspective:

> God the Father (who now pleads with mankind to accept the reconciliation that Christ's death secured for all) and God the Son (our appointed Judge, who wept over Jerusalem) will in a final judgment express wrath and administer justice against rebellious humans. God's holy righteousness will hereby be revealed; God will be doing the right thing, vindicating himself at last against all who have defied him. . . . (Read through Matt. 25; John 5:22-29; Rom. 2:5-16; 12:19; 2 Thess. 1:7-9; Rev. 18:1–19:3; 20:11-15, and you will see that clearly.) God will judge justly, and all angels, saints, and martyrs will praise him for it. So it seems inescapable that we shall, with them, approve the judgment of persons—rebels— whom we have known and loved.[15]

Of this we may be absolutely certain: Hell will have no power over Heaven, and none of Hell's misery will ever diminish any of Heaven's joy.

PRESENT AND FUTURE REST

❋

Excerpted from "Heavenly Rest"
Sermon #133

Delivered on Sabbath morning,
May 24, 1857, at the Music Hall, Royal Surrey Gardens

Are you weary, whether from your work, from the suffering you've endured, or simply from living in a world bogged down by sin? God offers us true rest, heart-level rest—both now and in eternity.

There remains a Sabbath rest for the people of God.

HEBREWS 4:9

———— ❋ ————

SPURGEON ☞ "*My* rest," says God (Hebrews 4:3-4), the rest of God! Something more wonderful than any other kind of rest. It is not the Sabbath, but the *rest* of the Sabbath—not the outward ritual of the Sabbath, which was binding upon the Jew, but the inward *spirit* of the Sabbath, which is the joy and delight of the Christian.

Now this rest, I believe, is partly enjoyed on Earth. "We who have believed enter that rest" (Hebrews 4:3), for we have ceased from our own works, as God did from his. But the full fruition and rich enjoyment of it remains in the future and eternal state of the blessed on the other side of the stream of death.

If God should help me to raise but one of his feeble saints on the wings of love to look within the veil and see the joys of the future, I shall be well contented to have made the joy-bells ring in one heart at least, to have set one eye flashing with joy, and to have made one spirit light with gladness. The *rest* of Heaven!

Here, too, on Earth, the Christian has to suffer. Here he has the aching head and the pained body. His limbs may be bruised or broken; disease may rack him with torture. He may be an afflicted one from his birth. He may have lost an eye or an ear, or he may have lost many of his powers. Or if not, being of a weakly constitution, he may have to spend most of his days and nights upon the bed of weariness.

Or if his body be sound, yet what suffering he has in his mind! Conflicts between depravity and gross temptations from the evil one, assaults of Hell, perpetual attacks of diverse kinds—from the world, the flesh, and the devil.

But in Heaven, no aching head, no weary heart. There, no palsied arm, no brow plowed with the furrows of old age. There, the lost limb shall be recovered and old age shall find itself endowed with perpetual youth. There, the infirmities of the flesh shall be left behind, given to the worm and devoured by decay.

There, they shall flit, as on the wings of angels, from pole to pole and from place to place, without weariness or anguish. There, they shall never need to lie upon the bed of rest or the bed of suffering, for day without night, with joy unflagging, they shall circle God's throne rejoicing and ever praise him who has said, "No inhabitant will say, 'I am sick'" (Isaiah 33:24).

There, too, they shall be free from persecution. There shall be none to taunt them with a cruel word or touch them with a cruel hand. They are in the society of saints; they shall be free from all the idle conversation of the wicked, and from their cruel jeers set free forever. Set free from persecution!

You army of martyrs: you were slain, you were torn apart, you were cast to wild beasts, tormented. I see you now, a mighty host. The clothing you wear is torn with thorns. Your faces are scarred with sufferings. I see you at your stakes and on your crosses. I hear your words of submission on your racks, I see you in your prisons, I behold you in your shackles. But

> *Now you are arrayed in white,*
> > *Brighter than the noonday-sun*
> *Fairest of the sons of light,*
> > *Nearest the eternal throne.**

These are they who for their Master died, who love the cross and crown. They waded through seas of blood in order to obtain the inheritance, and there they are, with the blood-red crown of martyrdom about their heads, that ruby brightness, far excelling every other. Yes, there is no persecution there. "There remains a Sabbath rest for the people of God."

Alas! In this mortal state the child of God is also subject to sin; he fails in his duty and wanders from his God; he does not walk in all the laws of his God blameless, though he desires to do it. Sin now troubles him constantly, but there sin is dead, there God's children have no temptation to sin, from without or from within, but they are perfectly free to serve their Master. Here God's children have sometimes to weep in repentance of their backslidings; but there they never shed tears of penitence, for they have never cause to do so.

And last of all, here, the child of God has to wet the cold ashes of his relatives with tears.

---

* From the hymn "What Are These Arrayed in White," by Charles Wesley, 1745.

But there never once shall be heard the toll of the funeral bell, no hearse with plumes has ever darkened the streets of gold. The immortal are strangers to the meaning of death; they cannot die—they live forever, having no power to decay and no possibility of corruption.

Oh, rest of the righteous, how blessed you are, where families shall again be bound up in one embrace. Where parted friends shall again meet to part no more. And where the whole church of Christ united in one mighty circle shall together praise God and the Lamb throughout eternal ages.

———————— ❁ ————————

ALCORN ☜ In 1649, Puritan pastor Richard Baxter wrote *The Saints' Everlasting Rest*, which Spurgeon read and treasured a few hundred years after its publication. It was for centuries the most influential book on Heaven ever written. Baxter, whom Spurgeon called "a man who above all other men loved the souls of men," marveled that we don't set everything else aside to consider Heaven and make sure we're going there. Somehow, he lamented, Heaven hasn't captured our imaginations or shaped our lives. Baxter and Spurgeon both latched onto the biblical picture of Heaven as a place of ultimate rest.

When God created the world, he rested on the seventh day (Genesis 2:2). That's the basis for the biblical Sabbath, when all people and animals were to rest (Exodus 20:9-11). God set aside days and weeks of rest, and he even called for the Earth itself to rest every seventh year (Leviticus 25:4-5). This is the rest we can anticipate on the New Earth—times of joyful praise and relaxed fellowship, "united," as Spurgeon writes, "in one mighty circle."

Our lives in Heaven will include rest (Hebrews 4:1-11). "Blessed are the dead who die in the Lord from now on." "'Yes,' says the Spirit, 'they will rest from their labor, for their deeds will follow them'" (Revelation 14:13, NIV).

Eden is a picture of rest—meaningful and enjoyable work, abundant food, beautiful environment, unhindered friendship with God and other people and animals. Even in Eden's perfection, one day was set aside for special rest and worship. Work will be refreshing on the New Earth, yet regular rest will be built into our lives.

Part of our inability to appreciate Heaven as a place of rest relates to our failure to enter into a weekly day of rest now. By rarely turning attention from our responsibilities, we fail to anticipate our coming deliverance from the Curse to a full rest.

Spurgeon speaks of another sort of rest—a rest from persecution: "There shall be none to taunt them with a cruel word or touch them with a cruel hand." Those who know Spurgeon's life will pick up the meaning behind lines like these. In a day when newspapers held sway over public opinion, Spurgeon was bitterly opposed by many newspaper editors, secular as well as religious.

For instance, in April 1855, the *Essex Standard* carried an article that described Spurgeon this way: "His style is that of the vulgar colloquial, varied by rant. . . . All the most solemn mysteries of our holy religion are by him rudely, roughly and impiously handled. Common sense is outraged and decency disgusted. His rantings are interspersed with coarse anecdotes."[16]

In 1857 Spurgeon wrote in one of his sermons, "Down on my knees have I often fallen, with the hot sweat rising from my brow under some fresh slander poured upon me; in an agony of grief my heart has been well-nigh broken."

Spurgeon's wife, Susannah, kept a scrapbook of the slanders spoken against her husband. She filled a huge volume with clippings and produced for Charles a framed wall text quoting

Matthew 5:11-12: "Blessed are you when others revile you and persecute you and utter all kinds of evil against you falsely on my account. Rejoice and be glad, for your reward is great in heaven, for so they persecuted the prophets who were before you."

This public criticism surely influenced Spurgeon's understanding of this text: "Make every effort to enter that rest" (Hebrews 4:11, NIV). He knew he needed to carve out rest for his body and his mind and step back from the battles on every front. Even so, he admitted that he did not excel at doing this.

It's ironic that it takes such effort to set aside time for rest. For many of us, myself included, it's difficult to guard our schedules, but it's worth it. A day of rest points us to Heaven and to Jesus, who says, "Come to me, all you who are weary . . . and I will give you rest" (Matthew 11:28, NIV).

What feels better than putting your head on your pillow after a hard day's work? (How about what it will feel like after a hard *life*'s work?) It's good to sit and have a glass of iced tea, feel the sun on your face, or tilt back in your recliner and close your eyes. It's good to have nothing to do but read a good book or take your dog for a walk or listen to your favorite music and tell God how grateful you are for his kindness. Rest is good, so good that God built it into his creation and his law.

Some people thrive on social interaction; others are exhausted by it. Some love solitude; others don't. On the New Earth, we'll likely all welcome the lively company of others but also crave times of restful solitude. We'll enjoy both.

God rested on the seventh day, before sin entered the world. He prescribed rest for sinless Adam and Eve, and he prescribed it for those under the curse of sin. Regular rest will be part of our future lives in God's new universe.

LONGING FOR HEAVEN'S REST

✤

Excerpted from "Heavenly Rest"
Sermon #133, May 24, 1857

If you've ever felt as if you were made for more than what this world
has to offer, you're right. Even the best moments from our past and our
present are merely hints of the future God has in store for us.

> *Let all who take refuge in you rejoice;*
> *let them ever sing for joy,*
> *and spread your protection over them,*
> *that those who love your name may*
> *exult in you.* PSALM 5:11

---------- ✤ ----------

SPURGEON ✑ The Christian has some rest here, but nothing compared with the rest which is to come (Hebrews 4:9).

There is the rest experienced by the church. When the believer
joins the church of God and becomes united with fellow believers,
he may expect to rest. The good old writer of *Pilgrim's Progress* says
that when the weary pilgrims were once admitted to the House
Beautiful, they were shown to sleep in a chamber called Peace.

The church member at the Lord's Table has a sweet enjoyment
of rest in fellowship with the saints, but up there in Heaven, the
rest of church fellowship far surpasses anything that is known

here. For there are no divisions there, no angry words at the church meetings, no harsh thoughts of one another, no bickering about doctrine, no fighting about practice.

There is, again, a rest of faith which a Christian enjoys—a sweet rest. Many of us have known it. We have known what it is, when the billows of trouble have run high, to hide ourselves in the breast of Christ and feel secure. We have cast our anchor deep into the rocks of God's promise, we have gone to sleep in our chamber and have not feared the tempest, we have looked at tribulation and have smiled at it, we have looked at death himself and have laughed him to scorn.

In the midst of defamation, reproach, slander and contempt, we have said, "I shall not be moved, for God is on my side." But the rest up there is better still—more unruffled, more sweet, more perfectly calm, more enduring, and more lasting than even the rest of faith.

And again, the Christian sometimes has the blessed rest of communion. There are happy moments when he puts his head on the Savior's breast—when, like John, he feels that he is close to the Savior's heart, and there he sleeps. God "gives to his beloved sleep" (Psalm 127:2)—not the sleep of unconsciousness, but the sleep of joy.

Happy, happy, happy are the dreams we have had on the couch of communion! Blessed have been the times when, like the spouse in Solomon's song, we could say of Christ, "His left hand is under my head, and his right hand embraces me!" (Song of Solomon 2:6).

When we shall have plunged into a very bath of joy, we shall have found the delights even of Communion on Earth to have been but the dipping of the finger in the cup, but the dipping of the bread in the dish, whereas Heaven itself shall be the participation of the whole of the joy and not the mere foretaste of it.

Here we sometimes enter into the doorway of happiness; there we shall go into the presence chamber of the King! Here we look over the hedge and see the flowers in Heaven's garden; there we shall walk between the flower beds of delight. We shall pluck fresh flowers at each step.

Here we just look and see the sunlight of Heaven in the distance, like the lamps of the thousand-gated cities shining far away. There we shall see them in all their blaze of splendor. Here we listen to the whisperings of Heaven's melody, borne by winds from afar. But there, entranced amid the grand melodies of the blessed, we shall join in the everlasting hallelujah to the great Messiah, *the* God, the I Am.

ALCORN ☞ I've never been to Heaven, yet I miss it. Eden's in my blood. The best things of life are souvenirs from Eden, appetizers of the New Earth. There are just enough of them to keep us going but never enough to make us satisfied with the world as it is or ourselves as we are. We live between Eden and the New Earth, pulled toward what we once were and what we yet will be.

As Spurgeon puts it, "Here we listen to the whisperings of Heaven's melody, borne by winds from afar." But there's a place Christ is preparing for us. Do you hear the final sounds of construction? Are you ready to live there with Jesus forever?

In Eden, God came down to Earth, the home of humanity, whenever he wished (Genesis 3:8). On the New Earth, God and mankind will be able to come to each other whenever they wish. We will not have to leave home to visit God, nor will God leave home to visit us. God and mankind will live together forever in the same home—the New Earth.

God declares this truth in Scripture: "I will put my dwelling place among you, and I will not abhor you. I will walk among you and be your God, and you will be my people" (Leviticus 26:11-12, NIV). "I will live with them and walk among them, and I will be their God, and they will be my people" (2 Corinthians 6:16, NIV).

Desire is a signpost pointing to Heaven. Every longing for better health is a longing for the perfect bodies we'll have on the New Earth. Every longing for romance is a longing for the ultimate romance with Christ. Every thirst for beauty is a thirst for Christ. Every taste of joy is but a foretaste of a greater and more vibrant joy than can be found on Earth now.

That's why we need to spend our lives cultivating our love for Heaven. That's why we need to meditate on what Scripture says about Heaven and to read books, have Bible studies, teach classes, and preach sermons on it. We need to talk to our children about Heaven. When we're camping, hiking, or driving or when we're at a museum, a sporting event, or a theme park, we need to talk about what we see around us as signposts of the New Earth.

When we think of Heaven as unearthly, our present lives seem unspiritual, as if they don't matter. When we grasp the reality of the New Earth, however, our present, earthly lives suddenly do matter. Conversations with loved ones matter. The taste of food matters. Work, leisure, creativity, and intellectual stimulation matter. Rivers and trees and flowers matter. Laughter matters. Service matters. Why? *Because they are eternal.*

Life on Earth matters, not because it's the only life we have, but precisely because it isn't—it's the beginning of a life that will continue without end on a renewed Earth. Understanding Heaven doesn't just tell us *what* to do, but *why*. What God tells us about our future enables us to interpret our past and serve him in our present.

MAKING CERTAIN OF HEAVEN

✸

Excerpted from "Heavenly Rest"
Sermon #133, May 24, 1857

Many people view Heaven as an uncertain gamble, spending their lives wondering if they will arrive at their desired destination. But it doesn't have to be this way. Through Christ, we can be assured of eternal life!

> *Bless the LORD, O my soul,*
> *and all that is within me,*
> *bless his holy name!*
> *Bless the LORD, O my soul,*
> *and forget not all his benefits,*
> *who forgives all your iniquity,*
> *who heals all your diseases,*
> *who redeems your life from the pit,*
> *who crowns you with steadfast*
> *love and mercy,*
> *who satisfies you with good*
> *so that your youth is renewed*
> *like the eagle's.* PSALM 103:1-5

———— ✸ ————

SPURGEON ⌐✎ Do we not wish to mount above and fly away, to enter into the rest which awaits the people of God?

This glorious rest is to be best of all commended for its

certainty. "There remains a Sabbath rest for the people of God"
(Hebrews 4:9). Doubter, you have often said, "I fear I shall never
enter Heaven." Fear not—all the people of God shall enter there.
There is no fear about it. I love the quaint saying of a dying man,
who, in his country brogue, exclaimed, "I have no fear of going
home; I have sent all before me. God's finger is on the latch of
my door, and I am ready for him to enter."

"But are you not afraid that you might miss your inheritance?"

"No," said he, "there is one crown in Heaven that the angel
Gabriel could not wear; it will fit no head but mine. There is one
throne in Heaven that Paul the apostle could not fill; it was made
for me, and I shall have it. There is one dish at the banquet that I
must eat, or else it will be untasted, for God has set it apart for me."

Oh Christian, what a joyous thought! Your portion is secure!
"There remains a Sabbath rest." "But cannot I forfeit it?" No, it
is secure. If I be a child of God, I shall not lose it. It is mine as
surely as if I were there.

Poor doubting one, see your inheritance—it is yours. If you
believe in the Lord Jesus, you are one of the Lord's people; if you
have repented of sin, you are one of the Lord's people; if you have
been renewed in heart, you are one of the Lord's people, and there
is a place for you, a crown for you. No one else shall have it but
you, and you shall have it before long.

I beg you to conceive of yourselves as being in Heaven. Is it not
a strange thing to think of—a poor clown in Heaven? Think, how
will you feel with your crown on your head? Weary mother, many
years have rolled over you. How changed will be the scene when
you are young again. Ah, toil-worn laborer, only think when you
shall rest. Can you conceive it? Could you but think for a moment
of yourself as being in Heaven now, what a strange surprise would
seize you.

You would say, "What! Are these streets of gold? What! Are these walls of jasper? What, am I here? In white? Am I here, with a crown on my head? Am I here singing—I who once groaned? I who once cursed God now praise him? What! I now lift up my voice in his honor? Oh, precious blood that washed me clean! Oh, precious faith that set me free! Oh, precious Spirit that made me repent, lest I'd have been cast away to Hell! Oh, joys that never fade!"

"Profusion of happiness! Wonder of wonders! Miracle of miracles! What a world I am in! And oh, that I am here—this is the greatest miracle of all!" And yet it's true. And that is the glory of it. It is true.

Then come, wings of faith. Come, leap with all power. Come, eternal ages. Come, and you shall prove that there are joys that the eye has not seen, which the ear has not heard, and which only God can reveal to us by his Spirit.

My earnest prayer is that none of you may fall short of this rest. May you enter into it and enjoy it forever and ever. God give you his great blessing, for Jesus' sake! Amen.

———— ✦ ————

ALCORN ✎ Not only did Spurgeon have a passion about the Heaven he had seen in his mind's eye, he also had an overwhelming longing for his congregation to come to faith in Christ and know for certain that Heaven awaited them when they died.

Can we really know in advance where we're going when we die? The apostle John, the same one who wrote about the new heavens and New Earth, said in one of his letters, "I write these things to you who believe in the name of the Son of God so that *you may know that you have eternal life*" (1 John 5:13, NIV, emphasis added).

What would keep us out of Heaven is universal: "All have sinned and fall short of the glory of God" (Romans 3:23, NIV). Sin separates us from a relationship with God (Isaiah 59:2). God is so holy that he cannot allow sin into his presence: "Your eyes are too pure to look on evil; you cannot tolerate wrongdoing" (Habakkuk 1:13, NIV). Because we are sinners, we are not entitled to enter God's presence as we are.

In the midst of these discussions about being with Jesus, being reunited with family and friends, and enjoying great adventures in Heaven, we dare not assume we will go there without asking ourselves how. We can't "wait and see" when it comes to what's on the other side of death! We shouldn't just cross our fingers and hope that our names are written in the Book of Life (Revelation 21:27). We can know—we *should* know—before we die. And because we may die at any time, we need to know *now*—not next month or next year.

Do you know?

People who want to get to Florida don't simply get in the car and start driving, hoping the road they're on will somehow get them there. Instead, they look at a map and chart their course. They do this in advance, rather than waiting until they arrive at the wrong destination or discover they've spent three days driving the wrong direction. The goal of getting to Heaven is worthy of greater advance planning than we would give to any other journey, yet some people spend far more time preparing for a trip to Disney World.

Only when our sins are dealt with in Christ can we enter Heaven. No other prophet or religious figure—only Jesus, the Son of God—is worthy to pay the penalty for our sins demanded by God's holiness (Revelation 5:4-5, 9-10). When Christ died on the cross for us, he said, "It is finished" (John 19:30). The Greek word translated "it is finished" means "paid in full." Christ died so that the certificate of debt, consisting of all our sins, could once and for all be marked "Paid in Full."

Because of Jesus Christ's sacrificial death on the cross on our behalf, God freely offers us forgiveness. "He does not treat us as our sins deserve or repay us according to our iniquities. . . . As far as the east is from the west, so far has he removed our transgressions from us" (Psalm 103:10, 12, NIV).

Forgiveness is not automatic. If we want to be forgiven, we must recognize and repent of our sins. Forgiveness is established by confession: "If we confess our sins, he is faithful and just and will forgive us our sins and purify us from all unrighteousness" (1 John 1:9, NIV).

Christ offers to everyone the gift of forgiveness, salvation, and eternal life: "Let the one who is thirsty come; and let the one who wishes take the free gift of the water of life" (Revelation 22:17, NIV). This is a text Spurgeon often quoted, and one each of us should ponder carefully.

This gospel gift, offered to us by God's sovereign grace, cannot be worked for, earned, or achieved in any sense. It's not dependent on our merit or effort, but solely on Christ's generous and sufficient sacrifice on our behalf.

Ultimately, God's greatest gift is himself. We don't need just salvation; we need Jesus, the Savior. It is the person, God, who graciously gives us the place, Heaven. A place purchased by his blood.

KNOWING OUR
LOVED ONES IN HEAVEN

Excerpted from "Heaven and Hell"
Sermon #39, 40

Delivered on Tuesday evening,
September 4, 1855, in a field, King Edward's Road, Hackney

When people we love die, we miss them and long to see them again. That's a big part of death's curse. But when your Christian loved ones die, if you know Christ you will see them again. In Heaven we will have eternal fellowship not only with God but also with the family of God.

> *I tell you, many will come from east and west and recline at*
> *table with Abraham, Isaac, and Jacob in the kingdom of heaven.*
>   MATTHEW 8:11

SPURGEON ⇜ To my mind, one of the best views of Heaven is that it is a land of rest—especially to the working man. Those who don't have to work hard think they will love Heaven as a place of service. That is very true. But to the working man, to the man who toils with his brain or with his hands, it must ever be a sweet thought that there is a land where we shall rest.

Soon this voice will never be strained again. Soon these lungs will never have to exert themselves beyond their power. Soon this brain shall not be racked for thought, but I shall sit at the banquet table of God. I shall recline on the bosom of Abraham and be at ease forever. Weary sons and daughters of Adam, you will not have to drive the plow into the unthankful soil in Heaven. You will not need to rise to daily toils before the sun has risen and labor still when the sun has long ago gone to his rest. But you shall be still, you shall be quiet, you shall rest yourselves, for all are rich in Heaven, all are happy there, all are peaceful. *Toil, trouble, travail,* and *labor* are words that cannot be spelled in Heaven; the saints have no such things there, for they always rest.

And mark the good company they sit with. Some people think that in Heaven we shall know nobody. But our text declares here that we shall sit down with Abraham and Isaac and Jacob. Then I am sure that we shall be aware that they are Abraham and Isaac and Jacob!

If we have known one another here, we shall know one another there. I have dear departed friends up there, and it is always a sweet thought to me that when I shall put my foot, as I hope I may, upon the threshold of Heaven, there will come my sisters and brothers to clasp me by the hand and say, "Yes, my loved one, at last you are here."

Dear relatives who have been separated from you, these you will meet again in Heaven. One of you has lost a mother—she is gone above. And if you follow the track of Jesus, you shall see her there.

We shall recognize our friends. Husband, you will know your wife again. Mother, you will know those dear babes of yours—you memorized their features when they lay panting and gasping for breath. You know how you hung over their graves when the cold sod was sprinkled over them and it was said, "Earth to earth. Dust to dust, and ashes to ashes." But you shall hear those sweet voices once more; you shall yet know that those whom you loved have been loved by God.

———————— ❋ ————————

ALCORN ✑ Amy Carmichael, a missionary to India in the early 1900s, wrote,

> Shall we know one another in Heaven? Shall we love and remember? I do not think anyone need wonder about this or doubt for a single moment. We are never told we shall, because, I expect, it was not necessary, for if we think for a minute, we know. Would you be yourself if you did not love and remember? . . . We are told that we shall be like our Lord Jesus. Surely this does not mean in holiness only, but in everything; and does not He know and love and remember? He would not be Himself if He did not, and we should not be ourselves if we did not.[17]

Bible scholar W. G. Scroggie echoes the sentiments of many believers: "If I knew that never again would I recognize that beloved one with whom I spent more than thirty-nine years here on earth, my anticipation of heaven would much abate. To say that we will be with Christ and that that will be enough is to claim that there we shall be without the social instincts and affections which mean so much to us here. . . . Life beyond cannot mean impoverishment, but the enhancement and enrichment of life as we have known it here at its best."[18]

Augustine said, "We have not lost our dear ones who have departed from this life, but have merely sent them ahead of us, so we also shall depart and shall come to that life where they will be more than ever dear as they will be better known to us, and where we shall love them without fear of parting."[19] He also said, "All of us who enjoy God are also enjoying each other in Him."[20]

Throughout the ages, Christians have anticipated eternal reunion with their loved ones.

Paul tells the Thessalonians that they'll be reunited with believing family and friends in Heaven: "Brothers and sisters, we do not want you to be uninformed about those who sleep in death, so that you do not grieve like the rest of mankind, who have no hope. . . . God will bring with Jesus those who have fallen asleep in him. . . . We who are still alive and are left will be caught up together with them. . . . And so we will be with the Lord forever. Therefore encourage one another with these words" (1 Thessalonians 4:13-14, 17-18, NIV).

Our source of comfort isn't only that we'll be with the Lord in Heaven but also that we'll be with one another. Christ is "the Alpha and the Omega, the First and the Last" (Revelation 22:13, NIV). He alone is sufficient to meet all our needs. Yet God has designed us for relationship not only with himself but also with others of our kind. After God created the world, he stepped back to look at his work and pronounced it "very good" (Genesis 1:31). However, before his creation was complete, he said there was one thing—and only one—that was not good: "It is not good for the man to be alone. I will make a helper suitable for him" (Genesis 2:18, NIV). God planned for Adam, and all mankind, to need human companionship.

Jesus rebuked the religious leaders for imagining they could love God without loving people (Luke 10:27-37). The spiritual-sounding "I will love just God and no one else" is not only unspiritual; it's impossible. If we don't love people, who are created in God's image, we can't love God (1 John 4:8).

Puritan Richard Baxter, whom Spurgeon regarded as a pastoral mentor, looked forward to being with Christ first, but he also anticipated being reunited with dear friends: "I know that Christ is all in all; and that it is the presence of God that makes Heaven to be Heaven. But yet it much sweetens the thoughts of that place to me that there are there such a multitude of my most dear and precious friends in Christ."[21]

On the New Earth we'll experience the joy of familiarity in old relationships and the joy of discovery in new ones. As we get to know one another better, we'll get to know God better. And as we find joy in one another, we'll find joy in him.

TOGETHER WITH EVERY NATION, TRIBE, AND TONGUE

✤

Excerpted from "Heaven and Hell"
Sermon #39, 40, September 4, 1855

Will there be more people in Heaven or in Hell? Spurgeon's answer may surprise you. Whether or not you agree, a close reading of Scripture indicates that Heaven will be filled with great multitudes of people from every culture, every nationality, and every language.

> *You are those who have stayed with me in my trials, and I assign to you, as my Father assigned to me, a kingdom, that you may eat and drink at my table in my kingdom and sit on thrones judging the twelve tribes of Israel.* Luke 22:28-30

———— ✤ ————

SPURGEON ✐ Would it not be a dreary Heaven for us to inhabit, if we should be both unknowing and unknown? I believe that Heaven is a fellowship of the saints. I have often thought I should love to see Isaiah, and as soon as I get to Heaven, I would like to ask for him, because he spoke more of Jesus Christ than all the rest.

I am sure I should want to find out good George Whitefield*—
he who so continually preached to the people and wore himself
out with a more than angelic zeal.

Oh yes! We shall have choice company in Heaven when we
get there. There will be no distinction of learned and unlearned,
clergy and laity, but we shall walk freely among one another. We
shall feel that we are family. The Jew and the Gentile will sit
down together. The great and the small shall feed in the same
pasture, and "many will . . . recline at table with Abraham, Isaac,
and Jacob in the kingdom of heaven" (Matthew 8:11).

But my text has a yet greater depth of sweetness, for it says,
that "*many* will come." Some think that Heaven will be a very
small place where there will be a very few people who went to
their chapel or their church. I confess, I have no wish for a very
small Heaven, and I love to read in the Scriptures that there are
many mansions in my Father's house (John 14:2, KJV).

How often do I hear people say, "The gate is straight and the
way is narrow, and there are few who find it. There will be very
few in Heaven; most will be lost."

My friend, I differ from you. Do you think that Christ will let
the devil beat him? That he will let the devil have more in Hell
than there will be in Heaven? No, it is impossible. For then Satan
would laugh at Christ. There will be more in Heaven than there
are among the lost. God says that there will be "a great multitude
no one could number who will be saved." But he never says that
there will be a multitude that no man can number that will be lost.

What glad tidings for you and for me! For if there are so many
to be saved, why shouldn't I be saved? Why shouldn't you? Why

---

* George Whitefield was an eighteenth-century minister who helped spread the Great
  Awakening in Britain and the American colonies.

shouldn't that man over there in the crowd say, "Can't I be one among the multitude?" And may not that poor woman there take heart and say, "Well, if there were but half a dozen saved, I might fear that I should not be one, but since many are to come, why shouldn't I also be saved?"

Cheer up, child of sorrow, there is hope for you still! I can never know that any man is past God's grace. There be a few who have sinned that sin that is unto death (Matthew 12:31-32), and God gives them up; but the vast host of mankind are yet within the reach of sovereign mercy. "Many will come from east and west and recline at table with Abraham, Isaac, and Jacob in the kingdom of heaven."

ALCORN ⌾⊷ Is there a biblical basis for Spurgeon's belief that God's eternal Kingdom will be inhabited by multitudes from all nations? I believe there is.

Most of us are unaccustomed to thinking of nations, rulers, civilizations, and culture in Heaven, but Isaiah 60 is one of many passages that demonstrate that the New Earth will in fact be earthly and full of the Earth's nations. God's people will have a glorious future in which the nations and their leaders will participate in and benefit from a renewed and glorious Jerusalem. It won't be only some nations but all of them: "All assemble and come to you" (verse 4, NIV).

This will be a time of unprecedented rejoicing: "Then you will look and be radiant, your heart will throb and swell with joy" (verse 5, NIV). On the renewed Earth, the nations will bring their greatest treasures into this glorified city: "The wealth on the seas will be brought to you, to you the riches of the nations will come" (verse 5, NIV).

Will we have ethnic and national identities? Yes. Is the risen Jesus Jewish? Certainly. Will we know he's Jewish? Of course. Our resurrected DNA will be unflawed, but it will preserve our God-designed uniqueness, racial and otherwise. The elders sing to the Lamb: "You are worthy.... Your blood has ransomed people for God from every tribe and language and people and nation. And you have caused them to become a Kingdom of priests for our God. And they will reign on the earth" (Revelation 5:9-10, NLT). Who will serve as the New Earth's kings and priests? Not people who were *formerly* of every tribe, language, people, and nation. Their distinctions aren't obliterated—they continue into the present Heaven and then into the eternal Heaven.

Tribe refers to a person's clan and family lineage. *People* refers to race. *Nation* refers to those who share a national identity and culture. Some scholars argue that the image of God has a corporate dimension: "There is no one human individual or group who can fully bear or manifest all that is involved in the image of God, so that there is a sense in which that image is collectively possessed. The image of God is, as it were, parceled out among the peoples of the Earth. By looking at different individuals and groups we get glimpses of different aspects of the full image of God."[22]

If this is true, and I believe it may be, then racism is not only an injustice toward people but also a rejection of God's very nature. On the New Earth we'll never celebrate sin, but we'll celebrate diversity in the biblical sense. We'll never try to keep people out. We'll welcome them in, exercising hospitality to every traveler. Peace on Earth will be rooted in our common ruler, Christ the King, who alone is the source of peace: "Glory to God in the highest, and on earth peace among men with whom He is pleased" (Luke 2:14, NASB).

Peace on Earth will be accomplished not by the abolition of our differences but by a unifying loyalty to the King, a loyalty that transcends differences—and is enriched by them. The kings and leaders of nations will be united because they share the King's righteousness, and with him they will rejoice in their differences as a tribute to his creativity and multifaceted character.

Consider this prophetic statement: "The kingdom of the world has become the kingdom of our Lord and of his Messiah, and he will reign for ever and ever" (Revelation 11:15, NIV). Scripture doesn't say that Christ will destroy or even replace this world's kingdom. No, the kingdom of this world will actually *become* the Kingdom of Christ. God won't obliterate earthly kingdoms but will transform them into his own. And it's that new earthly kingdom (joined then to God's heavenly Kingdom) over which "he will reign for ever and ever."

On the New Earth, "the nations will walk by [Christ's] light, and the kings of the earth will bring their splendor into [the New Jerusalem]. On no day will its gates ever be shut. . . . The glory and honor of the nations will be brought into it" (Revelation 21:24-26, NIV).

Pastor and author Bruce Milne says of this text, "Nothing of ultimate worth from the long history of the nations will be omitted from the heavenly community. Everything which authentically reflects the God of truth, all that is of abiding worth from within the national stories and the cultural inheritance of the world's peoples, will find its place in the New Jerusalem."[23]

Tribes, peoples, and nations will all make their own particular contribution to the enrichment of life in the New Jerusalem (Revelation 5:9; 7:9; 21:24-26). Daniel prophesied that the Messiah would be "given dominion and glory and a kingdom, that all peoples, nations, and languages should serve him"

(Daniel 7:14). Just as the church's diversity of gifts serves the good of others (1 Corinthians 12:7-11), so our diversity will serve everyone's good in the new universe.

Consider what it will be like to worship with Masai, Dinka, Hmong, Athabascan, Tibetan, Waodani, Icelandic, Macedonian, Moldovan, Moroccan, and Peruvian believers. In the sweeping breadth of his redemptive work, I believe that God may resurrect not only modern nations but also ancient ones, including, for instance, Babylon and Rome. Are ancient Assyrians, Sumerians, Phoenicians, Babylonians, and Greeks among God's redeemed? We know they are, for no nation, past or present, is excluded from "every nation, tribe, people and language" (Revelation 7:9, NIV).

Hundreds of nations, thousands of people groups, untold millions of redeemed individuals will gather to worship Christ. And many national and cultural distinctions, untouched by sin, will continue to the glory of God.

BEHOLD, THE LAMB OF GOD!

❋

Excerpted from "Heavenly Worship"
Sermon #110

Delivered Sabbath morning,
December 28, 1856, at the Music Hall, Royal Surrey Gardens

We have every reason to tremble when we think of facing a holy God. But Christ appears in Heaven as a Lamb—victorious and triumphant, yet also gentle. He is the Lamb of God who beckons us to his throne of grace.

> *I looked, and behold, on Mount Zion stood the Lamb, and with him 144,000 who had his name and his Father's name written on their foreheads. And I heard a voice from heaven like the roar of many waters and like the sound of loud thunder.* REVELATION 14:1-2

———— ❋ ————

SPURGEON ✑ Why should Christ in Heaven choose to appear as the figure of a lamb and not in some other of his glorious characters? Because it was as a lamb that Jesus fought and conquered, and therefore it is as a lamb he appears in Heaven.

I have read of certain military commanders, when they were conquerors, that on the anniversary of their victory they would never wear anything but the garment in which they fought. On that memorable day they say, "No, take away the robes. I will wear no other outfit but that in which I fought and conquered."

It seems as if the same feeling possessed the breast of Christ. "As a Lamb," says he, "I died and defeated Hell. As a Lamb I have redeemed my people, and therefore as a Lamb I will appear in Paradise."

But perhaps there is another reason: it is to encourage us to come to him in prayer. Ah, believer, we need not be afraid to come to Christ, for he is a Lamb. To a Lion-Christ we need fear to come, but the Lamb-Christ! Oh, children of the living God, should you ever fail to tell your griefs and sorrows into the breast of one who is a Lamb? Ah, let us come boldly to the throne of the heavenly grace, seeing that a Lamb sits upon it.

And you will further notice that this Lamb is said to stand. Standing is the posture of triumph. The Father said to Christ, "Sit at my right hand, until I put your enemies under your feet" (Mark 12:36). It is done; they are his footstool. And here he is said to stand erect, like a victor over all his enemies.

Many a time the Savior knelt in prayer, and once he hung upon the cross. But when the great scene of our text shall be fully accomplished, he shall stand erect, as more than conqueror, through his own majestic might. "I looked, and behold, on Mount Zion, stood the Lamb" (Revelation 14:1). Oh, if we could split the veil—if now we were privileged to see within it—there is no sight that would so enthrall us as the simple sight of the Lamb on the throne. My dear brothers and sisters in Christ Jesus, would it not be all the sight you would ever wish to see if you could once behold him whom your soul loves? Would it not be a Heaven to you if it were carried out in your experience—"My eyes shall behold [him], and not another" (Job 19:27)? Would you want anything else to make you happy but continually to see him?

And if a single glimpse of him on Earth affords you profound delight, it must be, indeed, a very sea of bliss and an abyss of Paradise, without a bottom or a shore, to see him as he is—to be lost in his splendors, as the stars are lost in the sunlight, and to hold fellowship with him, as did John the beloved, when he leaned his head upon his bosom. And this shall be your lot: to see the Lamb in the midst of the throne.

———————— ❁ ————————

ALCORN ☞ Revelation 5:1-10 depicts a powerful scene in the present Heaven. God the Father, the ruler of Heaven, sits on the throne with a sealed scroll in his right hand. What's sealed—with seven seals, to avoid any possibility of the document being tampered with—is the Father's will, his plan for the distribution and management of his estate—the Earth, which includes its people. God intended for the world to be ruled by humans. But who will come forward to open the document and receive the inheritance?

John writes, "I wept and wept because no one was found who was worthy to open the scroll or look inside" (Revelation 5:4, NIV).

Because of human sin, mankind and the Earth have been corrupted. No one is worthy to take the role God intended for Adam and his descendants. Adam proved unworthy, as did Abraham, David, and all other persons in history. But just when it appears that God's design for mankind and the Earth will forever be thwarted, the text continues in high drama: "Then one of the elders said to me, 'Do not weep! See, the Lion of the tribe of Judah, the Root of David, has triumphed. He is able to open the scroll and its seven seals.' Then I saw a Lamb, looking as if it had been slain, standing at the center of the throne, encircled by the four living creatures and the elders. . . . He went and took the scroll from the right hand of him who sat on the throne. And when he had taken it, the four living creatures and the twenty-four elders fell down before the Lamb. . . . And they sang a new song, saying: 'You are worthy to take the scroll and to open its seals, because you were slain, and with your blood you purchased for God persons from every tribe and language and people and nation'" (Revelation 5:5-9, NIV).

Spurgeon tells a remarkable story about an experience early in his ministry:

> In 1857, a day or two before preaching at the Crystal Palace, I went to decide where the platform should be fixed; and, in order to test the acoustic properties of the building, cried in a loud voice, "Behold the Lamb of God, which taketh away the sin of the world." In one of the galleries, a workman, who knew nothing of what was being done, heard the words, and they came like a message from heaven to his soul. He was smitten with conviction on account of sin, put down his tools, went home, and there, after a season of spiritual struggling, found peace and life by beholding the Lamb of God.

It was on his deathbed that this man told the story of his conversion, the result of God speaking to him through a single verse of Scripture uttered by Spurgeon. When Spurgeon preached in that building a day or two later, it was to a crowd of 23,654 people. But such is the power of Christ, the Lamb of God, who takes away the sin not only of the world, not only of a potential 23,654 people, but of one lone man working in a building when a preacher came to test the acoustics. This man will be forever grateful that when Spurgeon stood up front to do a sound check, he did not simply count to ten!

REHEARSING FOR HEAVEN

✹

Excerpted from "Heavenly Worship"
Sermon #110, December 28, 1856

Music has a great power to connect us to God. There is music in Heaven, but if we want to be part of the great song, we'll need to start practicing the melody now.

> *The voice I heard was like the sound of harpists playing*
> *on their harps, and they were singing a new song before*
> *the throne and before the four living creatures and before*
> *the elders. No one could learn that song except the 144,000*
> *who had been redeemed from the earth.* REVELATION 14:2-3

———— ✹ ————

SPURGEON ☞ It is said of all the worshipers in Heaven that they learned the song before they went there. At the end of the third verse it is said, "No one could learn that song except the 144,000 who had been redeemed from the earth."

Brothers and sisters, we must begin Heaven's song here below, or else we shall never sing it above. The choirs of Heaven have all had rehearsals upon Earth before they sing in that orchestra. You think that, die when you may, you will go to Heaven without being prepared. No, Heaven is a prepared place for a prepared people, and unless you are "qualified . . . to share in the inheritance of the saints in light" (Colossians 1:12), you can never stand there among them.

If you were in Heaven without a new heart and a right spirit, you would be glad enough to get out of it, for Heaven, unless a man is heavenly himself, would be worse than Hell. A man who is unrenewed and unregenerate would be miserable in Heaven. There would be a song—he could not join in it. There would be a constant hallelujah, but he would not know a note. And besides, he would be in the presence of the Almighty, even in the presence of the God he hates, and how could he be happy there?

No, you must learn the song of Paradise here, or else you can never sing it. You must learn to sing, "Jesus, I love Thy charming Name, 'tis music to my ears."*

Take that thought, whatever else you forget. Treasure it up in your memory, and ask God for grace that here you may be taught to sing the heavenly song, that afterward in the land of the hereafter, in the home of the blessed, you may continually chant the high praises of the One who loved you.

ALCORN ✎ Music is a bridge between this world and another. Spurgeon says, "We must begin Heaven's song here below, or else we shall never sing it above. . . . Ask God for grace that here you may be taught to sing the heavenly song."

It's not that we should literally learn to sing; it's that our lives here on Earth should be so in rhythm with God's will and plan that music will well up in our souls long before we cross over to our eternal home. In other words, learn how to praise him now. James says, "Are any of you happy? You should sing praises" (James 5:13, NLT).

---

* From the hymn "Jesus, I Love Thy Charming Name," by Philip Doddridge, 1717.

The Bible is full of examples of people praising God with singing as well as with musical instruments. In the Temple—a representation of God's presence—288 people sang and played a variety of instruments (1 Chronicles 25:1-8). The psalmist instructs the people to praise God with trumpets, harps, lyres, tambourines, strings, flutes, and cymbals (Psalm 150, NIV). Hezekiah says, "We will sing with stringed instruments all the days of our lives in the temple of the LORD" (Isaiah 38:20, NIV).

Jesus sang with his disciples (Mark 14:26), and the apostle Paul instructs Christians to sing to the Lord (Ephesians 5:19).

On Earth, creative, artistic, and skilled people sing and play instruments to glorify God. The apostle John speaks of trumpets and harps in the present Heaven (Revelation 8:7-13; 15:2). If we'll have musical instruments in our pre-resurrected state, how much more should we expect to find them on the New Earth? Scripture songs will endure, but other music from Earth may also be preserved. Consider Handel's *Messiah*, Luther's "A Mighty Fortress Is Our God," the spiritual "Swing Low, Sweet Chariot," and Isaac Watts's "Alas! and Did My Savior Bleed?"

What about the thousands of great hymns and praise songs from every world culture? Imagine a remote tribe singing praises in a beautiful language you've never heard. God is honored by our thankfulness, gratitude, and enjoyment of him. And these acts of worship now prepare us for worship in Heaven. Have you ever sat in stunned silence after listening to music beautifully performed? If you're like me, you don't want to leave the presence of greatness. On the New Earth we, the redeemed, never will. Our great God will be above all, beneath all, and at the center of all. Our praise will well up from within us, and we will sing!

THE WORSHIP OF MULTITUDES

Excerpted from "Heavenly Worship"
Sermon #110, December 28, 1856

When you picture Heaven, do you cringe at the thought of an eternal, boring church service? That notion doesn't come from God but from the devil. We will worship in Heaven, but there will be nothing boring about it. It will be a magnificent celebration!

> *Worship the LORD in the splendor of holiness;*
> *   tremble before him, all the earth;*
> *   yes, the world is established; it shall never be moved.*
> *Let the heavens be glad, and let the earth rejoice,*
> *   and let them say among the nations, "The LORD reigns!"*
> *Let the sea roar, and all that fills it;*
> *   let the field exult, and everything in it!*
> *Then shall the trees of the forest sing for joy*
> *   before the LORD, for he comes to judge the earth.*
> *Oh give thanks to the LORD, for he is good;*
> *   for his steadfast love endures forever!*   1 CHRONICLES 16:29-34

SPURGEON 🖙 Have you never heard the sea roar? Have you never walked by the seaside when the waves were singing and when every little pebble-stone turned choir member to make up music to the Lord God of hosts? Have you never heard the sea roar out his praise, when the winds were reveling—perhaps singing the funeral lament of mariners, wrecked far out on the stormy deep, but far more likely exalting God with their hoarse voice?

Have you never heard the rumbling and booming of the ocean on the shore when it has been lashed into fury and has been driven upon the cliffs? If you have, you have a faint idea of the melody of Heaven. It is like "the voice of many waters" (Revelation 14:2, KJV).

But do not suppose that this is the whole of the idea. It is not the voice of one ocean but the voice of many that is needed to give you an idea of the melodies of Heaven. You are to suppose ocean piled upon ocean, sea upon sea—the Pacific piled upon the Atlantic, the Arctic upon that, the Antarctic higher still—and so ocean upon ocean, all lashed to fury and all sounding with a mighty voice the praise of God. Such is the singing of Heaven.

Or if the illustration fails to strike, take another—the mighty falls of Niagara. They can be heard at a tremendous distance, so awesome is their sound. Now suppose waterfalls dashing upon waterfalls, Niagaras upon Niagaras, each of them sounding forth their mighty voices, and you have got some idea of the singing of Paradise.

"I heard a voice from heaven, as the voice of many waters" (Revelation 14:2, KJV). Can you not hear it? Ah! If our ears were opened, we might almost perceive the song. I have thought sometimes on summer evenings, when the wind has come in gentle breezes through the forest, you might almost think it was the floating of some stray notes that had lost their way among the harps of Heaven and come down to us to give us some faint foretaste of that song which sounds out in mighty peals before the throne of the Most High.

But why so loud? The answer is because there are so many

there to sing. Nothing is more grand than the singing of multitudes. Many have been the persons who have told me that they could but weep when they heard you sing in this assembly, so mighty seemed the sound when all the people sang, "Praise God from whom all blessings flow."

And, indeed, there is something very grand in the singing of multitudes. I remember hearing twelve thousand sing on one occasion in the open air. Some of our friends were then present when we concluded our service with that glorious hallelujah. Have you ever forgotten it? It was indeed a mighty sound; it seemed to make Heaven itself ring again. Think, then, what must be the voice of those who stand on the boundless plains of Heaven and with all their might shout, "To him who sits on the throne and to the Lamb be blessing and honor and glory and might forever and ever!" (Revelation 5:13).

ALCORN ☜ Spurgeon called upon his people to remember times of singing powerful songs to God, perhaps on those occasions when thousands gathered together and lifted their voices to the Lord in unbridled praise. Have you experienced such times of corporate praise in your life? I have.

Most people know that we'll worship God in Heaven. But many of us don't grasp how thrilling that will be. Multitudes of God's people—of every nation, tribe, people, and language—will gather to sing praise to God for his greatness, wisdom, power, grace, and mighty work of redemption (Revelation 5:13-14). Overwhelmed by his magnificence, we will fall on our faces in unrestrained happiness and say, "Praise and glory and wisdom and thanks and honor and power and strength be to our God for ever and ever. Amen!" (Revelation 7:12, NIV).

People of the world are always striving to celebrate—they just lack ultimate reasons to do that (and therefore find lesser reasons). As Christians, we have those reasons—our relationship with Jesus and the promise of Heaven. "Look! God's dwelling place is now among the people, and he will dwell with them. They will be his people, and God himself will be with them and be their God" (Revelation 21:3, NIV). Does this excite you? If it doesn't, you're not thinking correctly.

We'll never lose our fascination for God as we get to know him better. The thrill of knowing him will never subside. To imagine that worshiping God could be boring is to impose on Heaven our bad experiences of so-called worship. Satan is determined to make church boring, and when it is, we assume Heaven will be also. But church can be exciting, and worship exhilarating. That's what it will be in Heaven. We will see God and understand why the angels and other living creatures delight to worship him.

Theologian Sam Storms writes, "We will constantly be more amazed with God, more in love with God, and thus ever more relishing his presence and our relationship with him. Our experience of God will never reach its consummation. . . . It will deepen and develop, intensify and amplify, unfold and increase, broaden and balloon."[24]

Christ's desire for us to see his glory should touch us deeply. What an unexpected compliment that the creator of the universe has gone to such great lengths, at such sacrifice, to prepare a place for us where we can behold and participate in his glory.

Will we ever tire of praising him? Augustine writes, "As there is nothing greater or better than God himself, God has promised us himself. God shall be the end of all our desires, who will be seen without end, loved without cloy, and praised without weariness."[25]

CREATION RESTORED

Excerpted from "A Heavenly Pattern for Our Earthly Life"
Sermon #1778

The annual sermon of the Baptist Missionary Society
Preached on Wednesday morning, April 30, 1884, at Exeter Hall

We live under the Curse, and so does the whole creation we inhabit. But through the ultimate outworking of Christ's redemptive work, God has a grand design to restore this Earth, not just to what it once was, but to something far greater still.

> *Your kingdom come, your will be done, on earth as it is in heaven.* MATTHEW 6:10

SPURGEON ⟜ If the prayer of our text had not been dictated by the Lord Jesus himself, we might think it too bold. Can it ever be that this Earth, a mere drop in a bucket, should touch the great sea of life and light above and not be lost in it? Can it remain Earth and yet be made like Heaven? Will it not lose its individuality in the process?

This Earth is subject to vanity, dimmed with ignorance, defiled with sin, furrowed with sorrow. Can holiness dwell in it as in Heaven? Our divine Instructor would not teach us to pray for impossibilities. He puts such petitions into our mouths as can be heard and answered.

Yet certainly this is a great prayer. It has the hue of the infinite about it. Has not this poor planet drifted too far away to be reduced to order and made to keep rank with Heaven? Can your will, O God, be done on Earth as it is in Heaven?

It can be, and it must be, for a prayer wrought in the soul by the Holy Spirit is ever the shadow of a coming blessing, and he who taught us to pray after this manner did not mock us with vain words. It is a brave prayer, which only Heaven-born faith can utter, yet it is not the offspring of presumption, for presumption never longs for the will of the Lord to be perfectly performed.

That our present obedience to God should be like that of holy ones above is not a strained and fanatical notion. It is not far-fetched, for Earth and Heaven were called into being by the same Creator.

The empire of the Maker comprehends the upper and the lower regions. "The heavens are the Lord's heavens" (Psalm 115:16), and "The earth is the Lord's and the fullness thereof" (Psalm 24:1). He sustains all things by the word of his power both in Heaven above and in the Earth beneath.

If Earth were of the devil and Heaven were of God, and two self-existent powers were contending for the mastery, we might question whether Earth would ever be as pure as Heaven. But we expect to see the dragon cast out from Earth as well as Heaven.

Why shouldn't every part of the great Creator's handiwork become equally radiant with his glory? He who made can remake. The curse which fell upon the ground was not eternal; thorns and thistles pass away. God will bless the Earth for Christ's sake even as once he cursed it for man's sake.

"Your will be done, on earth as it is in heaven" (Matthew 6:10).

It was so once. Perfect obedience to the heavenly upon this Earth will only be a return to the good old times which ended at the gate of Eden. There was a day when no gulf was dug between Earth and Heaven; there was scarcely a boundary line, for the God of Heaven walked in Paradise with Adam. All things on Earth were then pure and true and happy. It was the Garden of the Lord.

Alas, the trail of the serpent has now defiled everything.

The Lord is King, and he has never left the throne. As it was in the beginning so shall it be yet again. History shall, in God's providence, repeat itself. The temple of the Lord shall be among men, and the Lord God shall dwell among them. "Truth shall spring out of the earth; and righteousness shall look down from heaven" (Psalm 85:11, KJV).

"Your will be done, on earth as it is in heaven." It will be so at the last.

This much, however, seems plain—there is to be "new heavens and a new earth in which righteousness dwells" (2 Peter 3:13). This creation which now "has been groaning . . . in the pains of childbirth" (Romans 8:22), in sympathy with man, is to be brought forth from its bondage into the glorious liberty of the children of God.

ALCORN ☞ Spurgeon says, "God will bless the Earth for Christ's sake even as once he cursed it for man's sake." God has never given up on his original creation. Yet somehow we've managed to overlook an entire biblical vocabulary that makes this point clear: *Reconcile. Redeem. Restore. Recover. Return. Renew. Regenerate. Resurrect.* Each of these biblical words begins with the *re-* prefix, suggesting a return to an original condition that was ruined or lost. *Redemption* means to buy back what was formerly owned. Similarly, reconciliation means the restoration or reestablishment of a prior friendship or union.

These words emphasize that God always sees us in light of what he intended us to be, and he always seeks to restore us to that design. Likewise, he sees the Earth in terms of what he intended it to be, and he seeks to restore it to its original design.

It's impossible to understand the ministry of Christ without the larger view of redemption's sweeping salvage plan.

Religion professor Albert Wolters says it is "particularly striking that all of Jesus' miracles (with the one exception of the cursing of the fig tree) are miracles of restoration—restoration to health, restoration to life, restoration to freedom from demonic possession. Jesus' miracles provide us with a sample of the meaning of redemption: a freeing of creation from the shackles of sin and evil and a reinstatement of creaturely living as intended by God."[26]

God placed mankind on Earth to fill it, rule it, and develop it to God's glory. But that plan has never been fulfilled. Should we therefore conclude that God's plan was ill conceived, thwarted, or abandoned? No. These conclusions do not fit the character of an all-knowing, all-wise, sovereign God.

In *Creation Regained*, Wolters writes, "[God] hangs on to his fallen original creation and salvages it. He refuses to abandon the work of his hands—in fact, he sacrifices his own Son to save his original project. Humankind, which has botched its original mandate and the whole creation along with it, is given another chance in Christ; we are reinstated as God's managers on earth. The original good creation is to be restored."[27]

God hasn't changed his mind; he hasn't fallen back to Plan B or abandoned what he originally intended for us at the creation of the world. When Christ says, "Take your inheritance, the kingdom prepared for you since the creation of the world" (Matthew 25:34, NIV), it's as if he's saying, "This is what I wanted for you all along. This is what I went to the Cross for and defeated death to give you. Take it, rule it, exercise dominion over it, enjoy it. And in doing so, share my happiness."

God doesn't throw away his handiwork and start from scratch—instead, he uses the same canvas to repair and make more beautiful the painting marred by the vandal. God makes an even greater masterpiece out of what his enemy sought to destroy. And for that, we will worship and praise him for all eternity!

THE THIN PARTITION BETWEEN HEAVEN AND EARTH

Excerpted from "A Heavenly Pattern for Our Earthly Life" Sermon #1778, April 30, 1884

From our Earth-bound perspective, Heaven may seem impossibly far away. But in reality, Earth is merely a shadow of Heaven, a place made in the image of Heaven—and the two are much closer than we might think.

> *The one who conquers, I will make him a pillar in the temple of my God. Never shall he go out of it, and I will write on him the name of my God, and the name of the city of my God, the new Jerusalem, which comes down from my God out of heaven, and my own new name.* REVELATION 3:12

SPURGEON ☞ One day the material world shall become a proper temple for the Lord of hosts. The New Jerusalem shall come down from God out of Heaven, prepared as a bride is prepared for her husband. We are sure of this. Therefore, toward this consummation let us strive mightily, praying evermore, "Your will be done, on earth as it is in heaven" (Matthew 6:10).

There is an analogy between Earth and Heaven, so that the

one is the type of the other. You could not describe Heaven except by borrowing the things of Earth to symbolize it, and this shows that there is a real likeness between them.

What is Heaven? It is Paradise, or a garden. Walk amid your fragrant flowers and think of Heaven's bed of spices. Heaven is a kingdom: thrones, crowns, and palms are the earthly emblems of the heavenlies. Heaven is a city, and there again, you fetch your metaphor from the dwelling places of men. It is a place of "many mansions" (John 14:2, KJV)—the homes of the glorified. Houses are of Earth, yet is God our dwelling place.

The tables are spread here as well as there, and it is our privilege to go forth and bring in the vagabonds and the highwaymen, that the banqueting hall may be filled. While the saints above eat bread in the marriage supper of the Lamb, we do the like below in another sense.

Between Earth and Heaven there is but a thin partition. The home country is much nearer than we think. Heaven is by no means the far country, for it is the Father's house.

Heaven is, at any rate, so near that in a moment we can speak with him that is King of the place, and he will answer to our call. Before the clock shall tick again you and I may be there. Can that be a far-off country which we can reach so soon?

Oh, brothers and sisters, we are within hearing of the shining ones; we are nearly home. A little while and we shall see our Lord. Perhaps another day's march will bring us within the city gate. And even if another fifty years of life on Earth should remain, what is it but the twinkling of an eye?

It's clear enough that the comparison between Earth and Heaven is not far-fetched. If Heaven and Heaven's God be, in truth, so near to us, our Lord has set before us a homelike model taken from our heavenly dwelling place.

———— ✦ ————

ALCORN ⌘ In his seventeenth-century classic *Paradise Lost*, John Milton describes Eden as a garden full of aromatic flowers, delicious fruit, and soft grass, lushly watered. Like Spurgeon, Milton connects Eden with Heaven, the source of earthly existence, portraying Heaven as a place of great pleasures and the source of Earth's pleasures. In Milton's story, the angel Raphael asks Adam,

> *What if Earth*
> *Be but the shadow of Heav'n, and things therein*
> *Each to other like, more than on Earth is thought?*[28]

Though the idea of Earth as Heaven's shadow is seldom discussed, it's a concept that has biblical support. For example, we're told there are scrolls in Heaven, elders who have faces, martyrs who wear clothes, and even people with "palm branches in their hands" (Revelation 7:9-13). There are musical instruments in the present Heaven (Revelation 8:6), horses coming into and out of Heaven (2 Kings 2:11; Revelation 19:14), and an eagle flying overhead in Heaven (Revelation 8:13). Perhaps some of these objects are merely symbolic, but surely not all of them.

The book of Hebrews seems to say that we should see Earth as a *derivative* realm and Heaven as the *source* realm. If we do, we'll abandon the assumption that something existing in one realm cannot exist in the other.

God created Earth in the image of Heaven, just as he created mankind in his image. C. S. Lewis proposed that "the hills and valleys of Heaven will be to those you now experience not as a copy is to an original, nor as a substitute is to the genuine article, but as the flower to the root, or the diamond to the coal."[29] Why do we imagine that God would pattern Heaven's holy city after an earthly city, as if Heaven knows nothing of community and culture and has to get its ideas from our world? Isn't it more likely that earthly realities, including cities, are derived from heavenly counterparts?

We tend to start with Earth and reason up toward Heaven, when instead we should start with Heaven and reason down toward Earth. It isn't merely an accommodation to our earthly familial structure, for instance, that God calls himself a father and us children. On the contrary, he created father-child relationships to display his relationship with us, just as he created human marriage to reveal the love relationship between Christ and his bride (Ephesians 5:25-32). God's plan is that there will be no more gulf between the spiritual and physical worlds. There will be one cosmos, one universe united under one Lord—forever. This is where history is headed. This is the unstoppable plan of God.

When God walked with Adam and Eve in the Garden, Earth was Heaven's backyard. The New Earth will be even more than that—it will be Heaven itself. And those who know Jesus will have the privilege of living there. What Spurgeon calls the thin partition between Earth and Heaven will be forever broken through.

TO ENJOY HEAVEN IS TO ENJOY GOD

❀

Excerpted from "A Heavenly Pattern for Our Earthly Life"
Sermon #1778, April 30, 1884

If you've ever felt torn between a desire for Heaven and a desire for God, this text will calm your concerns. These yearnings are properly intertwined. The more we love God, the more we will love the place he has prepared for us. And the more we long for that place, the more we will find ourselves longing for him.

> *While we were living in the flesh, our sinful passions, aroused*
> *by the law, were at work in our members to bear fruit for death.*
> *But now we are released from the law, having died to that*
> *which held us captive, so that we serve in the new way of the*
> *Spirit and not in the old way of the written code.* ROMANS 7:5-6

——— ❀ ———

SPURGEON ☞ Heaven is the place of fellowship with God, and this is a blessed feature in its joy. But in this we are now participants for "indeed our fellowship is with the Father and with his Son Jesus Christ" (1 John 1:3). The fellowship of the Holy Spirit is with us all. It is our joy and our delight.

Having communion with the triune God—Father, Son, and Holy Spirit—we are uplifted and sanctified, and it is appropriate that the will of the Lord should be done by us on Earth as it is in Heaven (Matthew 6:10).

"Up there," says a brother, "they are all accepted, but here we are in a state of probation." Did you read that in the Bible? For I never did. A believer is in no state of probation. He has passed from death into life and shall never come into condemnation. We are already "accepted in the beloved" (Ephesians 1:6, KJV), and that acceptance is given in a way that can never be reversed. The Redeemer brought us up out of the horrible pit of depravity, and he has set our feet on the rock of salvation, and there he has established our paths. Therefore should we not, as the accepted of the Lord, do his will on Earth as it is done in Heaven?

"Yes," says one, "but Heaven is the place of perfect service, for his servants shall serve him." But is not this the place, in some respects, of a more extensive service still? Are there not many things which perfect saints above and holy angels cannot do? If we had a choice of a sphere in which we could serve God with widest range, we should choose not Heaven but Earth. There are no slums and overcrowded rooms in Heaven to which we can go with help, but there are plenty of them here. There are no jungles where missionaries may prove their unreserved consecration by preaching the gospel at the expense of their lives. In some respects this world has a preference beyond the heavenly state as to the extent of doing the will of God. Oh, that we were better men, and then the saints above might almost envy us! If we did but live as we should live, we might make Gabriel stoop from his throne and cry, "I wish I were a man!"

It is ours to be in the forefront in daily conflict with sin and Satan, and at the same time it is ours to bring up the rear, battling with the pursuing foe. God help us, since we are honored with so rare a sphere, to do his will on Earth as it is done in Heaven.

Then you say, "But Heaven is the place of overflowing joy." Yes, and have you no joy even now? A saint who lives near to God is so truly blessed that he will not be much astonished when he enters Heaven. He will be surprised to behold its glories more clearly, but he will have the same reason for delight as he possesses today. We live below the same life which we shall live above, for we are made alive by the same Spirit, are looking to the same Lord, and are rejoicing in the same security. Joy! Do you not know it? Your Lord says, "My joy may be in you, and that your joy may be full" (John 15:11). You will be larger vessels in Heaven, but you will not be fuller; you will be brighter, doubtless, but you will not be cleaner than you are when the Lord has washed you and made you white in his own blood.

Do not be impatient to go to Heaven. Hold lightly to the things of Earth, yet count it a great privilege to have a long life in which to serve the Lord on Earth. Mortal life is but a brief interval between the two eternities, and if we judged unselfishly and saw the needs of Earth, we might almost say, "Give us back the old days of human life, that through a thousand years we might serve the Lord in suffering and in reproach, as we cannot do in glory."

This life is but the entrance to glory. Clothe yourselves in the righteousness of Jesus Christ, for this is the royal robe of Earth and Heaven. Now begin the song which your lips shall sing in Paradise, or else you will never be admitted to the heavenly choirs.

None can unite in the music but those who have rehearsed it here below.

———— ❀ ————

ALCORN ☞ I'm often asked the following question: "Why talk about Heaven when we can just talk about Jesus?"

The answer, as I hope you're seeing from Spurgeon, is that

the two go together. The right kind of longing for Heaven *is* a longing for God, and longing for God is longing for Heaven. If we understand what Heaven is (God's dwelling place) and who God is, we will see no conflict between the two. A woman who longs to be reunited with her husband could well say, "I want to go home." By home, she means the place she shares with her beloved husband. There is no competition between Christ and Heaven. He loves Heaven, and he wants us to love Heaven and to long to be with him there.

Any bride in love with her husband wants to be with him more than anything. But if he goes away to build a beautiful place for her, won't she get excited about it? Won't she think and talk about that place? Of course. Moreover, he *wants* her to! If he tells her, "I'm going to prepare a place for you," he's implying, "I want you to look forward to it." Her love and longing for the place he's preparing—where she will live with him—is inseparable from her love and longing for her husband. If she says, "I love you but I have no interest in the place you're lovingly preparing for me," then in fact she is not loving him.

I've heard it said that God, not Heaven, is our inheritance. Well, God *is* called our inheritance (Psalm 16:5-6). But Heaven is also called our inheritance (1 Peter 1:3-4). Which is it? It's both. Every thought of Heaven should move our hearts toward God, just as every thought of God will move our hearts toward Heaven. That's why in Colossians 3:1 (NIV) Paul doesn't say to "set your hearts on Christ" but to "set your hearts on things above, where Christ is." To do one is to do the other.

A Christian leader once told me that people shouldn't look forward to Heaven; rather, they should look forward only to being with God. But Scripture knows nothing of this dichotomy. It says of Abraham that "he was looking forward to the city with foundations, whose architect and builder is God" (Hebrews 11:10, NIV). Or what about God's people, who are said to "desire a better country, that is, a heavenly one" (Hebrews 11:16)? Shouldn't they have been desiring just God, not Heaven? No! If they were doing something wrong, God wouldn't commend them for it in Scripture! In desiring Heaven, they *were* desiring God. In looking forward to Heaven, they *were* looking forward to seeing God.

Charles Spurgeon spoke a lot about Heaven, and he did so with passion. But isn't it clear that he was God centered in doing so? All the joys of Heaven are derived from the overflowing goodness of our God—to enjoy him will be to enjoy Heaven. To enjoy all the derivative goodness he shares with us in Heaven will be to enjoy God.

I've talked with people who erroneously assume that the wonders, beauties, adventures, and marvelous relationships of Heaven must somehow stand in competition with the One who has created them. But God has no fear that we'll get too excited about Heaven. After all, the wonders of Heaven aren't *our* idea, they're *his*. The wonders of the new heavens and New Earth will be a primary means by which God reveals himself and his love to us. When we love God's person, we will love God's place.

Picture Adam and Eve in the Garden of Eden. Eve says to Adam, "Isn't this place magnificent? The sun feels wonderful on my face. The blue sky's gorgeous. These animals are a delight. Try the mango—it's delicious!"

Can you imagine Adam responding, "Your focus is all wrong, Eve. You shouldn't think about beauty, refreshment, and mouth-watering fruit. All you should think about is God."

Adam would never have said that, because in thinking about these things, Eve *would be* thinking about God. Likewise, our enjoyment of what God has provided us should be inseparable from worshiping, glorifying, and appreciating him. God is honored by our thankfulness for his gifts and pleased by our anticipation of Heaven, that magnificent place the God-man is building with his own hands—the place for which he purchased our admission with his own blood.

HANDLING MONEY AS CITIZENS OF HEAVEN

❋

Excerpted from "A Heavenly Pattern for Our Earthly Life" Sermon #1778, April 30, 1884

When you get to Heaven, what kind of treasures will be waiting for you? Whether we realize it or not, what we do now with the money and possessions God has entrusted to us will have significant implications for all eternity.

> *No one can lay a foundation other than that which is laid, which is Jesus Christ. Now if anyone builds on the foundation with gold, silver, precious stones, wood, hay, straw—each one's work will become manifest, for the Day will disclose it, because it will be revealed by fire, and the fire will test what sort of work each one has done.* 1 CORINTHIANS 3:11-13

——— ❋ ———

SPURGEON ☞ Suppose that a man here has come fresh from Heaven. Some would be curious to see what his bodily form would be like. They would expect to be dazzled by the radiance of his countenance.

However, we will let that pass. We want to see how he would live. Coming newly from Heaven, how would he act? If he came

here to do the same as all men do on Earth, only after a heavenly
sort, what a father he would be, what a husband, what a brother,
what a friend! I would sit down and let him preach this morning,
most assuredly. And when he was done preaching, I would go
home with him and have a chat.

I should be very careful to observe what he would do with his
wealth. His first thought would be, if he had a shilling, to lay it out
for God's glory. "But," says one, "I have necessities to buy with my
shilling." So be it, but when you go, pray this: "Oh, Lord, help me
to lay it out to your glory." There should be as much piety in buying
your necessaries as in going to a place of worship.

I do not think this man coming fresh from Heaven would
say, "I must have this luxury; I must have this nice outfit; I must
have this grand house." But he would say, "How much can I save
for the God of Heaven? How much can I invest in the country
I came from?"

I am sure he would be pinching pennies to save money to serve
God with. And as he went about the streets and mingled with
ungodly men and women, he would be sure to find ways of getting at their consciences and hearts; he would always be trying to
bring others to the bliss he enjoyed.

Think that over, and live so—so as he did who really did come
down from Heaven. For after all, the best rule of life is, What
would Jesus do if he were here today and the world were lying
in the grip of the wicked one? If Jesus were in your business, if
he had your money, how would he spend it? For that is how *you*
ought to spend it.

Now think, my brother, you will be in Heaven very soon. Since
last year a great number have gone home; before next year many
more will have ascended to glory. Sitting up in those celestial
seats, how shall we wish that we had lived below?

It will not give any man in Heaven even a moment's joy to think that he gratified himself while here. It will give him no reflections suitable to the place to remember how much he amassed, how much he left behind to be quarreled over after he was gone. He will say to himself, "I wish I had saved more of my capital by sending it on before me, for what I saved on Earth was lost, but what I spent for God was really laid up where thieves do not break through and steal."

Oh, brothers, let us live as we shall wish we had lived when life is over; let us fashion a life which will bear the light eternal. Is it life to live otherwise?

<hr>

ALCORN ☞ Jesus spoke about where we should place our hearts and our treasures. "Do not store up for yourselves treasures on earth, where moths and vermin destroy, and where thieves break in and steal. But store up for yourselves treasures in heaven, where moths and vermin do not destroy, and where thieves do not break in and steal. For where your treasure is, there your heart will be also" (Matthew 6:19-21, NIV).

When we surrender our earthly treasures to care for the needy, love our neighbor, and further the purposes of God, what we do with money on Earth results in eternal rewards in Heaven. Giving transforms earthly treasures into heavenly ones.

We topple the money idol by giving away money and material things. Jesus always had two kingdoms in mind. He spoke of two treasuries, two perspectives, and two masters of those two kingdoms (Matthew 6:22-24). Each couplet presents two options and demands one choice. Unless the right choice is deliberately made and tenaciously clung to, we'll make the wrong choice by default.

There is truth in the old maxim "You can't take it with you." But when Jesus tells us to store up treasures in Heaven, he adds a new corollary. Essentially he is saying, "You can't take it with you, but you can send it on ahead."[30]

Material things on this fallen Earth just won't stand the test of time. Even if they escape moths and vermin and thieves, they cannot escape the coming fire of God that will consume the material world (2 Peter 3:7). Christ's primary argument against amassing material wealth isn't that it's morally wrong. It's that in light of the short time we spend here and the eternity we will spend in Heaven, storing up our treasures here instead of there is simply a poor investment.

Every day is one day closer to the day we will die. Therefore, those who store up treasures on Earth spend every day moving away from their treasures; they have reason to despair. Those who store up treasures in Heaven spend every day moving toward their treasures; they have every reason to rejoice.

REJOICING IN THE NEW CREATION

✺

Excerpted from "God Rejoicing in the New Creation"
Sermon #2211

Delivered on Lord's Day,
July 5, 1891, at the Metropolitan Tabernacle, Newington

As we see in so many Old Testament prophecies, God delights in transforming the old into the new. We can eagerly anticipate a new creation, a new Kingdom, a New Jerusalem, a New Earth.

> *Behold, I create new heavens and a new earth, and the former things shall not be remembered or come into mind. But be glad and rejoice forever in that which I create; for behold, I create Jerusalem to be a joy, and her people to be a gladness. I will rejoice in Jerusalem and be glad in my people; no more shall be heard in it the sound of weeping and the cry of distress.*
>
> ISAIAH 65:17-19

——— ✺ ———

SPURGEON ⚷ This passage, like the rest of Isaiah's closing chapters, will have its most complete fulfillment in the latter days when Christ shall come; when the whole company of his elect ones shall have been gathered out from the world; when the whole creation shall have been renewed; when new heavens and a New Earth shall be the product of the Savior's power; when,

forever and forever, perfected saints of God shall behold his face
and rejoice in him.

I hope and believe that the following verses actually describe
the condition of the redeemed during the reign of Christ upon
the Earth:

> "They shall build houses and inhabit them; they shall
> plant vineyards and eat their fruit. They shall not build
> and another inhabit; they shall not plant and another eat;
> for like the days of a tree shall the days of my people be,
> and my chosen shall long enjoy the work of their hands.
> They shall not labor in vain or bear children for calamity,
> for they shall be the offspring of the blessed of the LORD,
> and their descendants with them. Before they call I will
> answer; while they are yet speaking I will hear. The wolf
> and the lamb shall graze together; the lion shall eat straw
> like the ox, and dust shall be the serpent's food. They
> shall not hurt or destroy in all my holy mountain," says
> the LORD. (Isaiah 65:21-25)

But the work which is spoken of in the text is begun already among
us. There is to be a literal new creation, but that new creation has
commenced already, and I think, therefore, that even now we ought
to manifest a part of the joy. The Lord himself will rejoice, and we
who are in sympathy with him are exhorted and even commanded
to be glad. Let us not be slack in this heavenly duty.

Do you know what this work of creation is, which is here three
times promised in the words "I create. I create. I create."? It is
evidently a second creation, which is altogether to eclipse the first
and put it out of mind. Shall I tell the story?

The first creation was so fair that, when the Lord looked upon
it, with man as its climax and crown, he said, "It is very good"

(Genesis 1:31). But it failed in man, who should have been its glory. Man sinned, and in his sin he was so connected with the whole of the Earth that he dragged it down with him. The creation was made subject to vanity, and it groans in pain until now.

But the infinitely blessed God would not be defeated, and in infinite condescension he determined that he would make a new creation which should rise upon the ruins of the first. He resolved that under a second Adam something more than Paradise should be restored to the universe. He purposed that he would undo, through Jesus Christ, the Seed of the woman, all the mischief that had been wrought by the serpent. He has begun to undo this mischief and to work this new creation, and has so begun that he will never withdraw his hand until the work is done.

He has commenced it thus—by putting new hearts into as many as he has called by his Spirit, regenerating them and making them to become new creatures in Christ Jesus. These the apostle Paul tells us are a kind of firstfruits of this new creation. Our newborn spirits are the first ripe ears of corn out of a wonderful harvest that will come by and by. The saints' spirits are, first of all, newly created, but their bodily parts remain in the old creation. Hence we suffer pain, for though the Spirit is life because of righteousness, "the body is dead because of sin" (Romans 8:10).

By and by their bodies shall be newly created, when, from beds of dust and silent clay they shall rise into immortal beauty. The Resurrection will be to the body what regeneration is to the soul. When body and soul are thus created anew, the whole Earth around them, in which they dwell, shall be, at the same time, renewed also. And so God shall make the spirits, the minds, and the bodies of men all new.

Inasmuch as this ought to be the subject of joy, and the text invites us to it, I come to press upon you the sweet duty of present delight. Oh, when happiness is made a rule, when joy is made a command, I cannot but hope that God's people, to whom I am now speaking, will answer the call! Has gladness become the rule? Then we will gladly enough obey, and our hearts shall dance for joy.

———— ✲ ————

ALCORN ☞ God's people were right to expect the Messiah to bring an earthly kingdom. That's exactly what God had promised: "All kings shall fall down before Him; all nations shall serve Him" (Psalm 72:11, NKJV). An explicitly messianic passage tells us, "His rule will extend from sea to sea and from the River to the ends of the earth" (Zechariah 9:10, NIV).

God promises that he has a great future in store for Jerusalem, in which he will "extend peace to her like a river, and the wealth of nations like a flooding stream" (Isaiah 66:12, NIV). All the nations will bring their cultural treasures into a healed and peaceful Jerusalem, precisely as Revelation 21:24 portrays.

Isaiah 66 says that peace will come to Jerusalem and Jerusalem will become a center of all nations. The Lord says, "I . . . am about to come and gather the people of all nations and languages, and they will come and see my glory" (Isaiah 66:18, NIV). This prophecy is clearly fulfilled in the later chapters of Revelation. Jerusalem will again be a center of worship. Because this Jerusalem will reside on the New Earth, wouldn't we expect it to be called the New Jerusalem? That's exactly what it is called (Revelation 3:12; 21:2).

Scripture's repeated promises about land, peace, and the centrality of Jerusalem among all cities and nations will be fulfilled. On the New Earth, a host of Old Testament prophecies will ultimately be fulfilled. There the people of God will "possess the land [*erets*, the Earth] *forever*" (Isaiah 60:21, emphasis added).

Every time Jewish people greet one another with "Shalom"—loosely translated "Peace"—they express the God-given cry of the heart to live in a world where there's no sin, suffering, or death. There was once such a world, enjoyed by only two people and some animals. But there will again be such a world, enjoyed by all its inhabitants. Knowing that this glorious future awaits God's children can give us perspective and courage to face our present sufferings, which are very real, yet in view of eternity only fleeting.

GOD AS MASTER ARTIST

✦

Excerpted from "God Rejoicing in the New Creation"
Sermon #2211, July 5, 1891

When you see a purple sunset or a field full of daffodils or a breath-taking mountain vista, what does it tell you about the Creator? This world is far from perfect, but God has given us glimpses of himself—and of the New Earth—in the beauty of his creation.

> *When I look at your heavens, the work of your fingers,*
> *   the moon and the stars, which you have set in place,*
> *what is man that you are mindful of him,*
> *   and the son of man that you care for him?*
> *Yet you have made him a little lower than the*
> *   heavenly beings*
> *   and crowned him with glory and honor.*
> *You have given him dominion over the works of*
> *   your hands;*
> *   you have put all things under his feet,*
> *all sheep and oxen,*
> *   and also the beasts of the field,*
> *the birds of the heavens, and the fish of the sea,*
> *   whatever passes along the paths of the seas.*
> *O LORD, our Lord,*
> *   how majestic is your name in all the earth!*   PSALM 8:3-9

———— ✦ ————

SPURGEON ☞ Concerning the joy to which we are called, we would say, it is a joy in creation: "Behold, I create new heavens and a new earth. . . . I create Jerusalem to be a joy, and her people to be a gladness" (Isaiah 65:17-18).

I must confess that I think it a most right and excellent thing that you and I should rejoice in the natural creation of God. I do not think that any man is altogether beyond hope who can take delight in the nightly heavens as he watches the stars and feel joy as he treads the meadows all adorned with buttercups and daisies.

The man who is altogether bad seldom delights in nature. He cares little enough for the fields unless he can hunt in them, little enough for lands unless he can raise rent from them, little enough for living things except for slaughter or for sale. He welcomes night only for the indulgence of his sins, but the stars are not one half as bright to him as the lights that men have kindled. For him indeed the constellations shine in vain.

One of the purest and most innocent of joys, apart from spiritual things, in which a man can indulge is a joy in the works of God. I confess I have no sympathy with the good man, who, when he went down the Rhine, dived into the cabin that he might not see the river and the mountains, lest he should be absorbed in them and forget his Savior. I like to see my Savior on the hills and by the shores of the sea. I hear my Father's voice in the thunder and listen to the whispers of his love in the cadence of the sunlit waves. These are my Father's works, and therefore I admire them. I seem all the nearer to him when I am among them.

If I were a great artist, I should think it a very small compliment if my son came into my house and said he would not notice the pictures I had painted because he only wanted to think of me.

In doing so he would condemn my paintings, for if they were good for anything, he would rejoice to see my hand in them. Oh, but surely everything that comes from the hand of such a master artist as God has something of himself in it! The Lord rejoices in his works. Shouldn't his people do so? He said of what he had made, "It is very good." If a man thinks that what God has made is not very good, he cannot be very good himself. In this he contradicts his God. It is a beautiful world we live in.

There are lovely spots on this fair globe which ought to make even a blasphemer devout. I have said, among the mountains, "He who sees no God here is mad." There are things that God has made which overwhelm with a sense of his omnipotence: how can men see them and doubt the existence of the Deity? Whether you consider the anatomy of the body or the arrangement of the mighty heavens, you wonder that the scorner does not bow his head—at least in silence—and own up to the infinite supremacy of God.

ALCORN ⟜ I resonate with Spurgeon's story of the great artist whose son says he won't look at his father's paintings because he wants to think only of his father. There is a false spirituality among some believers who say "We must love God, not his gifts" and "We must worship the Creator, not his creation." They have forgotten the very purpose of God's gifts and what he created—to reveal his greatness to us! As Spurgeon says, we should look for God in what he has made and praise him for it.

If we take literally the earthly depictions of life on the New Earth, we can make a direct connection between our current lives and our future in Heaven. When I'm eating with people here, enjoying food and friendship, it's a bridge to when I'll be eating there, enjoying food and friendship at the banquet table God has prepared for us (Revelation 19:9). This isn't making a blind leap into a shadowy afterlife; it's just taking a few natural steps in the light Scripture has given us.

Every joy on Earth—including the joy of reunion—is an inkling, a whisper, of greater joy. The Grand Canyon, the Alps, the Amazon rain forests, the Serengeti Plain are but rough sketches of the New Earth.

All our lives we've been dreaming of the New Earth. Whenever we see beauty in water, wind, flower, deer, man, woman, or child, we catch a glimpse of Heaven. Just like the Garden of Eden, the New Earth will be a place of sensory delight, breathtaking beauty, satisfying relationships, and personal joy.

God himself prepared mankind's first home on Earth. "Now the LORD God had planted a garden in the east, in Eden; and there he put the man he had formed. The LORD God made all kinds of trees grow out of the ground—trees that were pleasing to the eye and good for food" (Genesis 2:8-9, NIV). The phrase "planted a garden" shows God's personal touch, his intimate interest in the creative details of our earthly home. If he prepared Eden so carefully and lavishly for the first people in the six days of Creation, imagine what he has fashioned in the place he has been preparing for us in the two thousand years since Jesus ascended from this world!

Just as Eden is our backward-looking reference point, the New Earth is our forward-looking reference point. Notice the Earth's restoration to Eden-like qualities prophesied in these passages:

> Indeed, the LORD will comfort Zion; He will comfort all her waste places and her wilderness He will make like Eden, and her desert like the garden of the LORD; joy and

gladness will be found in her, thanksgiving and sound of a melody. (Isaiah 51:3, NASB)

They will say, "This desolate land has become like the garden of Eden; and the waste, desolate and ruined cities are fortified and inhabited." (Ezekiel 36:35, NASB)

Instead of the thorn shall come up the cypress tree, and instead of the brier shall come up the myrtle tree. (Isaiah 55:13, NKJV)

Once we understand that all we love about the old Earth will be ours on the New Earth—either in the same form or another—we won't regret leaving all the wonders of the world we've seen or not yet seen. Why? Because we will yet be able to see them.

JOY IN THE NEW CREATION

Excerpted from "God Rejoicing in the New Creation" Sermon #2211, July 5, 1891

Emotions are not limited to our experience on Earth; in fact, we will feel things even more intensely in Heaven. The difference is that our feelings will be redeemed and no longer under the Curse. At last, our joy will be unbounded, our laughter unrestrained.

> *He set the earth on its foundations,*
>   *so that it should never be moved.*
> *You covered it with the deep as with a garment;*
>   *the waters stood above the mountains.*
> *At your rebuke they fled;*
>   *at the sound of your thunder they took to flight.*
> *The mountains rose, the valleys sank down*
>   *to the place that you appointed for them.*
> *You set a boundary that they may not pass,*
>   *so that they might not again cover the earth.*
> *You make springs gush forth in the valleys;*
>   *they flow between the hills;*
>   *they give drink to every beast of the field;*
>   *the wild donkeys quench their thirst.*
> *Beside them the birds of the heavens dwell;*
>   *they sing among the branches.*
> *From your lofty abode you water the mountains;*
>   *the earth is satisfied with the fruit of your work.*

You cause the grass to grow for the livestock
  and plants for man to cultivate,
that he may bring forth food from the earth
  and wine to gladden the heart of man,
oil to make his face shine
  and bread to strengthen man's heart.   PSALM 104:5-15

————————— ✻ —————————

SPURGEON ☞ These bodies, given life by his Spirit who
dwells in us and united to souls purified and refined, shall one
day tread upon an Earth delivered from the Curse, and shall
live beneath new heavens (Isaiah 65:17-19). Have they not new
desires? They shall tread a New Earth, for they have new ways.

In this first creation of God we still live in, there is something pure and elevating in enjoying God as the Creator of ordinary things. Much more is there something bright and pure and
spiritually exhilarating in rejoicing in God's higher works, in his
spiritual works, in his new creation. I believe that if a man feels
within him a new heart and rejoices in his new birth; if he sees
in others new and holier lives and rejoices in them; if he listens
to the preaching of the gospel and discovers in it new and better principles such as the old, worn-out world never could have
discovered—why, that man is a grace-filled man.

The heart that can rejoice in the new creation is a heart that
is itself renewed, or else it would not comprehend spiritual
things and could not rejoice in them. I invite you, therefore, dear
friends—you who see and know and somewhat appreciate the
new creation in its beginnings—to rejoice in it tonight.

It is a delightful thing that God should make a tree and bid it
come forth in the springtide with all its budding beauty. It is a far

better thing that God should take a poor, thorny heart like yours and mine and transform it till it becomes like the fir tree or the pine tree to his praise.

It is a charming sight when bulbs that have slept underground through the winter hold up their golden cups to be filled with the glory of the returning sun. But how much better that hearts that have lain dead in trespasses and sins should be moved by the secret touch of the Spirit of God to welcome the Sun of righteousness and to rejoice in him!

God's new creation, even in its beginnings here and now, is something to delight one's soul in. I pray you, delight yourselves therein. Behold, in the creation of a new heart, the manifest finger of God!

The attributes of God are to be seen in the visible creation, but they are to be seen in a brighter and superior light in the new creation. There is not one of the attributes of God which has no illustration under God's revelation of his grace. You shall be happy in your whole being if you can fully rejoice in that which God creates.

There is one reason why you are called upon to rejoice in it: namely, that you are a part of it. When the angels saw God making this world, they sang together and shouted for joy. But they were not a part of this lower world. They had nothing to do with man's estate, except as a matter of sympathy. But as for this new creation of our gracious God, you and I, beloved, who have believed in Jesus, are part of it.

That same grace, which has energized others into new life, has energized us. The same Spirit, who has given new principles and new desires to others, has given them to us also. The Father has regenerated us by the resurrection of Jesus Christ from the dead. We are the central beings of the new creation, and so let us rejoice in it with all our soul and mind and strength.

I know, when I lay sick and tormented in body, it seemed always to be such a joy to me that I myself—my inner self, my spirit—had been newly created. My nobler part could rise above the suffering and soar into the pure heavens of the spiritual realm. I said of this poor body, "You have not yet been newly created. The venom of the old serpent still taints you. But you shall yet be delivered. You shall rise again if you die and are buried, or you shall be changed if the Lord should suddenly come today. You, poor body, which drags me down to the dust in pain and sorrow, even you shall rise and be made remade in the redemption of the body. For the new creation has begun in me, with God's down payment of his Spirit."

Oh beloved, can't you rejoice in this? I encourage you to do so. Rejoice in what God is doing in this new creation! Let your whole spirit be glad! Leap down, you waterfalls of joy! Overflow with gladness! Let loose the torrents of praise!

ALCORN ⬅ Spurgeon spoke this message only six months before he died. For large parts of the previous twenty-two years he had lived with great physical pain. He suffered from gout, rheumatism, and Bright's disease (inflammation of the kidneys). He had even contracted smallpox. His first attack of gout came in 1869 at the age of thirty-five. His health became progressively worse so that nearly a third of his last twenty-two years were spent away from the pulpit, either suffering or convalescing. This physical hardship took a great emotional toll on him. At times he struggled with deep depression.

When he was twenty-two years old, Spurgeon preached for the first time in the Music Hall of the Royal Surrey Gardens because his own church wasn't large enough. The ten-thousand-person seating capacity was far exceeded by the crowds pressing in. Someone shouted, "Fire!" and panic took over. The stampede that followed resulted in many injuries and the deaths of seven people. Years later, Spurgeon said this horrifying incident resulted in taking him "near the burning furnace of insanity."

As no stranger to the suffering of body and mind, and with his own death looming, Spurgeon speaks here to the body, mind, and emotions about the promise of resurrection.

Many people have a hard time dealing with their emotions. In Heaven we'll be free to feel intensely. God has emotions, real ones, but they are not subject to whims and dips and inconsistencies. He made us in his image, so we have emotions too. But ours are under the Curse and subject to sin. In Heaven our emotions will be fully redeemed. There they will always be assets, never liabilities. Won't that be an incredible relief?

One writer says of our lives in Heaven: "We will live on a perpetual and exhilarating high akin to the feeling we have now when we shout 'Yes!' at a great victory."[31] I'm not so sure. Living constantly at a fever pitch of exhilaration would mean there wouldn't be special moments of greater joy. Certainly in Heaven we won't experience sadness, but that doesn't require each moment's joy to be exactly equal to the rest. We currently experience an ebb and flow to our lives. That rhythm is not part of being sinful but part of being human and finite—and we'll always be both of those, even when we're no longer subject to sin.

We know that people in Heaven have a range of feelings—all good ones. We're told of banquets, feasts, and singing. Remember, God assures those who mourn now, "You will laugh" (Luke 6:21, NIV). Laughter is an emotional response. Feasting, singing, and rejoicing involve feelings. Our present emotions are bent by sin, but they will be straightened forever when God removes the Curse.

Just two verses after Jesus promises, "You will laugh," he tells us precisely when the promise will be fulfilled: "Rejoice in that day and leap for joy, because great is your reward in heaven" (Luke 6:23, NIV).

Jesus doesn't say, "If you weep now, soon things on Earth will take a better turn, and then you'll laugh." Things won't always take a better turn on Earth. Just as our reward will come in Heaven, laughter (itself one of our rewards) will come in Heaven, compensating for our present sorrow. Yet by God's grace, we can laugh on Earth now, getting a head start on Heaven's laughter.

God won't only wipe away all our tears; he'll also fill our hearts with joy and our mouths with laughter. And just as laughter itself will be redeemed, so our emotions will be free at last of all sin, ill will, and lack of perspective.

If you are experiencing hard times that leave you physically and emotionally frail or drained, take heart. Spurgeon once said, "Glory be to God for the furnace, the hammer and the file. Heaven shall be all the more full of happiness because we have been filled with anguish here below; and Earth shall be better tilled because of our training in the school of adversity."

GODLY OPTIMISM

✳

Excerpted from "God Rejoicing in the New Creation"
Sermon #2211, July 5, 1891

Do you consider yourself an optimist or a pessimist? We have no guarantees about how our circumstances will turn out in this life. But when it comes to eternity, Christians have every reason for optimism—we know how the story will end!

> Open to me the gates of righteousness,
>   that I may enter through them
>   and give thanks to the LORD.
> This is the gate of the LORD;
>   the righteous shall enter through it.
> I thank you that you have answered me
>   and have become my salvation.
> The stone that the builders rejected
>   has become the cornerstone.
> This is the LORD's doing;
>   it is marvelous in our eyes.
> This is the day that the LORD has made;
>   let us rejoice and be glad in it.   PSALM 118:19-24

———— ✳ ————

SPURGEON ⚸ It is a present and a lasting joy: "Be glad and rejoice forever in that which I create" (Isaiah 65:18). Be now glad, and now rejoice: it is a present joy. Take a delightful interest in that which God is now creating in the spiritual realm. Be glad in anything that the Lord has created in you. Has he created in you so much of the new life as to have produced conviction, repentance, faith in Christ, hope in the promise, longing for holiness? Be glad in this even if you have other circumstances pressing upon you, and causing you to be heavy of heart.

Though you might be mourning because you are so sickly, yet be glad that you are born again. If somewhat distressed because you are so poor, yet be glad that you are a child of God and have a place in the new family of love. Let the old things go and grasp the new, the heavenly. The old creation—bear with it a little longer; for the time of your redemption from its bondage draws near. Find your joy where God would have you find it, namely, in that part of your nature which is new. Rejoice in the new principles, the new promises, the new covenant, and the blood of the new covenant which are yours—all of them. The Kingdom of God is within you; rejoice in it.

Find your joy in the new creation of God as you see it in others. The angels rejoice over one sinner who repents (Luke 15:10); surely you and I ought to do so! Try and do good, and bring others to Christ. And when a soul shows signs of turning to its God, let that be your joy.

"Be glad and rejoice *forever*." As long as you live, there will be something in the new creation that shall be to you a fresh joy and delight. Heaven will only enlarge this same joy. Be glad forever, because God will ever be creating something fresh in which you may be glad.

It may be said of the joy we ought to feel that it is a joy God intended for us: "Behold, I create Jerusalem to be a joy, and her people to be a gladness" (Isaiah 65:18). He has made the new city, the new people, the new world to be a source of joy.

We ought to be glad and rejoice forever in that which God creates. Ours is a heritage of joy and peace. My dear brothers and sisters, if anybody in the world ought to be happy, we are the people.

How large our obligations! How boundless our privileges! How brilliant our hopes!

What should make us miserable? Sin? That is forgiven. Affliction? That is working our good. Inward corruptions? They are doomed to die. Satanic temptations? We wear an armor which they cannot penetrate. We have every reason for delight, and we have moreover this command for it: "Delight yourself in the LORD, and he will give you the desires of your heart" (Psalm 37:4). May God bring us into that blessed condition and keep us there!

God intends not only that we should have joy but also that we should spread it among others. He intends that wherever we go we should be light bearers and set other lamps shining.

Help the widow, comfort the fatherless, assist the poor, cheer up the disheartened, tell the glad news to the weary heart. In the Father's hands, in Christ's hands, in the Spirit's hands, seek to break the prisoner's fetters and to bring him out into the light of liberty. You, too, are anointed to proclaim liberty to the captives (Luke 4:18). May the God of infinite mercy help you and me so to do!

When you and I see sin subdued, do we not feel happy? Whenever the news comes to me that a man has been reclaimed from drunkenness or a woman has been saved from the streets, or when I hear of a hard-hearted sinner repenting, I rejoice in the Lord. Conversion days are our high holidays. But eventually there will be a still greater joy. We shall enter into Heaven, and there will be joy among the angels and joy in our hearts over God's new creation work, which will proceed at a glorious rate. The day shall come when Christ shall reign from pole to pole. And what a joy that will be!

We shall indeed be glad in that which God creates, as the islands of the sea shall ring out his praise! Then Christ the Lord will come, and what joy and rejoicing there will be in that day when he has fully fashioned the New Earth and the new heavens.

Nothing prophesied should be dreaded by us. There is nothing foretold by a prophet or beheld in a vision that can alarm the Christian. He can stand serenely on the brink of the great eternity and say, "Come on! Let every event foretold become a fact! Pour out your vials, you angels! Fall, you star called Wormwood! Come, Gog and Magog, to the last great battle of Armageddon!" Nothing is to be feared by those who are one with Jesus. To us remains nothing but joy and rejoicing. For God has made his people a joy, and he has made them for rejoicing.

ALCORN ☙ Charles Spurgeon wrote this sermon near the end of his life, at a time when he was seldom able to preach. In the printed version of the sermon, distributed around the world later that same week, this statement was added, helping readers appreciate the context in which Spurgeon spoke his powerful words about joy and rejoicing:

> Mr. Spurgeon has been very seriously ill, but the prayers of the Lord's people, at the Tabernacle and elsewhere, have been graciously answered on his behalf. Hearty thanksgiving should be rendered to the Lord for his partial recovery, joined with earnest supplication for his complete restoration to health and strength. Both Mr. and Mrs. Spurgeon are deeply grateful for the widespread sympathy that has been manifested during this season of severe trial.

Spurgeon's partial recovery was brief. That he died only six months later makes all the more potent his words about the grounds for rejoicing.

Secular optimists are merely wishful thinkers. Discovering the present payoffs of optimism, they conduct seminars and write books on thinking positively. Sometimes they capitalize on optimism by becoming rich and famous. But then what happens? They eventually get old or sick, and when they die, if they haven't trusted Christ, they go to Hell forever. Their optimism is an illusion, for it fails to take eternity into account.

The only proper foundation for optimism is the redemptive work of Jesus Christ. Any other foundation is sand, not rock. It will not bear the weight of eternity.

If we build our lives on the redemptive work of Christ, we should all be optimists. Why? Because even our most painful experience in life is but a temporary setback. Our pain and suffering may or may not be relieved in this life, but they will certainly be relieved in the next. That is Christ's promise—no more death or pain. He will wipe away all our tears (Revelation 21:4). He took our sufferings on himself so that one day he might remove all suffering from us, which is the biblical foundation for our optimism. No Christian should be a pessimist. We should be realists, focused on the reality that we serve a sovereign and gracious God. Because of the certainty of Christ's atoning sacrifice and his promises, biblical realism is optimism.

We see the optimism in Spurgeon's teaching on the biblical text about God having made us for joy and rejoicing. Knowing that it will be relieved doesn't make suffering easy, but it does make suffering bearable. Hope allows us to have joy even in the midst of suffering. Paul says, "I rejoice in my sufferings" (Colossians 1:24), and James says, "Count it all joy, my brothers, when you meet trials of various kinds" (James 1:2). The apostles didn't enjoy their suffering, but they rejoiced in the midst of it because they trusted God's sovereign plan.

Our optimism is not that of the "health and wealth gospel," which claims that God will spare us from suffering here and now. Peter says, "Rejoice insofar as you share Christ's sufferings, that you may also rejoice and be glad when his glory is revealed" (1 Peter 4:13). Christ's future glory, in which we will participate, is the reason for our present rejoicing in the midst of suffering.

Anticipating Heaven doesn't eliminate pain, but it does lessen it and put it in perspective. Meditating on Heaven is a great pain reliever. Suffering and death are temporary conditions—they are but a gateway to eternal life of unending joy. The biblical doctrine of Heaven is about the future, but it has tremendous benefits here and now. If we grasp this truth, it will shift our center of gravity and radically change our perspective on life. This is what the Bible calls *hope*, a word used six times in Romans 8:20-25. In this passage, Paul says that all creation longs for our resurrection and the world's coming redemption.

Don't place your hope in favorable circumstances, which cannot and will not last. Place your hope in Christ and his promises. He *will* return. We *will* be resurrected to life on the New Earth. We *will* behold God's face and joyfully serve him forever and ever. We *will*, in fact, live happily ever after. That is not a fairy tale; it is the blood-bought promise of almighty God.

JOINING HEAVEN'S CELEBRATION NOW

❋

Excerpted from "God Rejoicing in the New Creation"
Sermon #2211, July 5, 1891

For all eternity we will rejoice in the redemptive work of Christ. But we don't have to wait until then to start the party. We should get a head start on Heaven by celebrating here and now.

> *The LORD your God is in your midst,*
> *a mighty one who will save;*
> *he will rejoice over you with gladness;*
> *he will quiet you by his love;*
> *he will exult over you with loud singing.* ZEPHANIAH 3:17

---------- ❋ ----------

SPURGEON ☞ I have often said to you that when the Lord made the material world, there was not much in it to touch his spiritual nature, so he simply spoke and said, in plain prose, "It is good." That was all: he said it was good. But when the Lord makes the new heavens and a New Earth, when he is finished, when the bride of Christ shall be brought to him, "he will exult over you with loud singing." Did you ever get into your hearts the idea of the Lord God singing? God singing over his church, over his Jerusalem, over his new creation! God singing!

I can understand the angels singing for joy over God's work, but here is God singing over his own work. I will tell you something more wonderful than that: it is that you should be a part of that work and that God should sing over you! Is he not the Father, and does not the Father sing over his prodigal son who wandered but came home? Is he not the Savior, and will not the Savior, who bought us with his blood, sing over us who were purchased with his agonizing death? He is the Spirit, and shall not the Spirit, who has striven with us and wrought all our works in us, sing when his work is done and we are sanctified?

Father, when your eternal purposes are all fulfilled, you will rejoice over your people! Son of God, Redeemer, when all your agonies shall have been rewarded in the salvation of your redeemed, you will rejoice over your chosen! Holy Spirit, when all your bending down and indwelling within us shall have accomplished its design, you will rejoice in your people!

Come now, beloved, rejoice in unity with the divine heart! When the father found his son, he made the whole household merry. Shouldn't we be merry? When the woman found her coin, she called together her friends and neighbors and said, "Rejoice with me, for I have found the coin that I had lost" (Luke 15:9). Shall not we rejoice with the Spirit over the lost that has been found? When the shepherd brought home his sheep, he said, "Rejoice with me, for I have found my sheep that was lost" (Luke 15:6). Come, then, rejoice with the Father, rejoice with the Son, rejoice with the Spirit.

And if the Lord God, as the Trinity in unity, invites us to be glad and rejoice in that which he creates, let us not hold back! Let us sing of his matchless love and new-creating power and infinite wisdom. I am sure you will sing—you must sing even now—if you know yourselves to be part of this celebration.

Nobody will ever rejoice in this new-creating work of God

while he is rejoicing in his own works and trusting in himself and boasting his own merits. It is a sign of grace when a man is sick of self and is in harmony with God. When he ceases to rejoice in what he can do and comes to rejoice in what God has done and is doing, then a change has been made in him.

Some of you are trying to save yourselves and make yourselves right before God. It cannot be done. You must be made new by a power you have not within yourself—by a divine power. You must be born again, and this is the work of God, not your work. We shall know this heavenly work is begun in you when you cease from rejoicing in anything that you are or can be of yourselves and then shall you with us rejoice in that which God creates in you.

ALCORN ☞ Spurgeon sees God's rejoicing over us, his redeemed people, as a prompting for us to rejoice: "Come now, beloved, rejoice in unity with the divine heart!" Sick as he was throughout his lifetime, Spurgeon emphasized all the more our reason to celebrate. God's redemptive work is what we will celebrate for eternity, and Spurgeon encourages his church not to delay the celebration, but to commence it here and now.

Always concerned about the souls of those who heard him preach, and even more concerned in light of his failing body and the likelihood that he wouldn't preach much longer, Spurgeon addresses those who haven't yet grasped the truth of the gospel: "Some of you are trying to save yourselves and make yourselves right before God. It cannot be done. You must be made new by a power you have not within yourself—a divine power. You must be born again, and this is the work of God, not your work."

Only God can offer forgiveness. Only God can empower people to receive his offer.

You may think that you don't deserve forgiveness after all you've done. That's exactly right. *No one* deserves forgiveness. If we deserved it, we wouldn't need it. That's the point of grace. On the cross, Jesus experienced the Hell we deserve so that for eternity we can experience the Heaven we don't deserve.

Once forgiven, we can look forward to spending eternity in Heaven with Christ and our spiritual family (John 14:1-3; Revelation 20:11–22:6). We need never fear that God will say, "If I'd known you did *that*, I wouldn't have let you into Heaven." Every sin is washed away by the blood of Christ. God has seen us at our worst and still loves us. No sin is bigger than the Savior. If God weren't willing to forgive sin on the basis of Christ's sacrifice, Heaven would be empty.

Our intimate link with Christ in his redemptive work makes us inseparable from him, even now. As we walk with him and commune with him in this world, we experience a faint foretaste of Heaven's delights and wonders.

Though it's true that Christ is with us and within us while we're on Earth, it also works in the other direction—we're so closely united with Christ that we are seated with him in Heaven: "God raised us up with Christ and seated us with him in the heavenly realms in Christ Jesus" (Ephesians 2:6, NIV).

Notice that the following description, written to believers alive on Earth, is in the present perfect (not future) tense, so it expresses a completed action: "You have come to Mount Zion, to the city of the living God, the heavenly Jerusalem. You have come to thousands upon thousands of angels in joyful assembly, to the church of the firstborn, whose names are written in heaven. You have come to God, the Judge of all, to the spirits of the righteous made perfect" (Hebrews 12:22-23, NIV).

In a metaphysical sense, as God's children we've already

entered Heaven's community. By seeing ourselves as part of the heavenly society, we can learn to rejoice *now* in what Heaven's residents rejoice in. They rejoice in God, his glory, his grace, and his beauty. They rejoice in repentant sinners, the faithfulness and Christlikeness of believers, and the beauty of God's creation. They rejoice in the ultimate triumph of God's Kingdom and the coming judgment of sin.

Heaven, then, isn't only our future home. It's our home already, waiting just over the next hill. If we really grasp this truth, it will have a profound effect on our holiness. People who see themselves seated with Christ in Heaven—in the very presence of a God to whom the angels cry out, "Holy, holy, holy" (Isaiah 6:3; Revelation 4:8)—won't spend their days viewing Internet pornography or gossiping on the phone or cutting corners on business deals.

No wonder the devil is so intent on keeping us from grasping our standing in Christ!

Have you confessed your sins to the Father? asked Christ to forgive you? responded to the Spirit's prompting and placed your trust in Christ's death and resurrection on your behalf? asked Jesus to be your Lord and empower you to follow him? "Seek the LORD while he may be found; call upon him while he is near" (Isaiah 55:6).

Wouldn't it be tragic if you read this book about Heaven but didn't end up going there?

AND THE SEA WAS NO MORE

❋

Excerpted from *Morning and Evening*
December 19 (evening)

If you've ever spent a leisurely day on a golden beach or sailed across the vast ocean or observed the beauty of God's underwater creatures, you may be surprised that John, taken in a vision to the far future, says that on the New Earth "the sea was no more." But when we take a closer look, we see that perhaps there will be great bodies of water there after all.

> *I saw a new heaven and a new earth, for the first heaven and the first earth had passed away, and the sea was no more. And I saw the holy city, new Jerusalem, coming down out of heaven from God, prepared as a bride adorned for her husband. And I heard a loud voice from the throne saying, "Behold, the dwelling place of God is with man. He will dwell with them, and they will be his people, and God himself will be with them as their God. He will wipe away every tear from their eyes, and death shall be no more, neither shall there be mourning, nor crying, nor pain anymore, for the former things have passed away."* REVELATION 21:1-4

———— ❋ ————

SPURGEON ⌛ "And the sea was no more." Scarcely could we rejoice at the thought of losing the glorious old ocean. The

new heavens and the New Earth are none the fairer to our imagination, if, indeed, there is literally to be no great and wide sea,
with its gleaming waves and shelly shores.

Is not the text to be read as a metaphor, tinged with the preju-
dice with which the Eastern mind universally regarded the sea in
the olden times? A real physical world without a sea is mournful
to imagine; it would be an iron ring without the sapphire which
made it precious.

There must be a spiritual meaning here. In the new dis-
pensation there will be no division—the sea separates nations
and separates peoples from each other. To John in Patmos the
deep waters were like prison walls, shutting him out from his
brethren and his work; there shall be no such barriers in the
world to come. Leagues of rolling waves lie between us and
many a kinsman whom tonight we prayerfully remember, but
in the bright world to which we go, there shall be unbroken
fellowship for all the redeemed family. In this sense there shall
be no more sea.

The sea is the emblem of change; with its ebbs and flows, its
glassy smoothness and its mountainous waves, its gentle murmurs
and its tumultuous roarings, it is never long the same. Slave of
the fickle winds and the moon, its instability is proverbial. In this
mortal state we have too much of this; Earth is constant only in
its inconstancy, but in the heavenly state all mournful change
shall be unknown, and with it all fear of storm to wreck our hopes
and drown our joys.

No tempest howls along the peaceful shores of Paradise. Soon
shall we reach that happy land where partings and changes and
storms shall be ended! Jesus will always keep us above water there.
Are we in him or not? This is the grand question.

———————— ✵ ————————

ALCORN ☞ When we read about no more seas, we think of God's doing away with the oceans that cover most of his beloved Earth. We think there will be no more surfing, tide pools, snorkeling, and fun on the beach, and there will be no more wonderful sea creatures. From Spurgeon's viewpoint, and most of us would feel the same way, that sounds like bad news. While Spurgeon's meditation from *Morning and Evening* is very brief, in tribute to him I'd like to further develop from Scripture the issue he raised, making a case I think he might have appreciated.

When Revelation 21:1 says that "the sea was no more," we must try to understand *sea* in exactly the way the writer and his readers of the book of Revelation would have understood it. To the great majority of them, the sea was devoid of the romantic properties many of us associate with it. Rather, the sea consisted of those vast, icy, treacherous, stormy waters that separated families, destroyed ships, and drowned loved ones. It posed a constant threat, with its great creatures that swallowed up seafarers and its salt waters that poisoned people on the open sea who craved freshwater. With that understanding, "no more sea" was a reassuring prospect!

Author and Bible teacher Steven Lawson points out, "To the ancient peoples, the sea was frightful and fearsome, an awesome monster, a watery grave. They had no compass to guide them in the open sea. On a cloudy day, their ships were absolutely lost without the stars or the sun to guide them. Their frail ships were at the mercy of the tempestuous ocean's fearsome, angry storms. The loss of human life in the sea was beyond calculation."[32]

But let's look at a larger picture. Of course, it was God who created the seas (Genesis 1:9-10). Like everything else he made, they were very good (Genesis 1:31). But the Curse had a devastating effect on creation, including the ocean waters.

Even if Revelation 21:1 is a literal promise of "no more ocean," this doesn't necessarily mean the absence of large bodies of water. Revelation tells us a great river flows right through the capital city (22:1-2). How much more water will there be outside the city? Flowing rivers go somewhere. Some of the world's lakes are huge and sealike, so theoretically the New Earth could have even larger lakes. Huge lakes could, in effect, be freshwater oceans.

Ezekiel 47 speaks of the water flowing from the Temple, which parallels the water flowing from the Messiah's throne on the New Earth (Revelation 22). Ezekiel says, "I saw a great number of trees on each side of the river" (47:7, NIV). Then he is told, "This water flows toward the eastern region and goes down into the Arabah, where it enters the Dead Sea. When it empties into the sea, the salty water there becomes fresh. Swarms of living creatures will live wherever the river flows. There will be large numbers of fish, because this water flows there and makes the salt water fresh; so where the river flows everything will live" (Ezekiel 47:8-9, NIV).

Ezekiel 47 goes on to say, "Fruit trees of all kinds will grow on both banks of the river. Their leaves will not wither, nor will their fruit fail. Every month they will bear fruit, because the water from the sanctuary flows to them. Their fruit will serve for food and their leaves for healing" (verse 12). This promise is applied directly to the New Earth in Revelation 22:2. Since this is clearly a New Earth passage, it appears that the reference to "no more sea" in Revelation 21 may simply mean "no more sea as we now know it."

In *The Voyage of the Dawn Treader*, one of C. S. Lewis's books in the classic Chronicles of Narnia series, the talking mouse Reepicheep is on a quest to find Aslan's country, which can be seen as a type of Heaven. As Reepicheep nears Aslan's country, the salt water transforms into pure, refreshing, life-giving "sweet" water. Will something similar happen on the New Earth?

Romans 8 suggests that "the whole creation," not just human beings, will experience a renewed existence on the New Earth. Since most of the Earth's species live in the ocean, it seems likely some of them will be re-created. Surely it would be easy for God to enable today's saltwater creatures to live in freshwater. I think this is more than wishful thinking, and there are biblical grounds to support Spurgeon's instinct that there may well be bodies of water of some sort on God's New Earth.

I've done enough snorkeling and diving to know it's exhilarating and worshipful to be immersed in the God-made undersea world. Twenty years ago I took out a boat and went snorkeling with one of my daughters and some friends. Suddenly, in very deep water, we heard the melodic sounds of whales calling to one another. We floated, nearly motionless, as the sounds grew louder and louder. We found ourselves absorbed in musical beauty and power that defied words. I felt indescribably close to God during that almost magical experience.

While I can't be sure, I believe we will swim and dive in large bodies of water, perhaps without tanks or masks, opening our eyes wide and playing with God's creatures of the deep. And if not, of course, God will have still better things in store for us, all of them for his glory and our delight!

THE FUTURE
REIGN OF CHRIST

❄

Excerpted from *Morning and Evening*
December 24 (evening)

In our present reality, we find ourselves in the midst of a battle between good and evil, between God's armies and the devil's strongholds. But we have the assurance that one day Christ will secure the ultimate victory . . . and that we will reign forever with him!

> *The glory of the LORD shall be revealed, and all flesh shall*
> *see it together, for the mouth of the LORD has spoken.*

ISAIAH 40:5

——— ❄ ———

SPURGEON ☞ We anticipate the happy day when the whole world shall know Christ; when the gods of the heathen shall be cast to the moles and the bats . . . and the crescent of Mohammed shall wane, never again to cast its baleful rays upon the nations; when kings shall bow down before the Prince of Peace, and all nations shall call their Redeemer blessed.

Some despair of this. We know that the world and all that is therein is one day to be burned up, and afterward we look for new heavens and for a New Earth. But we cannot read our Bibles without the conviction that

> *Jesus shall reign where'er the sun*
> *Does his successive journeys run.* *

We are not discouraged by the length of his delays; we are not disheartened by the long period he allots to the church in which to struggle with little success and much defeat.

We believe that God will never allow this world, which has once seen Christ's bloodshed upon it, to be always the devil's stronghold. What a shout shall that be when men and angels shall unite to cry, "Hallelujah! For the Lord our God the Almighty reigns" (Revelation 19:6).

What a satisfaction will it be in that day to have had a share in the fight, to have helped to break the arrows of the bow, and to have aided in winning the victory for our Lord!

Happy are they who trust themselves with this conquering Lord, and who fight side by side with him, doing their little in his name and by his strength! How unhappy are those on the side of evil! It is a losing side, and to lose is to lose and to be lost forever. Whose side are you on?

ALCORN ☞ Our present purpose is inseparable from God's eternal purpose for us to rule the Earth forever as his children and heirs. That truth is expressed in the Westminster Shorter Catechism's defining statement: "Man's chief end is to glorify God, and to enjoy him forever."[33] We will glorify God and find

---

* From the hymn "Jesus Shall Reign," by Isaac Watts, 1719.

joy in him as we do what he has made us to do: serve him as resurrected beings and carry out his plan for developing a Christ-centered, resurrected culture in a resurrected universe.

The apostle Paul describes Christ's reign—present and future—this way: "As in Adam all die, so in Christ all will be made alive. But each in turn: Christ, the firstfruits; then, when he comes, those who belong to him. Then the end will come, when he hands over the kingdom to God the Father after he has destroyed all dominion, authority and power. For he must reign until he has put all his enemies under his feet" (1 Corinthians 15:22-25, NIV).

Most scholars agree that the point of this passage is not that Christ will someday cease to reign but that his reign will continue after his enemies are conquered and judged. (According to royal tradition, when a prince handed over to his father a kingdom he had conquered, the king commonly entrusted rulership of that kingdom back to his son.)

When everything is put under his feet—when God rules all and mankind rules the Earth as kings under Christ, the King of kings—at last all will be as God intends. The period of rebellion will be over forever, and the universe, along with all who serve Christ, will participate in the Master's joy!

Today, while the battle still rages, may we join Spurgeon in his call to fight on the right side, looking to that day when humans and angels unite to cry, "Hallelujah! For the Lord our God the Almighty reigns" (Revelation 19:6).

HOMESICK FOR EDEN

✸

Excerpted from "Plenteous Redemption"
Sermon #351

Delivered on Sabbath evening,
December 16, 1860, at Exeter Hall, Strand

People are not the only ones who suffer under the Curse; the Earth itself experiences the devastation of the Fall in the form of thorns, blights, and disasters of every kind. But one day Christ will come to restore the Earth to its rightful state. Then it will no longer groan in the pains of childbirth but will live in joyful celebration of its new life, which will never again be taken from it.

> *Thorns and thistles it shall bring forth for you; and you shall*
> *eat the plants of the field. By the sweat of your face you shall*
> *eat bread.* GENESIS 3:18-19

——— ✸ ———

SPURGEON ☞ After the first humans sinned, God cursed the Earth.

When Christ came into the world, evil people twisted a crown made of the cursed thorn and put it on his head and made him king of the Curse, and in that day he purchased the redemption of the world from its curse. I believe, and I think it is warranted by Scripture, that when Christ shall come a second time, this world will become everywhere as fertile as the Garden of Paradise used to be.

I believe that the Sahara, the literal desert, shall one day blossom like Sharon* and rejoice like the garden of the Lord. I do not conceive that this poor world is to be a forlorn planetary wanderer forever.

Once mighty creatures far different from ours stalked through the Earth, and I firmly believe that luxurious vegetation such as this world once knew shall be restored to us and that we shall see again a garden such as we have not known—one no more cursed with blight and mildew, with no more parched withering. We shall see a land like Heaven itself—

> *Where everlasting spring abides,*
> *And never withering flowers.*†

When Christ returns he shall do this.

In the day of the Fall, too, animals for the first time received their ferocious temperament and began to fall on each other. If I read Scripture rightly, I find that the wolf shall lie down with the kid, and that the lion shall eat straw like the ox, and that the weaned child shall put his hand on the serpent's den. I do believe that in the millennial years that are coming, and coming soon, there shall be known no more devouring lions, no bloodthirsty tigers, no creatures that shall devour their kind. God shall restore to us again, and even to the beasts of the field, the blessing which Adam lost.

And, my friends, there is a worse curse than that which has fallen on this world. It is the curse of ignorance and sin. That, too, is to be removed.

---

* The Plain of Sharon is a coastal area in Israel near the Mediterranean Sea. It was known in biblical times as being particularly fertile.
† From the hymn "There Is a Land of Pure Delight," by Isaac Watts, 1707.

See that planet? It is whirling along through space—bright and glorious. Hear the morning stars sing together because this globe is made their new sister? That is the Earth; she is bright now.

See that shadow sweep across her? What caused it? The planet is dimmed, and on her path there lies a sorrowful shadow. I am speaking, of course, metaphorically. See there the planet; she glides along in dark night. The day has not come when that planet shall renew her glory, but it is hurrying full speed.

As the serpent escapes its swamp and leaves it behind, so that planet has slipped its clouds and shone forth bright as it was before. Do you ask who has done it? Who has cleared away the mist? Who has taken away the darkness? "I have done it," says Christ, the Sun of righteousness. "I have scattered darkness and made that world bright again."

Look, I see a New Heaven and a New Earth, where righteousness dwells. This world is now covered with sin, ignorance, mistakes, idolatry, and crime. The day is coming when the last drop of blood shall be drunk by the sword. God shall cause wars to cease to the ends of the Earth. The day is coming—oh, that it were now!—when the feet of Christ shall tread this Earth. Then down shall go idols from their thrones, down superstitions from their pinnacles; then slavery shall cease; then crime shall end; then peace shall spread its tranquil wings over all the world. And then shall you know that Christ has died for the world and that Christ has won it.

"The whole creation," says Paul, "has been groaning together in the pains of childbirth" (Romans 8:22). Groaning for what? Groaning and waiting for the redemption, when this world shall be washed of all her sin. Her curse shall be removed, her stains taken away, and this world shall be as fair as when God first formed her from his mind, as when, like a glowing spark,

forged from the anvil by the eternal hammer she first flashed
in her orbit. This Christ *has* redeemed; this Christ *shall* most
assuredly redeem.

———— ❋ ————

ALCORN ⇌ We are homesick for Eden. We're nostalgic for
what is implanted in our hearts. It's built into us, perhaps at a
genetic level. We long for what the first man and woman once
enjoyed—a perfect and beautiful Earth and free and unstained
relationships with God, one another, animals, and the environment. Every attempt at human progress has been an attempt to
overcome what was lost in the Fall. If God's plan were merely to
take mankind to the present Heaven or to a Heaven that is the
dwelling place of spirit beings, there would be no need for new
heavens and a New Earth. Why refashion the stars of the heavens
and the continents of the Earth? God could just destroy his original
creation and put it all behind him. But that is not his plan.

Upon creating the heavens and the Earth, God called them
"very good" (Genesis 1:31). Never once has he renounced his
claim on what he made. He isn't going to abandon his creation;
he's going to restore it. We won't go to Heaven and leave Earth
behind. Rather, God will bring Heaven and Earth together into
the same dimension, with no wall of separation, no armed angels
to guard Heaven's perfection from sinful mankind (Genesis 3:24).
God's perfect plan is "to bring unity to all things in heaven and
on earth under Christ" (Ephesians 1:10, NIV).

Albert Wolters says, "Redemption is not a matter of an addition of a spiritual or supernatural dimension to creaturely life that
was lacking before; rather, it is a matter of bringing new life and
vitality to what was there all along. . . . The only thing redemption

adds that is not included in the creation is the remedy for sin, and that remedy is brought in solely for the purpose of recovering a sinless creation. . . . Grace *restores* nature, making it whole once more."[34]

We have never seen the Earth as God made it. Our planet as we know it is a shadowy, halftone image of the original. But it does whet our appetites for the New Earth, doesn't it? If the present Earth, so diminished by the Curse, is at times so beautiful and wonderful and if our bodies, so diminished by the Curse, are at times overcome with a sense of the Earth's beauty and wonder, then how magnificent will the New Earth be?

Spurgeon speaks eloquently of what awaits this Earth: "Her curse shall be removed, her stains taken away, and this world shall be as fair as when God first formed her from his mind."

Earth cannot be delivered from the Curse by being destroyed. It can be delivered only by being *resurrected*. Christ's resurrection is the forerunner of our own, and our resurrection will be the forerunner of the Earth's.

THE PRESENT HEAVEN

Excerpted from "Justification and Glory"
Sermon #627

Delivered on Sunday morning,
April 30, 1865, at the Metropolitan Tabernacle, Newington

Do you know what happens when you die? Have you ever wondered whether there's a delay between Earth and Heaven, whether there is a preparation that needs to take place before your soul meets God? Spurgeon addresses these topics.

> *Those whom he predestined he also called, and those whom he called he also justified, and those whom he justified he also glorified.* ROMANS 8:30

SPURGEON ⟢ The moment that the believing soul leaves the body, that justified soul is in glory. We know that there is no preparatory process for it to pass through.

The case of the dying thief is to the point. He was no saint. He had not for many years performed works of moral superiority by which he reached perfection and could claim that the gates should be opened to him. He was a sinner up to the very last moment, and the only good deeds that we ever read of his doing were when he claimed Christ as Lord and rebuked his fellow thief for slandering the Savior. Yet hear the words: "Today you will be with me in Paradise" (Luke 23:43).

Nor is this the only instance. We find, when Lazarus died, according to the parable, that he was carried by angels into Abraham's bosom, a place of unspeakable rest and delight which the rich man greatly envied (Luke 16:19-31). Stephen expected the Lord Jesus to receive his spirit (Acts 7:59), and the apostle Paul was torn between life and death, being willing "to depart and be with Christ" (Philippians 1:23). He evidently did not anticipate any delay between Earth and Heaven, for he says, "We know that while we are at home in the body we are away from the Lord" (2 Corinthians 5:6).

Perhaps that word *Paradise*, which Christ uses to describe the state of disembodied spirits, may be a help to us in judging of the condition of the blessed. Paradise is a place of perfect peace, of sinlessness, of rest, of enjoyment, and freedom from evil.

Eden! Oh, how shall we talk of its glories long since faded? Let us, however, remember its winding walks among trees loaded with luscious fruits. Let us remember the glory of its rising and its setting sun, the immortality, the peace, the joy, the love, the brightness which our first parents enjoyed in their naked innocence.

The glory of Paradise was that God walked there in the cool of the evening with his creatures. The glory of Heaven is that "they will need no light of lamp or sun, for the Lord God will be their light" (Revelation 22:5) and that the days of their mourning shall be ended when God wipes away all tears from their eyes (Revelation 21:4) and the Lamb leads them to the springs of living water (Revelation 7:17). God is with them to be their God, and they are with him to be his happy people at his right hand, where there are pleasures forevermore.

The day will come when the Lord Jesus will descend from

Heaven with a shout, with the trump of the archangel and the voice of God. Some think that this descent of the Lord will be post-millennial—that is, after the thousand years of his reign. I cannot think so. I conceive that the advent will be premillennial—that he will come first and then will come the Millennium as the result of his personal reign upon Earth.

But this much is the fact: Christ will suddenly come, come to reign and to judge the Earth in righteousness. Now at that time, those of us who are alive and remain shall have no preference over them that sleep. It is true "we shall not all sleep, but we shall all be changed, in a moment, in the twinkling of an eye, at the last trumpet. For the trumpet will sound, and the dead will be raised imperishable, and we shall be changed" (1 Corinthians 15:51-52).

ALCORN   What we usually think of when we hear the word *Heaven* is what theologians call the *intermediate* Heaven. I prefer the term *present* Heaven, but in any case, it means the place God's children go when we die. It's the place we'll live until our bodily resurrection. As Spurgeon demonstrates from Scripture, our spirits go there immediately upon death. It is a conscious existence, even though it's an unnatural condition in that we are without our earthly bodies.

Our Christian loved ones who have died are now in this present Heaven. This is not the same as purgatory—some believe there is such a place where people pay the price for their own sin to become ready for Heaven, but it's not a biblical concept. The Bible teaches that Christ paid the complete price for our atonement, and thus we can do nothing to add to it.

Often we think of going to Heaven as departing from our earthly realm into an angelic realm to live with God where he is. But the Bible says that one day God will bring us down from his place to live with him in *our* place, the New Earth (Revelation 21:3).

In the present Heaven, God's people are with Christ and full of joy, and their lives there are "better by far" (Philippians 1:23, NIV). But still it is not their permanent home. They're looking forward to what Paul argues in 1 Corinthians 15 is vitally important to all of us: bodily resurrection.

RAISED IMPERISHABLE

❋

Excerpted from "Justification and Glory"
Sermon #627, April 30, 1865

Some people fear that we'll be absorbed into a sort of anonymous spiritual state in the afterlife. But nothing could be further from the truth. You will have the same soul and the same body for all eternity. You will be more you in Heaven than ever before.

> *I tell you this, brothers: flesh and blood cannot inherit the kingdom of God, nor does the perishable inherit the imperishable. Behold! I tell you a mystery. We shall not all sleep, but we shall all be changed, in a moment, in the twinkling of an eye, at the last trumpet. For the trumpet will sound, and the dead will be raised imperishable, and we shall be changed.*
>
> 1 CORINTHIANS 15:50-52

———— ❋ ————

SPURGEON ✐ My body is the same body that it was ten years ago, but I am told, and I believe it, that there is not a particle of matter in my body now that was in it ten years ago. Yet its identity is not disturbed thereby. Protect the seed, as God doubtless will, and you have protected identity. And though when we rise it will not be as flesh and blood, for "flesh and blood cannot inherit the kingdom of God, nor does the perishable inherit the imperishable" (1 Corinthians 15:50), yet it shall be the same body.

There are heavenly bodies and earthly bodies, and the glory is not the same, for there is the glory of the sun, the glory of the moon, and the glory of the stars. So I may have the same body—the same for identity, and yet as to its components, especially as to its qualities of weakness, mortality, and corruption, it may be as distinct and changed as light is distinct and changed from darkness.

Oh, my brothers and sisters, let this be an assured truth to us that we do not put the body into the grave to lose it. We put the body there as the chemist puts gold into the furnace; it shall come out the same as to its gold, but the dross shall be left behind. All that was precious in the fabric shall remain; that which was corruptible, defiled, sinful, shall have passed away.

According to our belief, the soul will then return to the body. There will be a joyful meeting. Soul and body often quarrel here, but they always hate to part, which proves how true is the marriage between them.

Will Christ reign? We shall reign with him. Will he judge the Earth? "Do you not know that the saints will judge the world?" (1 Corinthians 6:2). Will he be ruler over cities? He will make us ruler over many cities. All the splendor and triumph, the victory and shouting, we shall have a share in. And when the grand hallelujah shall go up from Earth and land and sea, and from the depths that are under the Earth, our tongues shall sing the tremendous chorus and our ears shall be partakers of the ever-blessed harmony.

Well, and what then? Then comes the end, when Jesus shall have delivered up the Kingdom to God the Father. Will the Earth be renovated and refitted as a New Heaven and a New Earth?

Will that New Jerusalem that is to come down at the coming of Christ be the future abode of saints?

This much we know: that we shall be forever with the Lord. With Christ shall be the Heaven of believers forever, according to the Lord's own prayer: "Father, I desire that they also, whom you have given me, may be with me where I am, to see my glory" (John 17:24). Life in its fullest sense; life with emphasis; eternal life; nearness to God; closeness to the divine heart; a sense of his love shed abroad in all its fullness; likeness to Christ; fullness of communion with him; abundance of the Spirit of God; being filled with all the fullness of God. An excess of joy; a perpetual influx of delight; perfection of holiness; no stain nor thought of sin; perfect submission to the divine will; a delight and agreement in, and conformity to, that will; absorption, as it were, into God— the creature still the creature but filled with the Creator to the brim; serenity caused by a sense of safety; continuance of heavenly service; an intense satisfaction in serving God day and night; bliss in the society of perfect spirits and glorified angels; delight in the retrospect of the past, delight in the enjoyment of the present, and delight in the prospect of the future; something ever new and evermore the same; a delightful variety of satisfaction and a heavenly sameness of delight; clear knowledge; absence of all clouds; ripeness of understanding; excellence of judgment; and, above all, an intense vigor of heart and the whole of that heart set upon him whom our eyes shall see to be altogether lovely!

I have looked at the crests of a few of the waves as I see them breaking over the sea of immortality; I have tried to give you the names of a few of the peaks of the long alpine range of glory. But, ah! Where are my words, and where are my thoughts? "No eye has seen, nor ear heard, nor the heart of man imagined, what God has prepared for those who love him" (1 Corinthians 2:9).

Our only satisfaction in thinking of it is that "these things God has revealed to us through the Spirit" (1 Corinthians 2:10). May his Spirit dwell in you and give you foretastes of the rest which remains, foretastes of the eternal banquet where Christ will drink the new wine with us in his heavenly Father's Kingdom.

ALCORN ⟜ Did you enjoy that 161-word sentence of Spurgeon's, the one with all the semicolons? In it he beautifully articulates scores of wonderful things awaiting us in Heaven.

When Spurgeon says, "We do not put the body into the grave to lose it," he is referring to the continuity of our personhood from this life to the next—the same soul and eventually the same body, for all eternity.

What makes you *you*? It's not only your body but also your memory, personality traits, gifts, passions, preferences, and interests. In the final resurrection, I believe all these facets will be restored and amplified, untarnished by sin and the Curse. You will be *you* in Heaven. Who else would you be? If Bob, a man on Earth, is no longer Bob—with his unique identity, history, and memory—when he gets to Heaven, then, in fact, Bob did not go to Heaven. The resurrected Jesus did not become someone else; he remained who he was before his resurrection: "It is I myself" (Luke 24:39).

Jesus said to his disciples, "*I* will not drink from this fruit of the vine from now on until that day when *I* drink it new with *you* in my Father's kingdom" (Matthew 26:29, niv, emphasis added). Think of it—in the world to come, the same Jesus will drink the same kind of wine with the same disciples.

If we weren't ourselves in the afterlife, then we couldn't be held accountable for what we did in this life. The Judgment would be meaningless. If Barbara is no longer Barbara, she can't be rewarded or held accountable for anything Barbara did. She'd have to say, "But that wasn't who I am now." The doctrines of judgment and eternal rewards depend on our retaining our distinct identities from this life to the next.

Bruce Milne writes, "We can banish all fear of being absorbed into the 'All' which Buddhism holds before us, or reincarnated in some other life form as in the post-mortem prospect of Hinduism. . . . The self with which we were endowed by the Creator in his gift of life to us, the self whose worth was secured forever in the self-substitution of God for us on the cross, *that self* will endure into eternity. Death cannot destroy us."[35]

Some of us read, "You may participate in the divine nature" (2 Peter 1:4, NIV) and imagine that we will lose our personal identities, but that's a page out of Eastern religions, not the Bible. This verse is actually saying not that we'll be indistinguishable from God but that we're covered with Christ's righteousness. We'll participate in God's holiness yet fully retain our God-crafted individuality.

Our personal histories and identities will endure from one Earth to the next. "As the new heavens and the new earth that I make will endure before me,' declares the LORD, 'so will your name and descendants endure'" (Isaiah 66:22, NIV).

A PREPARED PLACE
FOR A PREPARED PEOPLE

❋

Excerpted from "A Prepared Place for a Prepared People"
Sermon #2751

Delivered on Lord's Day evening,
May 25, 1879, at the Metropolitan Tabernacle, Newington

There is a certain longing for home that will be fulfilled only on the New Earth. Even now, Jesus is preparing our true home for us—a literal, physical place we can anticipate. As Spurgeon puts it, this place will be "the best of the best"!

> *The King will say to those on his right, "Come, you who are blessed by my Father, inherit the kingdom prepared for you from the foundation of the world."* MATTHEW 25:34

——————— ❋ ———————

SPURGEON ☞ My real text is not from the Bible; it is one of those Christian proverbs which are not inspired in words but the spirit of which is inspired: "Heaven is a prepared place for a prepared people."

Yet I shall have two texts from the Scriptures. The first will be our Savior's words to his disciples, "I go to prepare a place for you" (John 14:2), from which we learn that "Heaven is a prepared place." And the second will be Paul's words to the Colossians: "Giving thanks to the Father, who has qualified you to share in the inheritance of the saints in light" (Colossians 1:12), from which we learn that there is a prepared people, a people made fit to be partakers of the inheritance which Christ has gone to prepare for them.

When we get to Heaven, we shall know—perhaps it may take us a long while to find it all out—but we shall know and discover throughout eternity what he meant when he said, "I go to prepare a place for you."

I do not profess to be able to explain our Lord's words, but I am going simply to make a few remarks upon them. First, I ask you to notice that Heaven is already prepared for Christ's people. Christ has told us that, when he comes in his glory, he will say to those on his right hand, "Come, you who are blessed by my Father, inherit the kingdom prepared for you from the foundation of the world" (Matthew 25:34). So there is an inheritance which the Father has already prepared for the people whom he gave to his Son, and this inheritance is reserved for them.

But if it was prepared from the foundation of the world, how can it be said to be prepared by Christ? The explanation is probably that it was provided in the eternal arrangements of Jehovah that there should be a suitable place for his people to dwell in forever. He made the pavilion of the sun, and he gave the stars their appointed positions. Would he forget to prepare a place for his people?

He gave to angels their places, and even to fallen spirits he has appointed a prison house. So he would not forget, when he was arranging the entire universe, that a place would be needed for the heirs of grace.

Therefore, in purpose and plan and decree, long before God had laid the foundations of this poor world and the morning stars had sung together over creation's six days' work accomplished, he prepared a place for his people. It was not actually prepared, but it was in the purpose and plan of the eternal mind. Therefore it might be regarded as already done.

Our Lord Jesus Christ has gone to Heaven, he says, that he may prepare a place for his servants. We may be helped to form some idea of what he means by this expression if we just think a little about it. First, I am sure that must be a very great and glorious place which needs Christ to prepare it. If we do not know all that he means, we can get at least this much out of his declaration: he spoke this world into being. It was not; but he said, "Be," and it was at once made. Then he spoke it into order, into light, into life, into beauty. He had but to speak and what he willed was done.

But now that he is preparing a place for his people, he has gone to Heaven on purpose to do it. He used to stand still here on Earth and work miracles. But this was a miracle that he could not perform while he was here. He had to go back to his home above in order to prepare a place for his people. What sort of place, then, must it be that needs Christ himself to prepare it?

He might have said, "Angels, prepare a mansion for my beloved." He might have spoken to the firstborn sons of light and said, "Pile a temple of jewels for my chosen." But no, he leaves not the work to them.

Brothers and sisters, he will do it well, for he knows all about us. He knows what will give us the most happiness—and what will best develop all our spiritual faculties forever. He loves us so well that, as the preparing is left to him, I know he will prepare us nothing second rate, nothing that could possibly be excelled.

We shall have the best of the best, and much of it; we shall have all that even his great heart can give us.

———— ✸ ————

ALCORN ☞ When it comes to our eternal home, we often imagine that this world as it now is, under the Curse, is our ultimate home. C. S. Lewis writes, "Our Father refreshes us on the journey with some pleasant inns, but will not encourage us to mistake them for home."[36]

Theologian Donald Bloesch suggests, "Our greatest affliction is not anxiety, or even guilt, but rather homesickness—a nostalgia or continual yearning to be at home with God."[37]

Jesus says, "In my Father's house are many rooms. . . . I go to prepare a place for you" (John 14:2). The word *place* is singular, but *rooms* is plural. This suggests that Jesus has in mind for each of us an individual dwelling that is a smaller part of the larger place.

The word *room* is cozy and intimate. The term *house* can also be viewed as "estate"; either way, it suggests spaciousness. That is Heaven: a place both spacious and intimate. Some of us enjoy coziness, being tucked away in a private space. Some of us enjoy largeness, the freedom of a wide-open space. Most of us enjoy both at various times. The New Earth will offer both.

Think of it. The Carpenter from Nazareth promised us, his bride, that he was going to prepare a place for us and would one day come to take us there. Carpenters build things and fix things. Long ago he built a universe that later went wrong, and he's going to fix it. He has qualities that come in handy in building projects—including being all-knowing and all-powerful.

When this life is over—and particularly when we arrive on the

New Earth—God's children will truly be able to come home for the first time. Because our home in Heaven will never burn, flood, or be blown away, we'll never have to wonder whether home will still be there when we return. The new heavens and the New Earth will never disappear. They'll give a wonderful permanence to the word *home*.

If Heaven is truly our home, we should expect it to have the good qualities we associate with home. *Home* as a term for Heaven isn't simply a metaphor. It describes an actual, physical place—a place promised and built by our Bridegroom; a place we'll share with loved ones; a place of fond familiarity and comfort and refuge; a place of marvelous smells and tastes, fine food, and great conversation; a place of contemplation and interaction and opportunity to express the gifts and passions that God has given us.

Though many of us affirm a belief in the resurrection of the dead, we don't understand its implications in terms of *place*. Our truncated doctrine of the Resurrection, which fails to include eternal life on the New Earth, dresses up men and women in bodies, then gives them no place to go! This unbiblical stereotype of the eternal Heaven as a vague habitation of disembodied spirits hurts us far more than we realize. We envision an immaterial and utterly unfamiliar Heaven that might work for angels or ghosts but for human beings would be the *opposite* of home. No wonder there is such ambivalence and uneasiness about Heaven in our churches.

Bible scholar W. Graham Scroggie puts it this way: "Future existence is not a purely spiritual existence; it demands a life in a body, and in a material universe."[38]

When we see the particular place he has prepared for us— not just for mankind in general but for us in particular—we will rejoice. We will realize it is truly the perfect home, tailor made for us.

As Spurgeon says, "Brothers and sisters, he will do it well, for he knows all about us. He knows what will give us the most happiness. . . . I know he will prepare us nothing second rate, nothing that could possibly be excelled. We shall have the best of the best, and much of it; we shall have all that even his great heart can give us."

NOT JUST A STATE OF BEING

Excerpted from "A Prepared Place for a Prepared People"
Sermon #2751, May 25, 1879

When some people think of Heaven, they imagine disembodied souls floating around among the clouds. But that's not the picture the Bible paints of the New Earth. We, as both physical and spiritual beings, will inhabit a literal Heaven on Earth. The Bible says so!

He arose and came to his father. But while he was still a long way off, his father saw him and felt compassion, and ran and embraced him and kissed him. And the son said to him, "Father, I have sinned against heaven and before you. I am no longer worthy to be called your son." But the father said to his servants, "Bring quickly the best robe, and put it on him, and put a ring on his hand, and shoes on his feet. And bring the fattened calf and kill it, and let us eat and celebrate. For this my son was dead, and is alive again; he was lost, and is found." And they began to celebrate. LUKE 15:20-24

SPURGEON ☞ When the prodigal son came back to his father, there was the preparation of the fatted calf, the music and dancing, and the gold ring and the best robe. Then what will be the preparation when we come home not as prodigals but as the bride prepared for her husband or as the beloved children, without spot or wrinkle or any such thing, returning to the Father, who shall see his own image in us and rejoice over us with singing?

It is a grand place that Christ prepares for us, for never was there such a royal host as he is. It is a mansion of delights that Christ prepares, for never was there another architect with thought so magnificent as his. Never were other hands so skilled at quarrying living stones and putting them one upon another. This thought ought to cheer us much. It must be something very wonderful that Christ prepares as a suitable place for his people.

And it must be something very sweet when it is finally prepared. An honored guest cannot help observing that he is being treated with special recognition. That guest room appears newly furnished, and everything that was possible has been put there to do him honor. If you were such a guest, you would take pleasure in the fact that so much had been prepared for you. When you get to Heaven, you will be astonished to see this and that and the other joy that was prepared for you because Christ thought of you and provided just what you would most appreciate.

You will be no stranger there, beloved. You will say, "There has been over here a hand that helped me when I was in distress. There has been over here, I know, an eye that saw me when I was wandering far from God. There has been, in this place, a heart that cared for me—that very same heart that loved me and bled for me down below upon the cross. It is my Savior who has prepared this place for me!"

If Christ is preparing Heaven, then it will be what our Scotch friends call "a bonny place." And if it be prepared for us, when we get there, it will exactly fit us. It will be the very Heaven we wanted—a better Heaven than we ever dreamed of. A better Heaven than we ever pictured, even when our imagination took its loftiest flights. The Heaven of God, and yet a Heaven exactly suited to the happy creatures we shall then be.

Jesus Christ has gone to prepare a place for his people. Does this not refer, if we keep it to its strict meaning, to the ultimate place of God's people? You see, Christ mentions a place, not a state. And he speaks of going to it and coming back from it: "If I go and prepare a place for you, I will come again and will take you to myself, that where I am you may be also" (John 14:3). Christ is speaking of himself as fully human, without any figurative meaning to his words. He means that he is going, with all his human nature, away from this world and that he is going to prepare a place for us, intending to come again with all that glorified human nature to receive us to himself.

This does not mean his spiritual coming in death. I am persuaded that the clear meaning of the words involves our Lord's second advent, when he will come to receive us. Not you or me as individuals who, one by one, will enter into rest, but to receive his whole church into the place he shall then have prepared for her. After the Resurrection, you must remember, we shall need a place to live in—a literal, material place of residence. For these bodies of ours will be alive as well as our spirits, and they will need a world to live in, a New Heaven and a New Earth.

Christ is preparing a place not for disembodied spirits, for they are already before the throne of God perfectly blessed. No, a place for the entire personhood of his people, when spirit, soul, and body shall be again united and we as complete people shall receive the adoption—that is, the redemption of our bodies. Then the complete personhood of every believer shall be perfected in the glory of Christ.

———————— ❋ ————————

ALCORN ⟜ We shouldn't be surprised when Scripture speaks of Heaven in tangible and material ways. Nor should we feel it's necessary to take such references figuratively. Spurgeon says, "After the Resurrection, you must remember, we shall need a place to live in—a literal, material place of residence. For these bodies of ours will be alive as well as our spirits, and they will need a world to live in, a New Heaven and a New Earth."

Countless interpretations of Heaven have stemmed from an erroneous view of the eternal state, with the result that passages with clear, straightforward meanings, such as eating and drinking together in the eternal Kingdom, are viewed as metaphorical references to the communion of spirits. But Scripture is unwavering in its physical descriptions of the New Earth.

The writers of Scripture present Heaven in many ways, including as a garden, a city, and a kingdom. Because gardens, cities, and kingdoms are familiar to us, they afford us a bridge to understanding Heaven. When Marco Polo returned to Italy from the court of Kublai Khan, he was describing a world his audience had never seen, so he had to appeal to people's imaginations. China was not an imaginary realm, of course, but it was very different from Italy. He used Italy as a reference point to help people understand China. But if in the end his listeners thought China wasn't a literal place, Marco Polo's communication would have been in vain.[39]

We cannot anticipate or desire what we cannot imagine. That's why, I believe, God has given us glimpses of Heaven in the Bible to fire up our imaginations and kindle a desire for Heaven in our hearts. Rather than ignoring our imaginations, I believe we should fuel them with Scripture.

Our misguided attempts to make Heaven sound "spiritual" (i.e., nonphysical) merely succeed in making Heaven sound unappealing. As human beings, whom God made to be both physical and spiritual, we are not designed to live in a nonphysical realm. We are not, as Plato supposed, merely spiritual beings temporarily encased in bodies. Adam did not become a "living being" until he was both body *and* spirit (Genesis 2:7, NIV). We are physical beings as much as we are spiritual beings. That's why the bodily resurrection is so central in God's plan of redemption—it is essential that God endow us with eternal, righteous humanity. In doing so, he sets our minds and bodies free from sin, the Curse, and death and equips us to fulfill God's purpose for our lives. Only those with bodies can walk on and rule over the New Earth. A material world is occupied by material beings.

As Spurgeon puts it, "Christ is preparing a place not for disembodied spirits . . . [but] a place for the entire personhood of his people, when spirit, soul, and body shall be again united and we as complete people shall receive . . . the redemption of our bodies."

FRIENDSHIP IN HEAVEN

❁

Excerpted from "A Prepared Place for a Prepared People"
Sermon #2751, May 25, 1879

The Bible is clear that there will not be marriage in Heaven, but what about friendship? In this text, Spurgeon argues that we will continue the close relationships we've had on Earth and that these bonds will only grow stronger throughout eternity.

Nevertheless, I am continually with you;
*   you hold my right hand.*
You guide me with your counsel,
*   and afterward you will receive me to glory.*
Whom have I in heaven but you?
*   And there is nothing on earth that I desire*
*   besides you.*
My flesh and my heart may fail,
*   but God is the strength of my heart and*
*   my portion forever.* PSALM 73:23-26

——————— ❁ ———————

SPURGEON ☞ I do not know what better world, in many respects, there could be than this, so far as material nature is concerned. It is so full of the beauty and loveliness that God pours upon it on every side. It is a wonderful world.

But I could not reconcile myself to the idea that this world would be Heaven. It will do well enough for the thousand years of glory, if it shall literally be that we shall reign with Christ upon it during the millennial age. But it is a drossy thing, and if it is ever to be the scene of the new heavens and the New Earth, it must first pass through the fire. The very smell of sin is upon it, and *God will not use this globe as a vessel unto honor until he has purified it with fire as he once did with water.*

Do you not think, dear friends, that our Lord Jesus Christ prepares Heaven for his people by going there? Supposing you were to be lifted up to a state which was supposedly Heaven but that Jesus was not there. It would be no Heaven to you. But wherever I may go, when I do go, if Jesus is already there, I do not care where it is! Wherever he is shall be my Heaven. For that is our very first and last thought about Heaven: to be with Christ where he is. To be with Christ is far better than to be anywhere else.

The first thing that Christ had to do in order to prepare Heaven for his people was to go to Heaven, for that made it Heaven. Oh, how I long to see him in his glory! I would part with all the joys of time and sense to gaze upon him seated upon his throne. Oh, what will it be to see him? You have seen how painters have failed when they have tried to depict him. The bravest artist may well tremble and the brightest colors fade when anyone tries to paint him even in his humiliation. There is no other face so marred as his face was. But what will it be in Heaven when it is marred no more? No tear in his eye! No spittle running down his cheeks! But, oh, the glory of humanity perfected and allied with deity! "The king in his beauty!" (Isaiah 33:17).

It struck me as I turned this subject over in my mind that our Lord Jesus Christ knew that there was a place to be prepared for each one of his people. It may be—I cannot tell—that in some part of the society of Heaven, one spirit will be happier than it might have been in another part. You know that, even though you love all the brothers and sisters, you cannot help feeling most at home with some of them.

Our blessed Lord and Master had no sinful favoritism, yet he did love twelve men better than all the rest of his disciples. And out of the twelve, he loved three whom he introduced into mysteries from which he excluded the other nine. And even out of the three, there was one, you know, who was that disciple whom Jesus loved (John 13:23). Now everybody here has his likings. I do not know if we shall carry anything of that spirit to Heaven. If we do, Christ has so prepared a place for us that you shall be nearest, in your position and occupation, to those who would contribute most to your happiness.

You shall be where you can most honor God and most enjoy God. But depend upon it: if there be any association—any more intimate connection—between some saints than among others, Jesus Christ will so beautifully arrange it that we shall all be in the happiest places.

If you were to give a dinner party and you had a number of friends there, you would like to pick the seats for them. You would say, "Now, there is So-and-so. I know that he would like to sit next to So-and-so," and you would try so to arrange it. Well, in that grand wedding feast above, our Savior has so prepared a place for us that he will find us each the right position.

We know that there have been bonds of spirit that may still continue. I sometimes think that if I could have any choice as to those I should live near in Heaven, I should like to live in the region of such distinctive folk as Rowland Hill and John Berridge.* I think I would

---

* Rowland Hill was a popular preacher in London who died a year before Spurgeon was born, and John Berridge was an English revivalist and hymn writer in the eighteenth century.

get on best with them, for we could talk together of the way God led us and how he brought souls to Christ by us. Though some said that we were a good deal too merry when we were down below and that the people laughed when they listened to us, and some spoke as if that were a great sin, we will make them laugh up yonder, I warrant you, as we tell again the wonders of redeeming love and of the grace of God—their mouths shall be filled with laughter and their tongues with singing! And then—

> *Loudest of the crowd I'll sing,*
> *While heaven's resounding mansions ring*
> *With shouts of sovereign grace.**

And I expect each of you who love the Lord will say the same.

Let me just say this to you: The place is prepared. Are you prepared for it? Do you believe on the Lord Jesus Christ? If so, your preparation has begun. Do you love the Lord and love his people? If so, your preparation is going on. Do you hate sin, and do you long for holiness? If so, your preparation is progressing. Are you nothing at all, and is Jesus Christ your all in all? Then you are almost ready. May the Lord keep you in that condition and before long swing up the gates of pearl and let you in to the prepared place! May the Lord bring us all safely there, for Jesus' sake! Amen.

———————— ❋ ————————

ALCORN ☞ For Christians, to die is to "be present with the Lord" (2 Corinthians 5:8, NKJV). The apostle Paul says, "I desire to depart and be with Christ, which is better by far" (Philippians

---

* From the hymn "When Thou, My Righteous Judge, Shall Come," by Selina Shirley Huntingdon.

1:23, NIV). He could have said, "I desire to depart and be in Heaven," but he didn't—his mind was on being with his Lord Jesus, which is the most significant aspect of Heaven.

Seventeenth-century Scottish theologian Samuel Rutherford says, "O, my Lord Jesus Christ, if I could be in heaven without thee, it would be a hell; and if I could be in hell, and have thee still, it would be a heaven to me, for thou art all the heaven I want."[40] Martin Luther said, "I had rather be in hell with Christ, than be in heaven without him."[41]

When Jesus prays that we will be with him in Heaven, he explains why: "Father, I want those you have given me to be with me where I am, and *to see my glory*, the glory you have given me because you loved me before the creation of the world" (John 17:24, NIV, emphasis added). When we accomplish something, we want to share it with those closest to us. Likewise, Jesus wants to share with us his glory—the glory of his accomplishments and his being.

Our greatest pleasure, our greatest satisfaction, is to behold his glory. As John Piper says, "God is most glorified in us when we are most satisfied in him."[42]

We'll worship Jesus as the Almighty and bow to him in reverence, yet we'll never sense his disapproval in Heaven—because we'll never disappoint him. He'll never be unhappy with us. We'll be able to relax fully—the other shoe will never drop. No skeletons will fall out of our closets. Christ bore every one of our sins. He paid the ultimate price so we would be forever free from sin—and the fear of sin.

All barriers between us and him will be gone forever. He will be our best friend there.

I love that Spurgeon expresses his desire to live near Rowland Hill and John Berridge in Heaven, two men who died before he was born. When he talks of the three of them being "a good deal too merry," we see not only Spurgeon's spunk but also the sense of camaraderie he anticipates in Heaven. Spurgeon had an astounding number of critics who reproached him about everything from his doctrine to his humor to his weight to his cigar smoking. Spurgeon says of himself and his as-yet-unmet friends Hill and Berridge, "We will make them laugh up yonder, I warrant you, as we tell again the wonders of redeeming love and of the grace of God—their mouths shall be filled with laughter."

The Bible doesn't directly address the concept of special friendships in Heaven, but is there any basis for Spurgeon's position? I think so. First, since we remain human in the Resurrection—since we maintain our identities and since our memories are part of who we are—shouldn't I expect to be particularly close to my wife and daughters and sons-in-law and dearest friends? Is there any reason to believe we won't pick right up in Heaven where our relationships from Earth left off?

True, there won't be marriage as we know it here (Matthew 22:30), but there will be *one* marriage—our marriage to Christ. That means as fellow members of the body of Christ, my wife, Nanci, and I will be *part of the same marriage forever*—our marriage to Jesus. Wouldn't it be fitting and in keeping with God's ways, given our many years of growing in Christ and serving him together here, that we would be close friends when we're with him?

I think we'll especially enjoy connecting with those we faced tough times with on Earth and saying, "Did you ever imagine Heaven would be so wonderful?" We all have our own Rowland Hills and John Berridges, don't we? Enjoying God and enjoying one another go hand in hand. Augustine said, "All of us who enjoy God are also enjoying each other in Him."[43]

The odd notion that relationships with family and friends won't continue in Heaven flies in the face of Paul's encouragement to the Thessalonians in 1 Thessalonians 4:13-18 to look forward to rejoining their loved ones in the presence of Jesus and his encouragement to comfort one another with those words. The comfort is *not* "Don't worry—you won't remember or care about them anyway." The comfort comes from the anticipation that we will actually see our loved ones again.

Do you have a close friend who has had a profound influence on you? Do you think it is a coincidence that she was in your dorm wing or became your roommate? Was it accidental that your desk was near his or that his family lived next door or that your father was transferred when you were in third grade so that you ended up in his neighborhood? "From one man he made all the nations, that they should inhabit the whole earth; and he marked out their appointed times in history and the boundaries of their lands" (Acts 17:26, NIV).

Since God determined the time and places where you would live, it's no accident which neighborhood you grew up in, who lived next door, who went to school with you, who was part of your church youth group, who was there to help you and pray for you. It's no accident that Charles Spurgeon heard about and read about Rowland Hill and John Berridge and was touched by God through their stories. It's no accident that God gave me the friends and the profound influences he has given me. Some of these men and women are from different times and places, and I have not yet met them except through books. Our relationships, past and present, direct and indirect, were appointed by God, and there's every reason to believe they'll not only continue but expand in Heaven.

God's plan won't stop on the New Earth. He doesn't abandon

his purposes; he extends and fulfills them. Friendships begun on Earth will continue in Heaven, growing richer than ever.

Notice Spurgeon's point that Jesus loved twelve men more than the rest of his disciples and that he loved three most out of those and that one, John, was his most-beloved disciple. While Spurgeon isn't certain we'll have favorite relationships in Heaven, he clearly hopes we will. He says, "If we do, Christ has so prepared a place for us that you shall be nearest, in your position and occupation, to those who would contribute most to your happiness."

If, as you walk about the New Jerusalem, you see Adam and Eve holding hands as they look at the tree of life, would you begrudge them their special friendship? Of course not. And no one will begrudge you yours.

Perhaps you're disappointed that you've never experienced the close friendships you long for. In Heaven you'll have much closer relationships with some people you know now. But it's also true that you may not have met your closest friends yet. Maybe your future best friend, after Jesus himself, will be someone sitting next to you at the first great feast. Don't be surprised. After all, as Spurgeon suggests, the sovereign God, who orchestrates and redeems friendships, will be in charge of the seating arrangements.

THE RESURRECTION OF GOD'S CHILDREN

❋

Excerpted from "The First Resurrection"
Sermon #391

Delivered on Sunday morning,
May 5, 1861, at the Metropolitan Tabernacle, Newington

The redemption we look forward to is not one dimensional, nor is it sur-
face level. Our resurrection will be like Christ's, with the full flourishing
of bodies and spirits. We will experience at last what God intended for
us all along.

> *I saw thrones, and seated on them were those to whom the*
> *authority to judge was committed. Also I saw the souls of those*
> *who had been beheaded for the testimony of Jesus and for the*
> *word of God, and those who had not worshiped the beast or*
> *its image and had not received its mark on their foreheads or*
> *their hands. They came to life and reigned with Christ for a*
> *thousand years. The rest of the dead did not come to life until*
> *the thousand years were ended. This is the first resurrection.*
> *Blessed and holy is the one who shares in the first resurrection!*
> *Over such the second death has no power, but they will be*
> *priests of God and of Christ, and they will reign with him*
> *for a thousand years. . . . And I saw the dead, great and small,*
> *standing before the throne, and books were opened. Then*
> *another book was opened, which is the book of life. And the*

dead were judged by what was written in the books, according to what they had done.   REVELATION 20:4-6, 12

———————— ❀ ————————

SPURGEON ☞ I think some ministers would do far more for the profit of God's people if they would preach more about the first coming of Christ and less about the second. But I have chosen this topic because I believe it has practical bearings and may be useful, instructive, and rousing to us all. I find that the most earnest of the Puritan preachers did not resist dwelling upon this mysterious subject. I turn to Charnock,* and in his discussion upon the unchanging nature of God, he does not hesitate to speak of the fiery destruction of the world, of the millennial reign, and of the new heavens and New Earth.

I turn to Richard Baxter,† a man who above all other men loved the souls of men—who, perhaps more than any man, with the exception of the apostle Paul, agonized in birth for souls—and I find him making a barbed arrow out of the doctrine of the coming of the Lord and thrusting this great truth into the very hearts and consciences of unbelievers as though it were Heaven's own sword.

And John Bunyan‡—plain, honest John, who preached so simply that a child could comprehend him and was certainly never guilty of having written upon his forehead the word *mystery*. He, too, speaks of the coming of Christ and of the glories which shall

---

* Stephen Charnock was a Puritan clergyman in the seventeenth century who at one time served as a chaplain to Henry Cromwell; he was best known for his classic work *The Existence and Attributes of God.*

† Richard Baxter was a Puritan church leader, theologian, and hymn writer in seventeenth-century England. He was best known for his classic work on Heaven, *The Saints' Everlasting Rest.*

‡ John Bunyan was a writer and preacher in seventeenth-century England, best known for his classic allegory, *The Pilgrim's Progress.*

follow and uses this doctrine as a stimulus to the saints and as a warning to the ungodly. I do not think, therefore, I need tremble very much if the charge should be brought against me of bringing before you an unprofitable subject. It shall profit if God shall bless the word, and if it is God's word, we may expect his blessing if we preach it all. But he will withdraw it if we refrain from teaching any part of his counsel because in our pretended wisdom we fancy that it would not have practical effect.

Turn to the first letter to the Thessalonians: "We do not want you to be uninformed, brothers, about those who are asleep, that you may not grieve as others do who have no hope. For since we believe that Jesus died and rose again, even so, through Jesus, God will bring with him those who have fallen asleep. For this we declare to you by a word from the Lord, that we who are alive, who are left until the coming of the Lord, will not precede those who have fallen asleep. For the Lord himself will descend from heaven with a cry of command, with the voice of an archangel, and with the sound of the trumpet of God. And the dead in Christ will rise first. Then we who are alive, who are left, will be caught up together with them in the clouds to meet the Lord in the air, and so we will always be with the Lord" (1 Thessalonians 4:13-17).

Here is nothing said whatever about the resurrection of the wicked. It is only stated that the dead in Christ shall rise first. The apostle Paul is evidently speaking of a first resurrection. And since we know that a first resurrection implies a second, and since we know that the wicked dead are to rise as well as the righteous dead, we draw the conclusion that the wicked dead shall rise at the second resurrection, after the interval between the two resurrections shall have been accomplished.

Everyone will rise—no orthodox Christian doubts that. The doctrine of a general resurrection is received by all the Christian church. What, then, is this resurrection after which Paul is exerting himself, if by any means he might attain unto it? It could not be the general resurrection. He would attain to that however he might live. It must be some superior resurrection of which only those shall be partakers who have known Christ and the power of his resurrection, having become like him in his death. I think you cannot interpret this passage, or give it any force of meaning, without admitting that there is to be a prior resurrection of the just before the resurrection of the unjust.

In chapter 14 of the Gospel of Luke, in verses 13-14, you have a promise made to those who, when they host a feast, do not do it with the intention of getting anything in return. "When you give a feast, invite the poor, the crippled, the lame, the blind, and you will be blessed, because they cannot repay you. For you will be repaid at the resurrection of the just."

I would not insist upon it that this would prove that the just rose at a different time, but still there is to be a resurrection of the just, and on the other hand, there is to be a resurrection of the unjust. And the time of reward for the righteous is to be the resurrection of the just, which is spoken of as being a particular period.

There is a passage in Hebrews where the apostle, speaking of the trials of the godly and their noble endurance, speaks of them as "refusing to accept release, so that they might rise again to a better life" (11:35). The better life is not in the after results of Resurrection, but in the Resurrection itself. How then could it be a better resurrection unless there be some distinction between the resurrection of the saint and the resurrection of the sinner? Let the one be a resurrection of splendor, let the other be a resurrection of gloom and horror, and let there be a marked division between the two. As it was in the beginning, it may be even to the end—the Lord has put a difference between him who fears God and him who fears him not.

I have no purpose to serve except to make the Scripture as plain to you as possible. And I say it yet again: I have not the shadow of a doubt in my own soul that these passages teach us that there shall first of all be a resurrection concerning which it shall be said: "Blessed and holy is the one who shares in the first resurrection! Over such the second death has no power, but they will be priests of God and of Christ, and they will reign with him for a thousand years" (Revelation 20:6).

———————— ✵ ————————

ALCORN ⬳ Spurgeon says, "If it is God's word, we may expect his blessing if we preach it all. But he will withdraw it if we refrain from teaching any part of his counsel." He spoke critically of pastors who compromised their biblical teaching to accommodate the newly popularized theories of Charles Darwin (which were the talk of London at the time) and opposed various higher critics who taught that the Bible wasn't reliable.

Spurgeon takes delight in referring to the men whose books God used to mold his thinking. He refers here to John Bunyan, author of *The Pilgrim's Progress*, with great fondness. In fact, *The Pilgrim's Progress* was Spurgeon's favorite book—he read it over a hundred times. His many comments on it were collected into a book called *Pictures from Pilgrim's Progress*, his own commentary on Bunyan's great work of fiction. Spurgeon often spoke of the writers who were his mentors as if they were old friends—Baxter, Bunyan, John Owen,* and Charnock among them. He talks about these men as if he knew them well—he

———————————

* John Owen was a seventeenth-century English Puritan pastor and reformed theologian.

calls Bunyan "plain, honest John"—for they had a formational role in his thinking, just as Spurgeon has had in my life and in the lives of numerous others.

Spurgeon's meditation demonstrates his understanding that our anticipation of eternal life as resurrected beings in a resurrected universe has present, practical implications. "Therefore [in light of our eventual resurrection], my dear brothers and sisters, stand firm. Let nothing move you. Always give yourselves fully to the work of the Lord, because you know that your labor in the Lord is not in vain" (1 Corinthians 15:58, NIV).

How do we know that our labor in the Lord is not in vain? Because of our bodily resurrection. Just as we will be carried over from the old world to the new, so will our labor. In a sense, not only our bodies but also our service for Christ will be resurrected. J. B. Phillips renders 1 Corinthians 15:58 as follows: "Let nothing move you as you busy yourselves in the Lord's work. Be sure that nothing you do for him is ever lost or ever wasted."[44]

Bruce Milne writes, "Every kingdom work, whether publicly performed or privately endeavored, partakes of the kingdom's imperishable character. Every honest intention, every stumbling word of witness, every resistance of temptation, every motion of repentance, every gesture of concern, every routine engagement, every motion of worship, every struggle toward obedience, every mumbled prayer, everything, literally, which flows out of our faith-relationship with the Ever-Living One, will find its place in the ever-living heavenly order which will dawn at his coming."[45]

Paul says, "In this hope we were saved" (Romans 8:24). What hope? The words of the previous verse tell us: "the redemption of our bodies" (verse 23). That's the final resurrection—when death will be swallowed up and sin will be reversed, never again to touch us. This is what we should long for and live for.

Is resurrected living in a resurrected world with the resurrected Christ and his resurrected people *your* daily longing and hope? Is it part of the gospel you share with others? Paul says that the resurrection of the dead is the hope for which we were saved. It will be the glorious climax of God's saving work that began at our new birth. In liberating us from sin and all its consequences, the Resurrection will free us to live with God, gaze on him, and enjoy his uninterrupted fellowship forever, with no threat that anything will ever again come between us and him.

May God use our mentors, the pastors and friends we talk to, and the books we read to preserve us from embracing lesser hopes. May we rejoice as we anticipate the height, depth, length, and breadth of our Savior's redemptive work.

DEATH HAS NO POWER

Excerpted from "The First Resurrection"
Sermon #391, May 5, 1861

For those who don't have the assurance of eternal life, death is a terrifying enemy. But for the believer, death does not have the final say. It remains a difficult passageway, but a thoroughfare to a magnificent destination.

> *He who has an ear, let him hear what the Spirit says to the churches. The one who conquers will not be hurt by the second death.* REVELATION 2:11

SPURGEON ⟨⟨ Note the privilege here promised to the godly: "The one who conquers will not be hurt by the second death." This is a literal death, none the less literal because its main terror is spiritual, for a spiritual death is as literal as a physical death.

The death which shall come upon the ungodly without exception can never touch the righteous. Oh, brothers and sisters, this is the best of all. As for the first resurrection, if Christ has granted that to his people there must be something glorious in it if we cannot perceive it. "What we will be has not yet appeared; but we know that when he appears we shall be like him, because we shall see him as he is" (1 John 3:2).

On this point we can understand what Scripture states and understand this much well: that damnation, the second death, shall have no power on those who rise at the first resurrection. How should it? How can damnation fall on any but those who are sinners and are guilty of sin? But the saints are not guilty of sin. They were by nature the children of wrath even as others. But their sin has been lifted from them. It was laid upon the scapegoat's head in the Old Testament account. The eternal substitute, our Lord Jesus, carried all their guilt and their iniquity into the wilderness of forgetfulness, where it shall never be found against them forever. They wear the Savior's righteousness, for they have been washed in his blood.

There shall be a second death, but over us it shall have no power. Do you understand the beauty of the picture? As if we might walk through the flames of Hell and they should have no power to devour us, any more than when Shadrach, Meshach, and Abednego paced with ease over the hot coals of Nebuchadnezzar's seven-times heated furnace.

Death may bend his bow and fit the arrow to the string. But we laugh at you, oh death! And you, oh Hell, we will despise! For over both of you enemies of mankind we shall be more than conquerors through him who loved us (Romans 8:37). We shall stand invulnerable and invincible, defying and laughing to scorn our every foe. And all this because we are washed from sin and covered with a spotless righteousness.

But there is another reason why the second death can have no power over the believer. Because when the prince of this world comes against us then, we shall be able to say what our Master did: "He has no claim on me" (John 14:30). When we shall rise again, we shall be freed from all corruption. No evil tendencies shall remain in us.

We shall be as pure as Adam before his fall, as holy as the immaculate manhood when it first came from the divine hand. We shall be better than Adam, for Adam might sin; but we shall be so established in goodness, in truth, and in righteousness that we shall not even be tempted again, much less have any fear of falling. We shall stand spotless and faultless at the last great day.

Brothers and sisters, lift up your heads. Contending with sin and cast down with doubts, lift up your heads and wipe the tears from your eyes. There are days coming, the likes of which angels have not seen, but you shall see them.

And when his followers rise, they shall leave the old Adam behind them. Blessed day! One of the happiest aspects of Heaven will be freedom from the tendency to sin, a total death to that old nature which has been our plague and woe.

ALCORN ⟁ Christ promises this about eternal life on the New Earth: "Death shall be no more, neither shall there be mourning, nor crying, nor pain anymore, for the former things have passed away" (Revelation 21:4).

The prophet Isaiah says of God, "On this mountain he will destroy the shroud that enfolds all peoples, the sheet that covers all nations; he will swallow up death forever. The Sovereign LORD will wipe away the tears from all faces" (Isaiah 25:7-8, NIV).

God guarantees that death will die. He himself will kill it.

Meanwhile, though dying is still difficult for the believer, death itself is radically changed. Death is the means by which God's children enter his presence. Death is not a wall but a turnstile, a last obstacle that marks a great beginning. Pastor and author Calvin Miller puts it beautifully:

I once scorned ev'ry fearful thought of death,
  When it was but the end of pulse and breath,
But now my eyes have seen that past the pain
  There is a world that's waiting to be claimed.
Earthmaker, Holy, let me now depart,
  For living's such a temporary art.
And dying is but getting dressed for God,
  Our graves are merely doorways cut in sod.[46]

When it came to Heaven and Hell, Spurgeon's contemporary across the Atlantic, Samuel Clemens (Mark Twain), never got it. Under the weight of age, he says in his autobiography, "The burden of pain, care, misery grows heavier year by year. At length ambition is dead, pride is dead, vanity is dead, longing for release is in their place. It comes at last—the only unpoisoned gift Earth ever had for them—and they vanish from a world where they were of no consequence; where they achieved nothing; where they were a mistake and a failure and a foolishness."[47]

What a contrast to Charles Spurgeon's perspective on death: "To come to you is to come home from exile, to come to land out of the raging storm, to come to rest after long labor, to come to the goal of my desires and the summit of my wishes."

For the Christian, death is a difficult means to an incredibly wonderful end.

You may be troubled, feeling uncertain or unready to finish this life. Then make sure of your relationship with Jesus Christ. Be certain that you're trusting him alone to save you—not anyone or anything else, and certainly not any good works you've done. And then, like Spurgeon, allow yourself to get excited about what's on the other side of death's door.

THE REALITY OF GOD'S WRATH

Excerpted from "The First Resurrection"
Sermon #391, May 5, 1861

In this sermon Spurgeon specifically addresses unbelievers. His message about the reality of Hell is not a popular one, and it's not easy to swallow in our day, when tolerance trumps holiness. But it's solidly grounded in the truth of God's Word, and we need to pay attention to it.

> *The kings of the earth and the great ones and the generals and the rich and the powerful, and everyone, slave and free, hid themselves in the caves and among the rocks of the mountains, calling to the mountains and rocks, "Fall on us and hide us from the face of him who is seated on the throne, and from the wrath of the Lamb, for the great day of their wrath has come, and who can stand?"* REVELATION 6:15-17

SPURGEON Sinner, you have heard us speak of the resurrection of the righteous. To you the word *resurrection* has no music. There is no flash of joy in your spirit when you hear that the dead shall rise again. But, oh, I pray you lend me your ear while I assure you in God's name that you shall rise. Not only shall your soul live—you have perhaps become so brutish that you forget you have a soul—but your body itself shall live.

Those eyes that have been full of lust shall see sights of horror. Those ears which have listened to the temptations of the evil one shall hear the thunders of the Day of Judgment. Those very feet that lead you to the worthless pleasures shall attempt but utterly fail to sustain you when Christ shall sit in judgment.

Don't think that when your body is put into the soil you will be done with it. It has been partner with your soul in sin. It shall share with your soul in punishment. [God] is able to "destroy both soul and body in hell" (Matthew 10:28).

God's book tells me that the dead, both small and great, shall rise. When the archangel's trumpet shall sound, the whole of the old inhabitants of the world before the Flood shall rise out of the ocean. The buried palaces, the sunken homes shall all give up the once-buried multitude.

Up shall rise from the great deeps of the fathomless sea thousands upon thousands of men who have slept now these three and four thousand years. Every churchyard, too, where men have been quietly buried with Christian rites but were un-Christian still, shall yield up its dead. The battlefield shall yield a mighty harvest, a harvest which was sown in blood and which shall be reaped in violence. Every place where man has lived and man has died shall see the dying raised to life once again, and flesh and blood once more instilled with life.

But the main thing with you is that you will be there. The most awful curse that could fall on you, with the exception of the damnation of your soul, is the sure and certain resurrection of your body. Go and pamper your body. Go and luxuriate and indulge it in ease. You may well pamper your bodies, for there is short enough time for your bodies to have mirth in. And when that short time is over, you shall drink another wine—the dregs of the cup of God's wrath, which the wicked shall drain to the last drop.

Satisfy your ears with music now. You shall soon hear nothing but the howling of the damned! Go your way—eat, drink, and be merry. But for all these the Lord shall bring you into judgment—sevenfold for all your sinful pleasures, yes seventy times seven. For all your joys of lust and wickedness and crime shall the Lord be avenged on you in the great and terrible day of his wrath. Sinner, when you sin, think of the Resurrection!

But after the Resurrection, according to Revelation 20, comes the Judgment. You have cursed God. You have entered the chamber of immorality or the hall of infidelity. You have walked through the stews of grime and through the stench and filth of the brothel. You have wandered into sin and plunged into it, thinking it would all die with the day, that as the night covers up the sights of the day, so the night of death should cover up the deeds of your day of life. Not so. The books shall be opened.

I think I see you closing your eyes because you dare not look upon the Judge when he opens that page where stands your history. I hear a sinner, boldest among you all. He is crying, "You rocks fall on me." There they stand, majestic and fearful, those granite rocks. This sinner would rather be crushed by them than stand there before the avenging eye. But the mountains will not give way; their flinty insides will feel no pangs of sympathy. They will not move. You stand while the fiery eye pierces you through and through and the dread voice reads on and on and on, accounting your every act and word and thought.

I see you as the shameful crime is read, and men and angels hear. I see your horror as a nameless deed is told, in terms explicit which none can misunderstand. I hear your thought brought out—that lust, that murder which was in thought but never grew into deed. And you are all this while astonished like Belshazzar when he saw the writing on the wall and his knees knocked together and he was terribly afraid.

So shall it be with you; and yet again, and again, and again, shall you send up that awful shriek: "Hide us! Hide us from the face of him who sits upon the throne and from the wrath of the Lamb!"

ALCORN ⬤⇢ "You shall soon hear nothing but the howling of the damned. . . . When you sin, think of the Resurrection!"

If you are like me, you shudder at Spurgeon's words. I shudder not because they are bold but because they are true. They are confirmed by the Word of God. I'm sure Spurgeon got more pleasure speaking about Heaven than Hell. I know I do. But because he preached the *whole* counsel of God, not just part of it, Spurgeon *had* to speak about Hell, and he often did.

If I had a choice—that is, if Scripture were not so clear and conclusive—I would not believe in Hell. Trust me when I say I do not *want* to believe in it. But if I make what I want—or what others want—the basis for my beliefs, then I am a follower of myself and my culture, not a follower of Christ. Were I as holy as I ought to be, I would want there to be a Hell, given the reality of unrepentant sinners. After all, our holy God has determined it should be so.

"There seems to be a kind of conspiracy," writes novelist Dorothy Sayers, "to forget, or to conceal, where the doctrine of Hell comes from. The doctrine of Hell is not 'mediaeval priest-craft' for frightening people into giving money to the church: it is Christ's deliberate judgment on sin. . . . We cannot repudiate Hell without altogether repudiating Christ."[48]

In *The Problem of Pain*, C. S. Lewis writes of Hell, "There is no doctrine which I would more willingly remove from Christianity than this, if it lay in my power. But it has the full support of Scripture and, specially, of our Lord's own words; it has always been held by Christendom; and it has the support of reason."[49]

Spurgeon says of the unbeliever, "To you the word *resurrection* has no music." How sad that the skeptic has no interest in the gift of salvation offered by the Savior and will, instead, reap the sure alternative that awaits.

Contrary to popular belief, Heaven is *not* our default destination. Unless our sin problem is resolved, the place we will go is our default destination, Hell. The great danger is that people assume they are headed for Heaven. Judging by what's said at most funerals, you'd think nearly everyone's going to Heaven, wouldn't you? For every American who believes he's going to Hell, there are 120 who believe they're going to Heaven.[50] This optimism stands in stark contrast to Christ's words in Matthew 7:13-14 (NIV): "Enter through the narrow gate. For wide is the gate and broad is the road that leads to destruction, and many enter through it. But small is the gate and narrow the road that leads to life, and only a few find it."

Didn't Spurgeon say in an earlier meditation that multitudes will inhabit Heaven? Yes. But sadly, multitudes will also inhabit Hell. In C. S. Lewis's *The Screwtape Letters*, one demon says to another, "The safest road to hell is the gradual one—the gentle slope, soft underfoot, without sudden turnings, without milestones, without signposts."[51]

Hell will not be like it's often portrayed in comic strips— a giant lounge where people tell stories of their escapades on Earth between drinks. Rather, it will be a place of utter misery (Matthew 13:42, 50; 22:13; 24:51; 25:30; Luke 13:28). It will be a place of conscious punishment for sins, with no hope of relief.

This is why Dante, in *Inferno*, envisions this sign chiseled above Hell's gate: "Abandon every hope, you who enter."[52]

It's of paramount importance to make sure you are going to Heaven, not Hell. The voice that whispers, "There's no hurry. Put this book down—you can always think about it later," is not God's voice. God says, "Now is the day of salvation" (2 Corinthians 6:2, NIV) and "Choose for yourselves *this* day whom you will serve" (Joshua 24:15, NIV, emphasis added).

THE HORRORS OF HELL

Excerpted from "The First Resurrection"
Sermon #391, May 5, 1861

Hell isn't polite dinner-party conversation. Even Christians often downplay the topic or avoid it altogether. We might convince ourselves that it's more compassionate to assume that everyone will go to Heaven. But Spurgeon makes it clear why we need to affirm and declare to others the stark realities of Hell—and the fact that without Jesus, Hell is our default destination.

> *He has appeared once for all at the end of the ages to put away*
> *sin by the sacrifice of himself. And just as it is appointed for*
> *man to die once, and after that comes judgment, so Christ,*
> *having been offered once to bear the sins of many, will appear*
> *a second time, not to deal with sin but to save those who are*
> *eagerly waiting for him.* HEBREWS 9:26-28

SPURGEON ☞ After death, the judgment; after judgment, the damnation. If it be a dreadful thing to live again [when you thought you wouldn't], if it be a more dreadful thing still to spend the first day of that life in the courtroom of God, how much more awful shall it be when the sentence is pronounced and the terror of punishment shall begin!

We believe that the souls of the wicked are already tormented, but this judgment will cast both body and soul into the lake of fire. Men and women, you who fear not God, and have no faith in Jesus, I cannot picture to you damnation. Across it let me draw a curtain. But though we must not picture it, I pray you realize it.

This much we know: that Hell is a place of absence from God, a place where there is never sleep or rest or hope. It is a place where a drop of water is denied, though thirst shall burn the tongue; a place where pleasure never breathed, where light never dawned, where anything like consolation was never heard of; a place where the gospel is denied, where mercy droops her wings and dies; a place of fury and of burning; a place the likes of which imagination has not pictured.

May God grant that it may be a place which you shall never see and whose dread you shall never feel. When you die, sinner, flight from Hell becomes impossible. You are lost then, eternally. Oh, while yet you are on praying ground, I pray you, think on your end. Think! Think! This warning may be the last you shall ever hear. Perhaps while you sit here, the last sands are dropping from the hourglass, and then no more warning can be given because redemption and escape shall be impossible to you.

Sinner, I lift up before you now Christ the crucified one: "Whoever believes in him should not perish but have eternal life" (John 3:16). As Moses lifted up the serpent in the wilderness, so this morning the Son of Man is lifted up. Sinner, see his wounds. Look to his thorn-crowned head. See the nails in his hands and his feet. Do you perceive him? Pay attention. Listen again while he says, "It is finished!" (John 19:30). Salvation finished!

Believe on Christ and you shall be saved. Trust him and all the horrors of the future shall have no power over you. Oh, that today some of you may trust my Master for the first time in your lives. This done, you need not curiously inquire what the future shall be, but you may sit down calmly and say, "Come when it will, my soul is on the Rock of ages. It fears no ill; it fears no tempest; it defies all pain. Come quickly! Come quickly! Even so, come quickly, Lord Jesus."

※

ALCORN ✎ In my book *Lord Foulgrin's Letters*, inspired by C. S. Lewis's *The Screwtape Letters*, the demon Foulgrin writes instructions to Squaltaint, the evil spirit assigned to tempt a man named Jordan Fletcher: "It's long-term results we seek. Tactics count only insofar as they produce the desired impact on Fletcher—reality distortion, moral failure, thoughts, and actions displeasing to the Enemy. Whatever sends them to hell, we support. Whatever draws them toward heaven, we oppose."[53]

Spurgeon was as conscious of the devil's strategies as any man who ever preached. Satan has obvious motives for fueling not only procrastination about preparing for judgment but also our denial that there will even be a judgment or that eternal punishment will be a verdict. The enemy of our souls wants unbelievers to reject Christ without fear, he wants Christians to be unmotivated to share Christ, and he wants God to receive less glory for the radical nature of Christ's redemptive work.

Ironically, those who think themselves compassionate for denying Hell or not speaking of it are effectively ensuring that more people will go to Hell. Even some professed Christians are now, subtly or plainly, embracing a fashionable universalism—the belief that all people will ultimately be saved. Some consider Hell to be the invention of wild-eyed prophets obsessed with wrath. They argue that Christians should take the higher road of Christ's love.

But this perspective overlooks a conspicuous reality: Jesus says more about Hell than anyone else in the Bible does (Matthew 10:28; 13:40-42; Mark 9:43-48). He refers to it as a literal place and describes it in graphic terms—including raging fires and the worm that doesn't die (Mark 9:48). Christ says the unsaved "will be thrown outside, into the darkness, where there will be weeping and gnashing of teeth" (Matthew 8:12, NIV). In his story of the rich man and Lazarus, Jesus teaches that in Hell the wicked suffer terribly, are fully conscious, retain their desires and memories and reasoning, long for relief, cannot be comforted, cannot leave their torment, and are bereft of hope (Luke 16:19-31). The Savior could not have painted a bleaker picture.

How long will Hell last? "They will go away to eternal punishment," Jesus says of the unrighteous, "but the righteous to eternal life" (Matthew 25:46, NIV). Here, in the same sentence, Christ again uses the word translated "eternal" (*aionos*) to describe the duration of both Heaven and Hell. Thus, if Heaven will be consciously experienced forever, Hell must be consciously experienced forever as well.

Scripture says of those who die without Jesus, "They will be punished with everlasting destruction and shut out from the presence of the Lord and from the glory of his might" (2 Thessalonians 1:9, NIV). Because God is the source of all good and Hell is the absence of God, Hell must also be the absence of all good. Hell will have no community, no camaraderie, no friendship.

I don't believe Hell is a place where demons take delight in punishing people and where people commiserate over their fate. More likely, each person is in solitary confinement, just as the rich man is portrayed alone in Hell (Luke 16:22-23). Misery loves company, but there will be nothing to love in Hell.

Hell will be inhabited by people who haven't received God's

gift of redemption in Christ. Everyone whose name is not written in the Lamb's Book of Life will be judged by God according to the works they have done, which have been recorded in Heaven's books (Revelation 20:12-15). Because those works include sin, people on their own, without Christ, cannot enter the presence of a holy and just God and will be consigned to a place of everlasting destruction (Matthew 13:40-42; 2 Thessalonians 1:9, NIV). Christ will say to those who are not covered by his blood, "Depart from me, you who are cursed, into the eternal fire prepared for the devil and his angels" (Matthew 25:41, NIV).

If we understood Hell even the slightest bit, none of us would ever say, "Go to Hell." It's far too easy to go to Hell. It requires no navigational adjustments. We were born with our autopilot set toward Hell. It is nothing to take lightly—Hell is the single greatest tragedy in the universe.

One day we'll see clearly that God revealed himself to each person and that he gave opportunity for each heart or conscience to seek and respond to him (Romans 1:18–2:16). Those who have heard the gospel have a greater opportunity to respond to Christ (Romans 10:13-17), but every unbeliever, through sin, has rejected God and his self-revelation in Creation, conscience, or the gospel.

God loves us enough to tell us the truth. There are two eternal destinations, not one, and we must choose the right path if we are to go to Heaven. All roads do not lead to Heaven. Only one does: Jesus Christ. He said, "No one comes to the Father except through me" (John 14:6, NIV).

The high stakes involved in the choice between Heaven and Hell will cause us to appreciate Heaven in deeper ways. May we never take God's grace for granted—the grace that delivers us from what we deserve and grants us forever what we don't deserve.

We should emulate Spurgeon's commitment both to truth and to compassion and join him in saying to unbelievers, "May God grant that [Hell] may be a place which you shall never see and whose dread you shall never feel."

OBTAINING PROMISES

Excerpted from "Obtaining Promises"
Sermon #435

Delivered on Sunday morning,
February 16, 1862, at the Metropolitan Tabernacle, Newington

God has placed longings inside each human heart, longings for God and for Heaven and for a resurrected life on a resurrected Earth. We often confuse these as longings for something less. But our deepest desire is for precisely what God has promised us: to live as complete and righteous people, with the person we're made for, in the place we're made for.

> *Time would fail me to tell of Gideon, Barak, Samson, Jephthah, of David and Samuel and the prophets—who through faith conquered kingdoms, enforced justice, obtained promises, stopped the mouths of lions, quenched the power of fire, escaped the edge of the sword, were made strong out of weakness, became mighty in war, put foreign armies to flight.* HEBREWS 11:32-34

SPURGEON ☞ The promises of God are to the believer an inexhaustible mine of wealth. Happy is it for him if he knows how to search out their secret veins and enrich himself with their hidden treasures. They are to him an armory containing all manner of offensive and defensive weapons. Blessed is he who has learned to enter into the sacred arsenal, to put on the breastplate and the helmet, and to lay his hand to the spear and the sword.

The promises are the Christian's Magna Carta of liberty; they are the title deeds of his heavenly estate. Happy is he who knows how to read them well and call them all his own. Yes, they are the jewel room in which the Christian's crown treasures are preserved—the regalia, secretly his today, but which he shall openly wear in Paradise. He is already a king who has the silver key with which to unlock the treasury. He may even now grasp the scepter, wear the crown, and put upon his shoulders the imperial mantle.

Oh, how unutterably rich are the promises of our faithful, covenant-keeping God! See, then, my brothers and sisters, how necessary it is that you and I should know the heavenly art of obtaining promises by faith (Hebrews 11:33).

Life eternal is described as the *promise* of eternal life (1 John 2:25). We, brothers, look for the *promise* of his coming, and after that "according to his *promise* we are waiting for new heavens and a new earth in which righteousness dwells" (2 Peter 3:13, emphasis added).

It is certain that holy men of old and good men now do by faith obtain promises.

Obedient to the divine command, Abraham prepares to offer up his son Isaac, his only son on whom his hope of posterity depended, counting that God was able either to raise up children of stones or to raise up Isaac again from the dead.

Brothers and sisters, if you would obtain a promise, your faith must be accompanied by action. When you have made some sacrifice for God, and have been willing in the teeth of human reason to do God's Word as God bids you, you shall then stand in a place from which you may reach another and a higher promise than as yet you have ever been able to grasp in the hand of your faith.

I think it is Martin Luther who says that some passages of Scripture are like trees which bear fruit but the fruit does not easily drop. You must get hold of the tree and shake it again and again, and sometimes you will need to exhaust all your strength. But at the last shake, down drops the luscious fruit. So you do with the promise—shake it to and fro by meditation, and the apples of gold will fall.

To doubt an honest man is to cast a slur upon him. But to doubt God, who cannot lie, who has sworn by an oath, is to make God a liar or even a perjurer! Our souls shrink back from infamy so cursed. Did ever fiend in Hell commit a more detestable sin than that of doubting the truthfulness of a God of perfection and truth? Come, soul, there is the promise; there it stands before you.

You say, "I dare not believe it." But I say, "How dare you doubt it? Where did you get your arrogance from? How can you speak so exceeding proudly as thus to think of God and say of him, that he has promised what he cannot or what he will not perform?"

And you! Saints of God, look to your noble ancestors. What a pedigree you have! Through what a host of martyrs, confessors, prophets, and apostles has our blood descended, and all these bear their testimony that not one good thing has failed of all that the Lord God has promised. Among them all there is no exception. Not one of them will question the truthfulness of God. They tried him on the rack, in the gloomy dungeon, and at the stake. They tried him in the Roman amphitheater, when their bones were cracking between the jaws of lions.

They tried him in Nero's garden,* when the pitch smeared on

---

* Nero was Rome's emperor, AD 54–68. He soaked Christians in oil, attached them to poles, and then ignited them for use as torches to light his garden at night.

them was flaming up, an awful sacrifice to God. They tried him when then they lay in moldy dungeons rotting or burning with fever. They tried him in the tracks of the wild goats, when they wandered about in sheepskins and goatskins, destitute, afflicted, tormented.

They tried him in the bitterness of life and in the agonies of death, and they all say to you, "Trust in the Lord; believe in him. So shall he bring it to pass, and you shall attain the promise. Falter not, hesitate not, waver not, but with the unstaggering faith of Abraham, say, 'He that has promised is able also to perform,' and you shall see it with your eyes and you shall eat thereof. You shall have his presence and blessing in this world, and in the world to come life everlasting." God help us so to do for Jesus' sake. Amen.

ALCORN ⟞ What God made us to desire, and therefore what we *do* desire if only we recognize it, is exactly what he promises to those who follow Jesus Christ: a resurrected life in a resurrected body, with the resurrected Christ on a resurrected Earth. Desiring something doesn't make it true or false. But because the God who put desires in us determined to correspond them to his plans, they do in fact find their fulfillment in the very things God has promised us.

Paul doesn't just say that if there's no Heaven, the Christian life is futile. He says that if there's no resurrection of the dead, the hope of Christianity is an illusion, and we're to be pitied for placing our faith in Christ (1 Corinthians 15:17-19). Ultimately, there is no Heaven for human spirits unless Heaven is also for human bodies.

Our deep longing for a resurrected life is not based on wishful thinking. Rather, it is a longing placed in our hearts by God himself, precisely because he intends for us to be raised to new life on the New Earth. It is God who "set eternity in the human heart" (Ecclesiastes 3:11, NIV). It is God who designed us to live on Earth and to desire not only spiritual fulfillment but also the earthly life. And it is our bodily resurrection that will allow us to return to an earthly life—this time freed from sin and the Curse.

"If anyone is in Christ, the new creation has come: The old has gone, the new is here!" (2 Corinthians 5:17, NIV). That's a promise!

If we are tempted to doubt such a promise, Spurgeon asks a question as pertinent to us as it was to his audience in 1862: "How dare you doubt it? Where did you get your arrogance from? How can you speak so exceeding proudly as thus to think of God and say of him, that he has promised what he cannot or what he will not perform?"

DRAWN FROM HELL INTO HEAVEN

❈

Excerpted from "Christ Lifted Up"
Sermon #139

Delivered on Sabbath morning,
July 5, 1857, at the Music Hall, Royal Surrey Gardens

If we're to escape the fires of Hell, who will get the credit? In this sermon, Spurgeon appeals to people to repent and turn to Christ, but he clearly affirms God's drawing and empowering grace, without which no sinner can come to the Savior.

> *[Jesus said,] "I, when I am lifted up from the earth, will draw*
> *all people to myself."* JOHN 12:32

───── ❈ ─────

SPURGEON ◑⊶ I would prefer that the most prominent feature in my ministry should be the preaching of Christ Jesus. Christ should be most prominent, not Hell and damnation.

God's ministers must preach God's terrors as well as God's mercies. We are to preach the thunder of God's law. If men will sin, we are to tell them that they must be punished for it. If they will transgress, woe to the watchman (Ezekiel 33:6-8) who is ashamed to say, "The Lord comes, he who takes vengeance."

Does God say, "The wicked shall be turned into hell, and all the nations that forget God" (Psalm 9:17, KJV)? It is our business to say so. Did the loving Savior talk of the pit that burns, of the worm that never dies, and of the fire that can never be extinguished? It is ours to speak as he spoke and not to mince words.

It is no mercy to men to hide their doom. But my brothers, terrors never ought to be the prominent feature of a minister's preaching. Many old preachers thought they would do a great deal of good by speaking like this. I do not believe it. Some souls are awakened and terrified by such preaching. However, they are but few.

Sometimes, solemnly, the sacred mysteries of eternal wrath must be preached, but far more often let us preach the wondrous love of God. There are more souls won by wooing than by threatening. It is not Hell but Christ we desire to preach. Oh sinners, we are not afraid to tell you of your doom, but we do not choose to be forever dwelling on that doleful theme. We rather love to tell you of Christ, and him crucified. We want to have our preaching rather full of the frankincense of the merits of Christ than of the smoke and fire and terrors of Mount Sinai. We are not come to Mount Sinai but to Mount Zion—where milder words declare the will of God and rivers of salvation are abundantly flowing.

Again, the theme of a minister should be Christ Jesus in opposition to mere doctrine. Some of my good brothers are always preaching doctrine. Well, they are right in so doing, but I would not care myself to have as the characteristic of my preaching doctrine only. I would rather have it said, "He dwelled much upon the person of Christ and seemed best pleased when he began to tell about the atonement and the sacrifice. He was not ashamed of the doctrines; he was not afraid of threatening. But he seemed as if he preached the threatening with tears in his eyes, and the doctrine solemnly as God's own Word. But when he preached of Jesus, his tongue was loosened, and his heart was at liberty."

Brothers, there are some men who preach the doctrine only, who are an injury, I believe, to God's church rather than a benefit. I know of men who have set themselves up as umpires over all spirits. Wisdom will die with them. If they were once taken away, the great standard of truth would be removed.

If you want to be made drunkards, if you want to be made dishonest, if you want to be taught every vice in the world, go and hear a moral preacher. These gentlemen, in their attempts to reform and make people moral, are the men that lead them from morality. Hear the testimony of holy Bishop Lavington:* "We have long been attempting to reform the nation by moral preaching. With what effect? None. On the contrary, we have skillfully preached the people into downright infidelity. We must change our voice. We must preach Christ and him crucified. Nothing but the gospel is the power of God for salvation."

"I, when I am lifted up from the earth, will draw all people to myself" (John 12:32). Then Christ Jesus will draw all his people to Heaven. He is in Heaven; then Christ is the chariot in which souls are drawn to Heaven. The people of the Lord are on their way to Heaven—they are carried in everlasting arms, and those arms are the arms of Christ.

Christ is carrying them up to his own house, to his own throne. By and by his prayer—"Father, I desire that they also, whom you have given me, may be with me where I am" (John 17:24)—shall be wholly fulfilled. And it is being fulfilled now, for he is like a strong, swift horse drawing his children to himself in the chariot of the covenant of grace.

Oh, blessed be God, the cross is the plank we hold to as we

* Bishop Lavington was a chaplain to King George I and was appointed Bishop of Exeter in 1746.

swim to Heaven. The cross is the great covenant ship which will weather out the storms and reach its desired Heaven.

And now, poor sinner, I desire before God that Christ would pardon you. Remember his death on Calvary; remember his agonies and bloody sweat. All this he did for you, if you feel yourself to be a sinner. Does not this draw you to him?

> *Though you are guilty he is good,*
> *He'll wash your soul in Jesus' blood.*

You have rebelled against him and revolted, but he says, "Return, backsliding children." Will not his love draw you? I pray that you may be drawn to Christ now and at last be drawn to Heaven.

———— ❊ ————

ALCORN ⟜ Spurgeon says, "It is not Hell but Christ we desire to preach." He sometimes speaks of Christ without speaking of Hell, but he never speaks of Hell without speaking of Christ.

As a young Christian I recited memory verses printed on small cards. One of them said, "Him who comes to me I will not cast out" (John 6:37, RSV). But the first part of the same verse apparently didn't fit someone's theology, since it wasn't on the card: "All that the Father gives me will come to me."

Jesus makes an obvious case that God calls souls to him. He goes on to say, "No one can come to me unless the Father who sent me draws him" (verse 44). And if we still don't get the message, he adds, "No one can come to me unless it is granted him by the Father" (verse 65).

Spurgeon, who loved the doctrine of election, continually called upon sinners to choose Christ, to yield to him as Savior and Lord, to turn from sin and Hell to Christ and Heaven. The hyper-Calvinists of his day were severely critical of Spurgeon's pulpit evangelism. Yet he continued to make his pleas, following the biblical model of preaching to saints and sinners alike. He believed people can make a meaningful choice to turn to Christ because God empowers us to do so. He saw it as his job to implore sinners to make the good choice. Sovereignty and free will may remain mysterious to us, but when we compare all the Scriptures, discarding none, we are plainly instructed to ask God to save people and also to tell people of their need for salvation. Spurgeon did both, since he was less concerned about reconciling doctrines than about believing and acting on them.

God calls us spiritually dead without Christ (Ephesians 2:1). We did not, by acts of our will, make ourselves alive. Lazarus serves as an illustration of what it means to be dead, then made alive. Who's more helpless than a dead man? When Jesus said, "Lazarus, come out" (John 11:43), the dead man lacked the capacity to obey until Jesus made him alive.

Still, God extends a genuine invitation to people to come to him. They can do so as he sovereignly empowers them.

Sometimes as Christians we assume we have a full capacity to respond to God. But this doesn't square with any number of Scriptures, including this one: "Just as the Father raises the dead and gives them life, even so the Son gives life to whom he is pleased to give it" (John 5:21, NIV). It appears that a person doesn't simply choose life; Jesus gives it to him.

Romans 8:7 tells us the sinful mind "does not submit to God's law, nor *can* it do so" (NIV, emphasis added). In our sinful state, we have no innate ability to follow God. People who lack the Spirit cannot begin to understand spiritual things (1 Corinthians 2:14).

Our problem is both our unwillingness to understand *and* our incapacity to turn our wills toward God. Without acknowledging those truths, we might imagine ourselves in Heaven congratulating one another that we had the savvy and strength of will to turn to Christ. But God leaves no room for such boasting (Ephesians 2:8-9; Titus 3:5).

God's amazing grace doesn't end at our conversion. Even the regenerated human will depends upon the divine will to live as it should. Philippians 2:12-13 corrects those who understate and those who overstate the role of the human will: "Continue to work out your salvation with fear and trembling, for it is God who works in you to will and to act in order to fulfill his good purpose" (NIV). We must will and work, *and* God must will and work.

Sinners should choose to repent, yet only God grants saving repentance. God calls upon us not only to surrender and lay down our arms but to switch sides. Without God's empowerment, no sinner could ever do this. Thank God for his sovereign grace!

WEDDING PREPARATIONS

❊

Excerpted from "The Barrier"
Sermon #1590

Delivered on Lord's Day morning,
March 27, 1881, at the Metropolitan Tabernacle, Newington

Of all the analogies God could use to describe his church, one of his favorites is a bride preparing for marriage. If we're going to love Christ, we must love his bride. And if we're to be ready for the wedding, we need to make sure we are dressed accordingly.

> *Nothing unclean will ever enter [the New Jerusalem, on the New Earth], nor anyone who does what is detestable or false, but only those who are written in the Lamb's book of life.*
>
> REVELATION 21:27

——— ❊ ———

SPURGEON ☞ It is the glorified church that is here spoken of, and hence the text may be said to refer to Heaven. For at the present moment the nucleus of the glorified church is in Heaven, and from Heaven every defiled thing must be shut out.

It may also refer to the Kingdom of the millennial age, when the saints will reign with Christ upon the Earth for a thousand years, when even upon this battlefield our conquering Leader shall be crowned with victory, and where his blood was shed, his throne shall be set up.

The text may also be read as including the eternal world of future happiness [the New Earth], for the glorified church will one day possess that glorious, endless, undefiled inheritance. But out of her shall long before have been gathered all things that offend and those that do iniquity. From Heaven and from all heavenly joys and states sin must be shut out. Into the perfected church there nothing that contaminates shall ever enter.

I should like you for a minute or two to think of that perfected church as she is described in Revelation 21, for it is a description worthy of the most profound study. What glory will surround the risen saints in their role in the city of God: "having the glory of God," says the eleventh verse. What a glory of glories is this! Even now, my brothers and sisters, you who are in Christ possess the grace of God, but by and by you shall conspicuously shine with the glory of God.

At present you share in the dishonor which falls on your Master and his cause among a wicked generation, but then you shall share in the glory which is the reward of the anguish of his soul. "Then the righteous will shine like the sun in the kingdom of their Father" (Matthew 13:43).

How glorious will that church be whose light shall be the presence of God himself—light in which the nations of the redeemed shall rejoice. Oh my God, write my name among them! And to that end, write me among your persecuted saints below. We should be content to endure what little shame shall come upon the active church on Earth if we may participate in the honor of the church glorified above, for this is an excellent glory.

What a church will the church of God be in those happier days! We watch the church of God sometimes with apprehension and alarm, for though we know that the gates of Hell shall not prevail against her, yet her feebleness makes the timid tremble.

But in her state after the Resurrection there shall remain no signs of feebleness, for that which was sown in weakness shall be raised in power. She shall be a city the like of which has never been beheld, whose foundation shall be deeper than the depths beneath and whose towers shall reach above the clouds.

No institution shall exist so long or flourish so abundantly as the church of the living God. When you think of the church of God, settled in her place by the Almighty himself who has established her, remember her vastness, for a multitude that no man can number shall be seen among her inhabitants. Her census shall prove her citizens to be as the stars of Heaven in their multitudes. From her vast foundation the living stones shall rise course upon course, twelve foundations of jewels, till "the mountain of the house of the LORD . . . shall be lifted up above the hills" (Isaiah 2:2).

I say again, write my name down among the dwellers in the great city! What higher honor can I crave? To be numbered with princes, to be named with emperors—think of it! Your beautiful pieces of royal clothing are but poor toys. True glory lies in being part and parcel of the church, today despised and rejected of men, which shall before long look forth fair as the sun and astonish the world with the brightness of her rising.

———— ❀ ————

ALCORN ✎ These days many Christians bend over backward to criticize the church—in some cases to berate her in the most scathing terms. They distance themselves from the bride of Christ to the point that they no longer are part of local churches, confident they are better off on their own.

Spurgeon acknowledges the church's "feebleness" but believes

Christ's promise that Hell itself won't prevail against it. So he says, "True glory lies in being part and parcel of the church, today despised and rejected of men, which shall before long look fair as the sun and astonish the world with the brightness of her rising."

Spurgeon would decry the low regard and dismissive attitudes many Christians today have for the church, Christ's body. It's trendy for people to say, "I love Jesus, but I hate the church." But the church is Christ's bride, and even with all her flaws, he loves her and will never give up on her. If you came to me and said, "Randy, I want to be your friend; I love you, but I hate your wife," I would say, "If you hate Nanci, you cannot be my friend. She and I are one. I am deeply loyal to her. I would die for her." Christ would say the same of his bride, except he would add, "In fact, I *did* die for her."

As the church, we're part of the ultimate Cinderella story— we'll be rescued from a home where we labor, often without appreciation or reward. One day we'll be taken into the arms of the Prince and whisked away to live in his palace. When "the wedding of the Lamb has come" (Revelation 19:7, NIV), the New Jerusalem, consisting not only of buildings but also of God's people, will come down out of Heaven, "prepared as a bride beautifully dressed for her husband" (Revelation 21:2, NIV). The eyes of the universe will be on the Bridegroom, yes, but also on the bride for whom he died. "His bride has made herself ready. Fine linen, bright and clean, was given her to wear" (Revelation 19:7-8, NIV).

It takes faith, but we must learn to look at our local churches, even with all their problems, and say, "Many of these people are redeemed; they are Christ's bride, though now they are as imperfect as I am. Help me, Jesus, not to dismiss and berate and ridicule them but to love them as you do. Help me to see that you call me to be your bride, not as an individual, but as part of a church."

I have vivid memories of my wife's and my daughters' pure beauty in their wedding dresses. The church, Christ's bride, should likewise be characterized by purity—a fitting gift for our Bridegroom, the Crown Prince who has been utterly faithful to us.

If we were to guess what the bride's fine linen stands for, our first instinct might be to assume it's the righteousness of Christ that covers us. Significantly, however, the text says something different: "Fine linen stands for the righteous acts of God's holy people" (Revelation 19:8, NIV). It's only because of the Bridegroom's work that the chosen princess, the church, can enter the presence of her Lord. Yet her wedding dress is woven by her many acts of faithfulness while away from her Bridegroom on the fallen Earth.

The picture is compelling. Each prayer, each gift, each hour of fasting, each kindness to the needy—all these are the threads that have been woven together into this wedding dress. Her works have been empowered by the Spirit, and she has spent her life on Earth sewing her wedding dress for the day when she will be joined to her beloved Bridegroom.

This gives us a wonderful reason to remain here on this Earth, even though we long to be with our beloved Jesus. The wedding approaches, yet there's more for us to do to present ourselves pure before our Lord. Part of us wants fewer days between now and the wedding, because we're so eager to be with our Beloved in our new home. But another part wants more days to better prepare for the wedding, to sew our dress by acts of faithful service to God.

The imagery is beautiful but potentially disturbing. A pure bride doesn't want to appear scantily clothed or dressed in rags at the altar before her beloved Bridegroom and a crowd of guests. But if she has been diligent to prepare, her dress will be substantial, beautiful, and complete. May God help us to be his church, to build his church, and to love his church.

NO PLACE FOR SIN IN HEAVEN

❋

Excerpted from "The Barrier"
Sermon #1590, March 27, 1881

Would Heaven still be Heaven if sin had a place there? According to
Spurgeon, the answer is no! We will be entirely and forever free, not
only from the consequences of sin, but from our sin natures that plague
us now by pulling us away from God.

> *He who was seated on the throne said, "Behold, I am making
> all things new." Also he said, "Write this down, for these words
> are trustworthy and true." And he said to me, "It is done! I am
> the Alpha and the Omega, the beginning and the end. To the
> thirsty I will give from the spring of the water of life without
> payment. The one who conquers will have this heritage, and I
> will be his God and he will be my son. But as for the cowardly,
> the faithless, the detestable, as for murderers, the sexually
> immoral, sorcerers, idolaters, and all liars, their portion will be
> in the lake that burns with fire and sulfur, which is the second
> death."* REVELATION 21:5-8

——— ❋ ———

SPURGEON ☞ How holy the church will be. She shall have
no temple within her walls, for this simple reason: she shall be the
temple. She shall have no spot reserved for sacred uses because

all shall be "holiness unto the LORD" (Zechariah 14:20, KJV). The divine presence shall be in all and over all. And this shall be her joy: "The glory of God gives it light, and its lamp is the Lamb" (Revelation 21:23).

Brothers and sisters, the glory of the church even here below is the presence of God in her midst. But what will that presence be when it shines forth in noonday brightness, when spirits strengthened for the vision shall behold the full splendor of Jehovah's throne? Tongue cannot tell the glory, for thought cannot conceive it.

Write my name among the blessed who shall see Jehovah's face. Oh, you living God, my soul thirsts after you. To dwell in your presence is the summit of the soul's delight. To be with you where you are and to behold your glory is the Heaven of Heaven. To what beyond this can thoughts aspire?

It is not fitting that so royal and divine a body as the glorified church of God should be ruined by being defiled. God forbid that her light, which is "like unto a stone most precious, even like a jasper stone, clear as crystal" (Revelation 21:11, KJV) should ever be dimmed by the breath of sin.

How beautiful was this fair world in the early morning of her creation, when the dew of her youth glistened upon her, and the sunlight of God made her face to shine. Keep watch and stand guard, you shining ones, that this beauty be not marred! Sad was the hour when with dragon wing the fallen spirit descended into Eden, advanced to mother Eve, and whispered in her ear the fatal temptation.

Oh, you guardian angels, if only your fiery swords had kept out the arch deceiver, that this world might never have fallen, that we might have dwelled here amid sunny glades, by pure rivers rippling over golden sands. If only we had remained a holy and happy race, making every hill reverberate with the praise of God.

Now, oh Earth, you are a field of blood, but you might have been a garden of delights. Now are you one vast cemetery, where all the dust was once a part of the living fabric of mortal men. But you might have been as the heavens filled with stars, all shining to their Creator's praise. Alas that Eden should now remain only as a name—gone as a vision of the night!

As much as we could heartily wish that evil had never entered into the original world, we earnestly reject the idea that it will ever contaminate the new. Shall those new heavens ever look down with amazement upon the flight of a rebellious spirit, flying, beneath their serene blue sky, on an errand of destruction? Shall the jeweled walls of the Holy City be betrayed by an enemy of the King who is there enthroned? Shall the serpent leave his horrid trail upon the heavenly Eden, twice made of the Lord? God forbid!

The purity of a world twice made, the perfection of the church of the regenerate, the majesty of the presence of God—all demand that every sinful thing should be excluded. All Heaven and heavenly things cry, "Write the decree and make it sure; there is no way anything that defiles shall enter into it." It would be horrible indeed if a second time evil should destroy the work of God!

Into the church of the Jesus above the breath of iniquity must not enter. It cannot be that the work which cost the Redeemer's blood should yet be defiled. The eternal purpose of the Father and the love of the Spirit forbid that the Lord's own perfected church should be invaded by any unholy thing.

Brothers and sisters, there can be no entrance of evil into the Kingdom of God, for it is the very essence of the happiness of the glorified church that evil should be excluded. Imagine for a moment that the decree of our text were reversed or suspended and that it were allowed that a few unregenerate men and women should enter into the glorified church of God. Suppose, in addition, that those few should be of the gentler sort of sinners—not those who would profanely blaspheme the name of God, but a few who are indifferent to God's glory and cold and formal in his praise. How could Heaven bear with these?

These, who are neither cold nor hot are sickening both to Christ and to his people. As in a living body, the existence of a dead piece of bone breeds worry and pain and disease, so would the presence of these few unholy ones cause I know not what trouble and sorrow. It must not be. Love to the saints demands that they be no more troubled by sin or sinners. Pity, mercy, even the partiality of kindred love, dare not ask that it may be. All Heaven is up in arms at the very thought.

Holy people are alarmed at the idea that they should be again tempted by the presence of evil. Speedily bar the gates of pearl and never open them again rather than that there should come upon that pure street of transparent gold a foot that will not walk in the ways of God's commandments. God forbid that the halls of Zion be disgraced by a single spirit that shall refuse to love the holy and exalted name.

Heaven would not be Heaven if it were possible for evil of any sort to enter there. Therefore, stand firm, God's decree, for it would be cruelty to saints and destruction to Heaven if anything unholy would ever enter it.

ALCORN ⟨— I'm convinced that the Bible is clear on the exact point Spurgeon is making: though we will have freedom to choose in Heaven, we will have no ability to sin. Consider Revelation 21:4-5: "Death shall be no more, neither shall there be mourning, nor crying, nor pain anymore, *for* the former things have passed away. And he who was seated on the throne said, 'Behold, I am making all things new'" (emphasis added).

What follows the word *for* explains why the evil that causes death, mourning, crying, and pain will no longer exist. It's because the old order will have once and for all passed away, and God will replace it with a new order—one that is fundamentally transformed. Deception, sin, and rebellion against God will be things of the past. Those in Heaven need never fear another Fall.

Since "the wages of sin is death" (Romans 6:23, NIV), the promise of no more death on the New Earth is synonymous with a promise of no more sin. Since sinners always die, those who are promised they will never die are being promised they will not sin anymore.

Sin causes mourning, crying, and pain. If those will never occur again, then sin, their cause, can never occur again either.

But, some argue, "Adam and Eve were sinless, yet they fell into sin. Why shouldn't the same thing happen again?"

Adam and Eve's situation was very different from that of God's resurrected saints. The first man and woman were innocent, but not righteous. That is, they had not been made righteous by the atoning work of Christ. All people who will be in Heaven, on the other hand, have been made righteous through Christ: "As by the one man's disobedience the many were made sinners, so by the one man's obedience the many will be made righteous" (Romans 5:19).

To suggest we could have Christ's righteousness yet one day sin in Heaven is to say Christ could one day sin. God completely delivers us from sin and vulnerability to sin. Scripture emphasizes that Christ died once to deal with sin and will never again need to die (Hebrews 9:26-28; 10:10; 1 Peter 3:18). We'll have the full experience of our new nature, so we will in Christ "become the righteousness of God" (2 Corinthians 5:21). Possessing God's own righteousness, we won't sin in Heaven for the same reason God doesn't: he cannot. Christ purchased with his blood our eternal inability to sin: "By a single offering [himself] he has perfected for all time those who are being sanctified" (Hebrews 10:14).

Consider Spurgeon's text: "Nothing unclean will ever enter it [the New Jerusalem], nor anyone who does what is detestable or false, but only those whose names are written in the Lamb's book of life" (Revelation 21:27). The passage doesn't say, "If someone becomes impure or shameful or deceitful, they will be evicted." No eviction will be necessary, because nothing impure can ever enter in the first place.

The fact that evil will have no footing in Heaven and no leverage to affect us is further indicated by Jesus when he says, "The Son of Man will send his angels, and they will gather out of his kingdom *all causes of sin* and all law-breakers, and throw them into the fiery furnace. . . . *Then* the righteous will shine like the sun in the kingdom of their Father" (Matthew 13:41-43, emphasis added).

Even in the present Heaven, prior to the Resurrection, people cannot sin, for they are "the spirits of the righteous made perfect" (Hebrews 12:23). Ultimately, we'll be raised "incorruptible" (1 Corinthians 15:52, NKJV). *Incorruptible* is a stronger word than *uncorrupted*. Our risen bodies, and by implication all that we are, will be immune to corruption.

We will have true freedom in Heaven, but a righteous freedom that never sins.

Heaven will harbor no evil desires and no corruption, and we will fully participate in the sinless perfection of Christ. What does this mean in terms of human freedom? Remember, though God can't sin, no being has greater free choice than he does. That we won't be able to sin does not mean we won't have free choice.

Once we become what the sovereign God has made us to be in Christ, and once we see him as he is, we'll see all things—including sin—for what they are. God won't need to take away our ability to choose; he won't need to restrain us from evil. Sin will have absolutely no appeal to us. It will be, literally, unthinkable. The memory of evil and suffering in this life will serve as an eternal reminder of sin's horrors and emptiness. *Sin? Been there, done that. And have seen how ugly and disastrous it was.*

Theologian Paul Helm writes, "The freedom of heaven, then, is the freedom from sin; not that the believer just happens to be free from sin, but that he is so constituted or reconstituted that he cannot sin. He doesn't want to sin, and he does not want to want to sin."[54]

SINNERS COULD NEVER LOVE HEAVEN

❋

Excerpted from "The Barrier"
Sermon #1590, March 27, 1881

Spurgeon argues convincingly that sin and unrepentant sinners will have no place in a holy Heaven. Those who have rejected Christ would never be able to love Heaven—and those who have accepted him would never be able to love anything else.

> *The wicked boasts of the desires of his soul,*
>   *and the one greedy for gain curses and renounces the* Lord.
> *In the pride of his face the wicked does not seek him;*
>   *all his thoughts are, "There is no God." . . .*
> *His mouth is filled with cursing and deceit and oppression;*
>   *under his tongue are mischief and iniquity. . . .*
> *The helpless are crushed, sink down,*
>   *and fall by his might.*
> *He says in his heart, "God has forgotten,*
>   *he has hidden his face, he will never see it."*
> *Arise, O* Lord; *O God, lift up your hand;*
>   *forget not the afflicted.*
> *Why does the wicked renounce God*
>   *and say in his heart, "You will not call to account"?*
> *But you do see, for you note mischief and vexation,*
>   *that you may take it into your hands. . . .*

O LORD, you hear the desire of the afflicted;
    you will strengthen their heart; you will incline your ear
to do justice to the fatherless and the oppressed,
    so that man who is of the earth may strike terror no more.

PSALM 10:3-4, 7, 10-14, 17-18

———————— ❋ ————————

SPURGEON ⟨⟩ It is impossible for any defiled, sinful, unrenewed person to enter into the body of the glorified church of God—an impossibility that resides within the persons themselves. The reason wicked men cannot be happy is not alone because God will not let rebellion and peace dwell together but because they will not let themselves be happy. The sea cannot rest because it is the sea; the sinner cannot rest because he is a sinner.

How could you, an unregenerate man, ever enter into the Kingdom of Heaven as you are? You are not capable of it; it is not possible. Holiness has in it no attractions for you, since you love sin. You do not know God, and cannot see him, for this is the privilege of the pure in heart and of them alone.

You live in a world where everything has been made by the great Lord and yet you do not perceive his hand, so great is your blindness. Shall blind men grope through the streets of the New Jerusalem? You are unacquainted with the simplest elements of spiritual things, for they can only be spiritually discerned and you have no spiritual faculty.

You are blind and deaf, dead to God and heavenly things. You know you are. Well, then, of what benefit would it be that you should enter the spiritual realm? For if you were admitted into the place called Heaven, you would not be a partaker of the state of Heaven. And it is the state of mind and character which is, after all, the essence of the joy. To be in a heavenly place and not in a heavenly condition would be worse than Hell, if anything can be. What are songs to a sad heart? Such would Heaven be to an unrenewed mind. The element of glory would destroy rather than bless an unrenewed mind. No place would be so dreadful to a sinner as the place where God is most openly manifest.

That holy habitat of the newborn soul would be for the unholy soul the grave, the everlasting prison house, if it could enter there. To the wicked the Day of the Lord is darkness, not light, and the glory of the Lord is terror, not bliss. Oh, unconverted hearer, they sing in Heaven, but in their songs your ear would find no delight. They worship God in Heaven, but if divine worship is irksome to you, even when it lasts for an hour here, what would it be to dwell forever and ever in the world to come in the midst of hallelujahs? Oh soul defiled with sin, you are incapable of Heaven.

Suppose I were infected today with a deadly fever—an incurable typhus, which would bring death to any that touched me. The blasting wind is pitiless, and the snow is falling, and I stand shivering at the door of one of your houses longing for shelter. I see inside the room your little children, sporting in full health. Shall I venture among them?

I long to escape from the cold outside, but if I should enter your room I should bring to you fever, and death to your innocent little ones and to yourselves, and thus turn your happiness into misery. I would turn away and brave the storm and sooner die than bring such desolation into a friend's abode. And well might any honest spirit say at sight of the perfect family above, "Even if I might, I would not be admitted into a perfect Heaven while yet I might defile it and spread the deadly disease of moral evil."

You know, brothers and sisters, how a few rags from the East have sometimes carried a plague into a city. If you were standing at the wharf when a plague-laden ship arrived, you would cry, "Burn those rags; do anything with them—but keep them away from the people. Bring not the plague into a vast city where it may slay its thousands!"

So we cry, "Great God, forbid that anything which defiles should enter into your perfected church! We cannot endure such a thought." Draw your swords, you angels; stand in your closed, tight-formed ranks, you seraphim, and strike down every defiled one that would force a passage within Heaven's gates. It must be so: "Nothing unclean will ever enter it" (Revelation 21:27).

The decree of God has gone forth, and the fiery sword is set at the gate of the new Eden. Into the first paradise there came the serpent. But into the second paradise the tempter shall never enter. Into the first paradise there came sin, and God was driven from it as well as man. But into the second paradise there shall never come anything close to sin or falsehood. Rather, the Lord God shall dwell there forever, and his people shall dwell there with him.

ALCORN ⬤ C. S. Lewis says that the doors of Hell are locked on the inside. Of course, we know from Christ's account of the rich man and Lazarus that people in Hell do not want to stay there but would love to escape the punishment they endure (Luke 16:19-31). But Lewis's primary point may be that wanting to be relieved of Hell's fires is *not* the same as wanting to live in Heaven! And if there are no other options, what then?

In my novel *Deadline* I envision a character who has died:

> This was his first hour of Hell. How could he endure
> even a day, much less an eternal night? But if he could
> escape, what was the alternative? Heaven? The thought
> of being there sickened him. To be under those rules, that
> constant self-righteous oppression, would be intolerable.
> More intolerable, even, than this place. He thirsted for
> help, but not redemption. He hungered for hope, but not
> righteousness. He longed for friendship, but not with
> God or those who followed him.[55]

It appears that a sin nature would continue in Hell since only in Christ could it be removed. Professor D. A. Carson argues that Hell is eternal because sinful rebellion is eternal. If this is the case, Hell is a place where "sinners go on sinning and receiving the recompense of their sin, refusing, always refusing, to bend the knee."[56] Hell would be ever-ongoing punishment for ever-ongoing sins.

In contrast, those in Heaven will not sin because they will have been fully delivered from the old nature and granted a new and completely perfected one in Christ. But I am convinced we will *never* forget the ugliness of sin. People who have experienced severe burns aren't tempted to walk into a bonfire. We'll never be deceived into thinking God is withholding something good from us or that sin is in our best interest. Satan won't have any access to us. But even if he did, we wouldn't be tempted. We'll know what righteousness is but also what sin is—or was. We'll always know sin's true cost. Every time we see the scarred hands of King Jesus, we'll remember.

Because our hearts will be pure and we'll see people as they truly are, every relationship in Heaven will be pure. We'll all be faithful to the love of our lives: King Jesus. We couldn't do anything behind his back even if we wanted to. But we'll never want to.

We'll love everyone, men and women, but we'll be *in love* only with Jesus. We'll never be tempted to degrade, use, or idolize one another. We'll never believe the outrageous lie that our deepest needs can be met in any person but Jesus.

Often we act as if the universe revolves around us. We have to remind ourselves it's all about Christ, not us. In Heaven we'll never have to correct our thinking. What is true about God will be evident to all. Puritan preacher Jonathan Edwards says, "Even the very best of men, are, on Earth, imperfect. But it is not so in heaven. There shall be no pollution or deformity or offensive defect of any kind, seen in any person or thing; but everyone shall be perfectly pure, and perfectly lovely in heaven."[57]

In Heaven we'll be perfectly *human*. Adam and Eve were perfectly human until they bent themselves into sinners. Then they lost something that was an original part of their humanity—moral perfection. Since then, under sin's curse, we've been human but never perfectly human.

We can't remember a time when we weren't sinners. We've always carried sin's baggage. What relief we'll feel not to have to guard our eyes and our minds. We will not need to defend against pride and lust because there will be none.

Someone once asked me, "If we're sinless, will we still be human?" Although sin is part of us now, it's not essential to our humanity. In fact, it's *foreign* to it. It's what twists us and keeps us from being what we once were—and what we one day will be.

Our greatest deliverance in Heaven will be from ourselves. Our deceit, corruption, self-righteousness, self-sufficiency, hypocrisy—all will be gone forever. And we will never stop praising God for the miracle of his grace!

RESPONDING TO HEAVEN'S INVITATION

❁

Excerpted from "The Barrier"
Sermon #1590, March 27, 1881

Each one of us has been invited to the most exquisite wedding banquet we could imagine. But it is not enough to receive the invitation; we must respond. When the day of the celebration arrives, will our names be on the guest list?

> *At midnight there was a cry, "Here is the bridegroom! Come out to meet him." Then all those virgins rose and trimmed their lamps. And the foolish said to the wise, "Give us some of your oil, for our lamps are going out." But the wise answered, saying, "Since there will not be enough for us and for you, go rather to the dealers and buy for yourselves." And while they were going to buy, the bridegroom came, and those who were ready went in with him to the marriage feast, and the door was shut. Afterward the other virgins came also, saying, "Lord, lord, open to us." But he answered, "Truly, I say to you, I do not know you." Watch therefore, for you know neither the day nor the hour.* MATTHEW 25:6-13

——— ❁ ———

SPURGEON ☞ If Christ is God—if it is true that he, within that infant's body, contained the fullness of the deity and being thus God and man, took away my sin and in his own body on the cross did bear it and suffer its punishment for me—then I can understand how my transgression is forgiven and my sin is covered.

Short of this my conscience cannot rest. But this truth—Christ instead of me, God himself the offended one in the offender's place, bowing his majestic head to vengeance and laying his eternal majesty in the dishonor of a tomb—this is the fullness of consolation.

Oh Lamb of God, my sacrifice, I shall enter Heaven now! I shall not be afraid of the eyes of fire. I shall be without spot or wrinkle or any such thing—"washed . . . in the blood of the Lamb"! (Revelation 7:14). This is our first great comfort, brothers and sisters: "Whoever believes in him is not condemned" (John 3:18). He who believes in him is justified from all things from which he could not be justified by the law of Moses.

"There is therefore now no condemnation for those who are in Christ Jesus" (Romans 8:1). There can be no knowledge of God, no communion with God, no delight in God hereafter unless all sin is put away and our fallen nature is entirely changed. Can this be done? It can.

Faith in Christ tells us of something else beside the blood. There is a divine person—let us bow our heads and worship him—the Holy Spirit who goes out from the Father. He's the One who renews us in the spirit of our minds. When we believe in Jesus, the Spirit enters into the heart, creating within us a new life. That life struggles and contends against the old life, or rather, the old death. As it struggles, it gathers strength and grows. It masters the evil and puts its foot upon the neck of the tendency to sin.

Do you feel this Spirit within you? You must be under its power or perish. If any man doesn't have the Spirit of Christ, he doesn't belong to him. I would not have you imagine that in death everything is to be accomplished for us mysteriously in the last solemn moment. The sanctifying work of the Holy Spirit is not a sort of extreme ritual reserved for deathbeds; it is a matter for the walks of life and the activities of today.

I do not know how much is done in the saint during the last minute of his lingering here, but this I know: that in a true believer the conquest of sin is a matter to be begun as soon as he is converted and to be carried on throughout life. If the Spirit of God dwells in us, we walk not after the flesh but after the spirit, and we deny the lusts of the old nature. There must be now a treading underfoot of lust and pride and every evil thing, or these evils will tread us underfoot forever in the future state where character never changes.

Oh my hearers, suppose we should never enter there! No, do not be surprised, for the assumption will soon be a fact with many of you unless you repent. Suppose we should be in the next world what some of us are now—defiled and untruthful. What remains? That is an awful text in the parable of the virgins: "And the door was shut." You read of those who said, "'Lord, Lord, open to us.' But he answered, 'Truly, I say to you, I do not know you'" (Matthew 25:11-12).

Will any one of us who has a lamp and is thought to be a virgin soul be among the shut out ones, on whose ear shall fall the words, "I do not know where you come from"? (Luke 13:25). You see you cannot be anywhere else but out unless you are in. And you must be shut out if you are corrupted and corrupting.

I beg you to consider this question. You do not know how short a time you have left in which you may look into it. Some who were here but last Sunday are now gone from us. Eleven deaths reported at one church meeting among our members! We are a dying people. We shall all be gone within a very short time.

I charge you by the living God, and as you are dying men and women: see to it that you are not shut out, so as to hear the fatal cry, "Too late, too late—you cannot enter now." There shall be no purgatory in eternity and no possible way of entering in among the perfected, for it is written, "Nothing unclean will ever enter it" (Revelation 21:27). No crying, "Lord! Lord!" No striving to enter in, no tears, no, not even the pangs of Hell itself shall ever purge the soul so as to make it fit to join with the holy church above, should it pass into the future state uncleansed.

Shut out! Shut out! O God, may that never be true of anyone among us, for Christ's dear name's sake.

───────── ❀ ─────────

ALCORN ☞ Spurgeon's heart of compassion for the people of his church and the unbelieving masses prompted him to call upon them to examine their lives and their faith. He knew that every person is either Heaven bound or Hell bound.

Spurgeon was frustrated with church attenders who were picky about small things while not taking into consideration larger ones such as people's desire to hear the gospel or to be taught God's truth. In *Lectures to My Students*, he says, "What terrible blankets some professors are! Their remarks after a sermon are enough to stagger you. . . . You have been pleading as for life or death and they have been calculating how many seconds the sermon occupied and grudging you the odd five minutes beyond the usual hour."

Spurgeon's urgency in this particular sermon is great because, in that single church meeting, there had been reports of eleven people's deaths! It was a large church, true, but that is still a staggering number. Spurgeon says, "We are a dying people. We shall

all be gone within a very short time." This isn't cause for alarm for those who are ready, but it serves as a solemn warning for those who aren't.

Ancient cities kept rolls of their citizens as a safekeeping measure to keep out criminals and enemies. Guards were posted at the city gates, and they were responsible for checking people's names against the list. This is the context for Revelation 21:27: "Nothing unclean will ever enter [the city], nor anyone who does what is detestable or false, but only those who are written in the Lamb's book of life."

Ruthanna Metzgar, a professional singer, tells a story that illustrates the importance of having our names written in the Book. Several years ago she was asked to sing at the wedding of a very wealthy man. According to the invitation, the reception would be held on the top two floors of Seattle's Columbia Tower, the Northwest's tallest skyscraper. She and her husband, Roy, were excited about attending.

At the reception, waiters in tuxedos offered luscious hors d'oeuvres and exotic beverages. The bride and groom approached a beautiful staircase made of glass and brass that led to the top floor. Someone ceremoniously cut a satin ribbon draped across the bottom of the stairs. They announced that the wedding feast was about to begin. The bride and groom ascended the stairs, followed by their guests.

At the top of the stairs, a maître d' with a bound book greeted the guests outside the doors.

"May I have your name please?"

"I am Ruthanna Metzgar, and this is my husband, Roy."

He searched the *M*s. "I'm not finding it. Would you spell it, please?"

Ruthanna spelled her name slowly. After searching the book, the maître d' looked up and said, "I'm sorry, but your name isn't here."

"There must be some mistake," Ruthanna replied. "I'm the singer. I sang for this wedding!"

The gentleman answered, "It doesn't matter who you are or what you did. Without your name in the book, you cannot attend the banquet."

He motioned to a waiter and said, "Show these people to the service elevator, please."

The Metzgars followed the waiter past beautifully decorated tables laden with shrimp, whole smoked salmon, and magnificent ice sculptures. Adjacent to the banquet area, an orchestra was preparing to perform, the musicians all dressed in dazzling white tuxedos.

The waiter led Ruthanna and Roy to the service elevator, ushered them in, and pushed *G* for the parking garage.

After locating their car and driving several miles in silence, Roy reached over and put his hand on Ruthanna's arm. "Sweetheart, what happened?"

"When the invitation arrived, I was busy," Ruthanna replied. "I never bothered to RSVP. Besides, I was the singer. Surely I could go to the reception without returning the RSVP!"

Ruthanna started to weep—not only because she had missed the most lavish banquet she'd ever been invited to, but also because she suddenly had a small taste of what it will be like someday for people as they stand before Christ and find that their names are not written in the Lamb's Book of Life.[58]

Throughout the ages, countless people have been too busy to respond to Christ's invitation to his wedding banquet. Many assume that the good they've done—perhaps attending church, being baptized, singing in the choir, or helping in a soup kitchen—will be enough to gain entry to Heaven. But people who do not respond to Christ's invitation to forgive their sins are people whose names aren't written in the Lamb's Book of Life. To be denied entrance to Heaven's wedding banquet will mean being cast outside, into Hell, forever.

In that day, no explanation or excuse will count. All that will matter is whether our names are written in the Book. If they're not, we'll be turned away.

Have you said yes to Christ's invitation to join him at the wedding feast and spend eternity with him in his house? If so, you have reason to rejoice—Heaven's gates will be open to you.

If you have been putting off your response, or if you presume that you can enter Heaven without responding to Christ's invitation, one day you will deeply regret it.

BEHOLD THE FACE OF GOD

✦

**Excerpted from "The Heavenly Singers and Their Song"
Sermon #2321**

Delivered on Lord's Day evening,
July 14, 1889, at the Metropolitan Tabernacle, Newington

Heaven will be the furthest thing from dull! When we see God as he is, in all his glory, worship will never be monotonous. We will overflow with joy as we explore the depths of who God truly is.

> *When he had taken the scroll, the four living creatures and the twenty-four elders fell down before the Lamb, each holding a harp, and golden bowls full of incense, which are the prayers of the saints. And they sang a new song, saying, "Worthy are you to take the scroll and to open its seals, for you were slain, and by your blood you ransomed people for God from every tribe and language and people and nation, and you have made them a kingdom and priests to our God, and they shall reign on the earth."* REVELATION 5:8-10

———— ✦ ————

SPURGEON ☙ The blessed Lamb appears in Heaven as the mediator between God and men. At God's right hand is the Book of his eternal purposes. None dared even to look upon it; it was hopeless that any creature should be able to open its seven seals. But there came forward this glorious Lamb, who had the marks of his slaughter upon him, and he took the Book from the right hand of him who sat upon the throne. Thus he acted as interpreter, taking the will of God and translating it to us, letting us know the meaning of the writing which we could never have deciphered.

Jesus Christ is seen as our sacrifice. He is our mediator, and in that capacity he becomes the object of adoration first for the church, then for all the ten thousands of angels, and then for every creature God has made. It would be too large a subject to take in all those hallelujahs. Therefore, I select only these three verses to set forth the adoration of the church of God, rendered to the bleeding Lamb as the mediator between God and men.

Behold the worshipers, for we must be like them if we are to be with them. It is a well-known rule that Heaven must be in us before we can be in Heaven. We must be heavenly if we hope to sit in the heavenly places. We shall not be taken up to join the glorified choir unless we have learned their song and can join their sacred harmony. Look, then, at the worshipers. You are not yet perfectly like them, but you will be, by and by, if you already have the main points of likeness fashioned in you by the grace of God.

The first point about the worshipers is this: they are all full of life. I don't want to be dogmatic about the meaning of the four living creatures. But they seem to represent the church in its standing before God, made alive by the life of God. At any rate, they are living creatures, and the elders themselves are living persons. Those in Heaven are all full of life. There is no dead worshiper there, no dull, cold heart that does not respond to the praise by which it is surrounded.

And they are all of one mind. Whether they are twenty-four elders or four living creatures, they all move simultaneously. With perfect unanimity they fall on their faces or touch their harps or uplift their golden bowls full of incense.

Is there always real unanimity in our assembly? While one is praising, is another murmuring? While one is earnest, is another indifferent? Oh God, grant to our assemblies here below the harmony that comes of the one Spirit working in us the same result, for so we must be in Heaven.

If we are not of one mind here below, we are not like the heavenly beings above! When little bickerings come in, when denominational differences prevent our joining in the common adoration, it is a great pity. God heal his one church of all her unhappy divisions! And heal any one church of any latent differences that there may be, that our unity on Earth may be an anticipation of the unanimity of Heaven!

Note too that as the heavenly worshipers are full of life and full of unity, so they are all full of holy worship. "When he had taken the scroll, the four living creatures and the twenty-four elders fell down before the Lamb" (Revelation 5:8). All reverently fell down before the Lamb. And in the fourteenth verse, after their song is over and after the angels and the whole creation have taken their turn in the celestial music, we read, "The four living creatures said, 'Amen.'" It was all that they could say. They were overawed with the majestic presence of God and the Lamb. They did not say anything then; they simply fell down and worshiped.

It is a grand thing when, at last, we have broken the backs of words with the weight of our feelings, when expressive silence must come in to prove the praises which we cannot utter. It is glorious to be in this worshipful state of mind. We are not always so, but they are so in Heaven. They are all ready to fall down before the Lord.

Do you not think that we often come into our places of

worship with a great deal of carelessness? And while the service
is going on, are we not thinking of a thousand things? Or if we
are attentive, is there enough poor worship about us? In Heaven,
they fall down before the Lamb. Brothers and sisters, would we
not serve God better now if we did more of this falling down to
worship the Lamb?

In Heaven there is prayer. We must correct the common
mistake about that matter. And there is something to pray for.
Although we do not ask the intercession of saints and angels, we
believe that the saints do pray. Are they not crying, "O Sovereign
Lord . . . how long?" (Revelation 6:10). Why should they not
pray, "Your kingdom come, your will be done, on earth as it is in
heaven"? (Matthew 6:10). They would understand that prayer
better than we do.

We know how God's will is not done on Earth, but they know
how it is done in Heaven. And they could pray, "Thy kingdom
come . . . for thine is the kingdom, and the power, and the glory,
for ever. Amen" (Matthew 6:10, 13, KJV).

———— ⊛ ————

ALCORN ☞ Have you ever—in prayer or in corporate worship or during a walk on the beach—even for a few moments
experienced the very presence of God? It's a tantalizing encounter, yet for most of us it tends to disappear quickly in the distrac-
tions of life. What will it be like to behold God's face and never
be distracted by lesser things? And what will it be like when every
lesser thing unfailingly points our attention back to God?

Many Christians today have come to depreciate or ignore the
beatific vision—seeing the face of God—supposing that beholding God would be of mere passing interest, becoming monotonous
over time. But those who know God know that he is anything

but boring. Seeing God will be dynamic, not static. It will mean exploring new beauties, unfolding new mysteries—forever.

In Heaven we'll explore God's being, an experience that will be delightful beyond comprehension. The sense of wide-eyed wonder we see among Heaven's inhabitants in Revelation 4–5 suggests an ever-deepening appreciation of God's greatness. That isn't all there is to Heaven, but if it were, it would be more than enough.

Lovers aren't bored by one another. People who love God could never be bored in his presence. Remember, the members of the triune Godhead exist in eternal relationship with each other. To see God is to participate in the infinite delight of their communion.

I find it ironic that many people stereotype life in Heaven as an interminable church service. Apparently church attendance has become synonymous with boredom. Yet meeting God—when it truly happens—will be far more exhilarating than anything we might enjoy on Earth, including a great meal, hunting, gardening, mountain climbing, or watching the Super Bowl.

Even if it were true (it isn't) that church services must be dull, there will be no church services in Heaven. The church (Christ's people) will be there. But there will be no temple, and as far as we know, no services (Revelation 21:22).

Will we *always* be engaged in worship? I think the answer is yes and no. If we have a narrow view of worship, the answer is no. But if we have a broad view of worship, the answer is yes. As theologian Cornelis Venema explains, worship in Heaven will be all-encompassing:

> No legitimate activity of life—whether in marriage, family, business, play, friendship, education, politics, etc.—escapes the claims of Christ's kingship. . . . Certainly those who live and reign with Christ forever will find the diversity

and complexity of their worship of God not less, but richer, in the life to come. Every legitimate activity of new creaturely life will be included within the life of worship of God's people.[59]

Will we always be on our faces at Christ's feet, worshiping him? No, because Scripture says we'll be doing many other things— living in dwelling places, eating and drinking, reigning with Christ, and working for him. Scripture depicts people standing, walking, traveling in and out of the city, and gathering at feasts. When doing these things, we won't be on our faces before Christ. Nevertheless, all that we do will be an act of worship. At times this will crescendo into greater heights of praise as we assemble with the multitudes who are also worshiping him. God seeks worshipers (John 4:23). But he has no policy of compulsory adulation. Once we see God as he really is, no one will need to beg, threaten, or shame us into praising him. No matter what we're doing, we will overflow in gratitude and praise, and in that sense we will continuously worship God. Shouldn't we be getting a head start on this? As Spurgeon puts it, "Brothers and sisters, would we not serve God better now if we did more of this falling down to worship the Lamb?"

We were *created* to worship God. There's no higher pleasure. At times we'll lose ourselves in praise, doing nothing but worshiping him. At other times we'll worship him when we build a cabinet, paint a picture, cook a meal, eat and drink, talk with an old friend, take a walk, or throw a ball.

"Whether, then, you eat or drink or whatever you do, do all to the glory of God" (1 Corinthians 10:31, NIV). If we are commanded to do everything, including eating and drinking, to God's glory now, won't we do it all to God's glory then?

THE POWER AND GLORY OF OUR REDEEMER

✸

Excerpted from "The Heavenly Singers and Their Song"
Sermon #2321, July 14, 1889

This world is far from perfect, and we have reminders of that fact every day. But the brokenness we deal with isn't too much for God to handle, and it doesn't take him by surprise. One day he will fulfill his plan of redemption—for us and for this world.

> *I looked, and I heard around the throne and the living creatures and the elders the voice of many angels, numbering myriads of myriads and thousands of thousands, saying with a loud voice, "Worthy is the Lamb who was slain, to receive power and wealth and wisdom and might and honor and glory and blessing!" And I heard every creature in heaven and on earth and under the earth and in the sea, and all that is in them, saying, "To him who sits on the throne and to the Lamb be blessing and honor and glory and might forever and ever!" And the four living creatures said, "Amen!" and the elders fell down and worshiped.* REVELATION 5:11-14

———— ✸ ————

SPURGEON ☞ I pause a moment to ask whether we are prepared to go to Heaven and whether we are like those who are there. Remember that there is but one place for us besides. If we do not enter Heaven, to praise with those perfect spirits, we must be driven from the divine presence to suffer with the condemned.

You recoil at the idea of "Depart from me, you cursed!" (Matthew 25:41). I invite you to trust in him and find your sins forgiven, and so doing, you shall be prepared to meet the Lamb who sits upon the throne and there forever to adore his sacrifice while you enjoy the blessings that flow from it.

May we all meet in Heaven! It would be a dreadful thing if we could know the destiny of everybody here and find, among other things, that some here will never see the gates of pearl except from an awful distance, with a great gulf fixed between them.

May we be on the right side of that gulf! Get on the right side of it tonight, for Jesus' sake!

"They sang a new song, saying, 'Worthy are you to take the scroll and to open its seals, for you were slain, and by your blood you ransomed people for God from every tribe and language and people and nation, and you have made them a kingdom and priests to our God, and they shall reign on the earth'" (Revelation 5:9-10). I must take away the poetry for a moment and just deal with the doctrines of this heavenly hymn.

The first doctrine is that Christ is put in the front; his deity is affirmed. They sing, "Worthy are you." A strong-winged angel speeds his way over Earth and Heaven and down the deep places of the universe, crying with a loud voice, "Who is worthy to open the scroll?" (Revelation 5:2). But no answer comes, for no creature is worthy. Then came One of whom the church cries in its song, "Worthy are you."

Yes, beloved, he is worthy of all the praise and honor we can bring to him. He is worthy to be called equal with God; he himself *is* God, very God of very God. And no man can sing this song, or ever will sing it, unless he believes Christ to be true deity and accepts him as his Lord and God.

Next, the doctrine of this hymn is that the whole church delights in the mediation of Christ. Notice that it was when he had taken the scroll that they said, "Worthy are you to take the scroll" (Revelation 5:9). To have Christ standing between God and man is the joy of every believing heart. We could never reach up to God except that Christ has come to bridge the distance between us. He places one hand on man and the other upon God. He is the mediator who can lay his hand upon both, and the church greatly rejoices in this.

Remember that even the working of providence is not apart from the mediation of Christ. I rejoice in this, that if the thunders be let loose, if plagues and deaths around us fly, the child of God is still under the mediator's protection. No harm shall happen to the chosen, for Jesus always guards us. All power is given unto him in Heaven and in Earth, and the church rejoices in his role as mediator.

But now notice: in the church's song, what is her reason for believing that Christ is worthy to be a mediator? The church says, "Worthy are you . . . for you were slain" (Revelation 5:9). Ah, beloved, when Christ undertook to be her mediator, this was the extreme point to which his pledge to be her substitute could carry him—to be slain! Jesus is never more glorious than in his death. His substitutionary atonement is the culmination of his glory, as it was the very utmost depth of his shame. Beloved, we rejoice in our mediator because he died.

A thing that is redeemed belonged originally to the person who redeems it, and the redeemed of the Lord were always his. "Yours they were," said Christ, "and you gave them to me" (John 17:6). They always were God's. You cannot go and redeem a thing that does not belong to you. You may buy it, but you cannot redeem it. Now that which belonged originally to God became indebted through sin. We, having sinned, came under the curse of the law. And though God still held to it that we were his, we were yet under this embargo: sin had a claim upon us.

Christ came and saw his own, and he knew that they were his own. He asked what there was to pay to redeem them, to restore his ownership. It was his heart's blood, his life, himself that was required. He paid the price and redeemed them, and we tonight sing, "By your blood you ransomed people for God from every tribe and language and people and nation, and you have made them a kingdom and priests to our God, and they shall reign on the earth" (Revelation 5:9-10).

He has, by redeeming us, separated us to himself and made us a holy people, bought with blood in a special sense out of all the rest of mankind.

This redemption is the grounds for the distinction of God's holy people: "By your blood you ransomed people for God" (Revelation 5:9).

God never wearies of the precious blood, nor will his people who know where their salvation lies. They do not, even in Heaven, say that it is a dreadful word to mention. I heard a man the other day say of a certain minister, "Oh! We want another minister; we are tired of this man. He is always talking so much about the blood." In the last great day, God will be tired of the man who made that speech.

———————— ✦ ————————

ALCORN ✎ Spurgeon wrote some hymns and published a new collection of worship songs in 1866 called *Our Own Hymn-Book*. It was mostly a compilation of Isaac Watts's psalms and hymns. Spurgeon paid close attention to the doctrines contained in hymns. He was publicly critical of a particular hymnbook that portrayed God as distant and uninvolved in human affairs. As usual, his criticism gained him a great deal of negative press in return.

It is the hymn of Revelation 5 that Spurgeon chooses as his passage in this sermon, expressing that the entire physical universe was created for God's glory. But humanity rebelled, and the universe fell under the weight of our sin. Yet the serpent's seduction of Adam and Eve did not catch God by surprise. He had in place a plan by which he would redeem mankind—and all of creation—from sin, corruption, and death. Just as he promises to make men and women new, he promises to renew the Earth itself. How? By the blood of Christ, the Lamb of God. There is no other way.

If, due to the Fall, God would have given up on his original purpose for mankind to fill the Earth and rule it (Genesis 1:28), he surely wouldn't have repeated the same command to Noah after the Flood: "Be fruitful and increase in number and fill the earth" (Genesis 9:1, NIV). Still, until sin and the Curse are permanently removed, people are incapable of exercising proper stewardship of the Earth. Redemption buys back God's original design.

"God never wearies of the precious blood," Spurgeon says, "nor will his people who know where their salvation lies." The gospel is far greater than most of us imagine. It isn't just good news for us—it's good news for animals, plants, stars, and planets. It's good news for the sky above and the Earth below. Albert Wolters says, "The redemption in Jesus Christ means the restoration of an original good creation."[60]

God's redemptive plan climaxes not at the return of Christ nor in the millennial Kingdom but on the New Earth. Only then will all wrongs be made right. Only then will there be no more death, crying, or pain (Revelation 21:1-4). And only then will we all begin to see the breadth and depth of the universe-piercing power of the blood of God.

RULING THE EARTH FOREVER

Excerpted from "The Heavenly Singers and Their Song"
Sermon #2321, July 14, 1889

When you look back over the course of your life, you may find it hard to
imagine that God would choose you to one day be a ruler of the Earth.
But if you are redeemed by the blood of Christ, he declares that to be
your destiny.

> *I endure everything for the sake of the elect, that they also may*
> *obtain the salvation that is in Christ Jesus with eternal glory.*
> *The saying is trustworthy, for: If we have died with him,*
> *we will also live with him; if we endure, we will also reign*
> *with him.*   2 TIMOTHY 2:10-12

SPURGEON ⸎ It is redemption that makes us kings. We
cannot realize our kingship to the full extent here below, though
we do in a measure.

There is a poor man here who has but one room to live in. He
has no money in his pocket tonight, yet he is a king in the sight
of God.

There is one here, perhaps, who used to be a drunkard. He
could not overcome the evil. He signed the pledge, wore the blue
ribbon, and so on, but still he went back to the drink. By the

grace of God he has got his foot upon it now, for he has a new heart and a right spirit. That man is a king; he is a king over his drunken habits.

There is one here who used to have a very fierce temper. It was hard to live with him, but Christ has made him a changed man. Now he is a king, ruling over his temper. It is a grand thing to be made a king over yourself.

There are some who have dominion over millions of others, who have never ruled themselves. Poor creatures! Thank God if he has given you the mastery of your own nature. That is a glorious conquest, yet this is only the beginning of what is in this song of Heaven (Revelation 5:9-10).

And then they say, "You have made us priests." Christ has made every one of his people a priest, and every child of God is as much a priest as I am. And I am certainly a priest—a priest unto God to offer the spiritual sacrifice of prayer and praise and the ministry of the Word.

There is something to be expected: "They shall reign on the earth" (Revelation 5:10).

When that day will come, who can tell? But when it comes, the dead in Christ shall rise first. Arising at the midnight cry, they shall quit their beds of dust and silent clay, and the saints who are alive and remain shall join them.

"The rest of the dead did not come to life until the thousand years were ended" (Revelation 20:5). Then shall be a time of the saints' reigning upon the Earth. Their lives shall be regal; their delights, their joys, and their honors shall be equal to those of kings and princes—no, they shall far exceed them.

Do you and I expect to reign upon the Earth? It will seem very odd to one who is very poor, obscure, perhaps ignorant, but who knows his Lord, to find that Christ has made him a priest and a king, and that he shall reign on the Earth with him and then reign forever with him in glory.

But it would be perfectly monstrous if we were to assert of some persons, and of some here present, that they would reign on the Earth. The man who lives for himself shall never reign on the Earth. "Blessed are the meek, for they shall inherit the earth" (Matthew 5:5), not the men who, in their selfishness, trample down everybody else with iron heel. You shall not reign on the Earth—you have lived here simply to hoard money or to make a name for yourself or to indulge your passions or to revenge yourselves upon your fellow men. You reign, sir? You? God's prison house is the place for you, not a throne.

But when he has made us meek and humble and lowly and reverent and pure, then we shall become fit to be promoted to this high calling of being priests and kings for Christ unto God in glory, and even here on Earth in the day that is coming.

I wish that everybody here would take to searching himself as to whether he is likely to be of that blessed number. Do you with joy accept Christ as your mediator? Do you see clearly how worthy he is to be the mediator? Have you been redeemed from among men? Have you been taken away from old associations? Have you broken loose from habits that held you a slave?

Has God brought you into a New Heaven and a New Earth? Has he given you any measure of reigning power over yourself? Do you live as a priest, serving God continually?

If you are obliged to keep on saying, "No, no, no," to all these questions, then what shall I say but, "Come to Christ"? May you come to him tonight! May he tonight begin in you that blessed process that shall make you fit to be partaker of the inheritance of the saints in light, for Jesus' sake! Amen.

———————— ✳ ————————

ALCORN ☞ Human kingdoms will rise and fall until Christ sets up a kingdom that forever replaces them, where mankind rules in righteousness. In the context of earthly kingdoms, the Messiah's triumphant future reign is spoken of: "He was given authority, glory and sovereign power; all nations and peoples of every language worshiped him. His dominion is an everlasting dominion that will not pass away, and his kingdom is one that will never be destroyed" (Daniel 7:14, NIV).

The church father Irenaeus writes, "In the messianic kingdom the martyrs will reclaim the world as the possession which was denied to them by their persecutors. In the creation in which they endured servitude, they will eventually reign."[61]

In his parables, Jesus speaks of our ruling over cities (Luke 19:17). Paul addresses the subject of Christians ruling as if it were Theology 101: "Do you not know that the Lord's people will judge the world? . . . Do you not know that we will judge angels?" (1 Corinthians 6:2-3, NIV). The form of the verb in this question implies that we won't simply judge them a single time but will continually rule them.

If Paul speaks of this future reality as if it were something every child should know, why is it so foreign to Christians today?

Jesus said to his apostles, "I confer on you a kingdom, just as my Father conferred one on me, so that you may eat and drink at my table in my kingdom and sit on thrones, judging the twelve tribes of Israel" (Luke 22:29-30, NIV).

This is an astounding statement, one that should cause us to pause in wonder. Christ is conferring *a kingdom*? To human beings? But it is not just his apostles he promised would rule. Paul, speaking not to apostles but to Christians in general, says, "If we endure, we will also reign with him" (2 Timothy 2:12, NIV).

Mankind's reign on Earth is introduced in the first chapters of the Bible, mentioned throughout the Old Testament, affirmed by Jesus in the Gospels and by Paul in his letters, and repeated by John in the Bible's final chapters. With so much emphasis placed on this topic in Scripture, it's something we should not ignore—yet remarkably many Christians do.

Keeping in mind that *crown* and *throne*, both, indicate a ruling authority, consider the following examples from one small portion of the book of Revelation:

> If you remain faithful even when facing death, I will give you the crown of life. (2:10, NLT)

> To the one who is victorious and does my will to the end, I will give authority over the nations. (2:26, NIV)

> I am coming soon. Hold on to what you have, so that no one will take your crown. (3:11, NIV)

> To the one who is victorious, I will give the right to sit with me on my throne, just as I was victorious and sat down with my Father on his throne. (3:21, NIV)

> The twenty-four elders fall down before him who sits on the throne. . . . They lay their crowns before the throne. (4:10, NIV)

Earth is our land, our kingdom to govern, granted by our Father to Adam and Eve and their descendants. It's a kingdom once lost by us to a usurping pseudo-king, Satan, but which was won back for us by the mighty valor of Christ, who shed his blood to purchase our freedom—and with it our original inheritance, the Earth.

This is the drama of redemption. If we fail to understand our status as God's children and heirs and rulers of the Earth, we will fail to comprehend God's redemptive work. But if we understand our role in God's plan, we'll realize that he would not deliver us from Earth to live forever in a disembodied realm. In fact, the inheritance God grants us is the very same Earth over which epic battles have been fought since Satan's first attack in Eden. Our inheritance is not only physical but also eternal: "The blameless spend their days under the LORD's care, and their inheritance will endure forever" (Psalm 37:18, NIV).

Many people have told me they're uncomfortable with the idea that mankind will rule the Earth, govern cities, and reign forever. It sounds presumptuous and self-important. I would agree—if it were *our* idea! But it was not our idea; it was God's. And it's not a minor or peripheral doctrine; it's at the very heart of Scripture. This is God's plan and his promise, so if we're still uncomfortable with the idea, we'd better learn to get comfortable.

I love Spurgeon's illustrations of ordinary people whom God has designed to be royalty. I once gave one of my books to a delightful hotel bellman in Atlanta. I discovered he was a committed Christian, and he said he'd been praying for our group, which was holding a conference at the hotel. Later I gave him a little gift—a rough wooden cross. He seemed stunned, overwhelmed. With tears in his eyes he said, "You didn't need to do that. I'm only a bellman."

The moment he said it, God spoke to me. This brother had spent his life serving, and he had come from a line of people who had been slaves for many generations. It will likely be someone like him I'll have the privilege of serving under in God's Kingdom. He was "only a bellman" who spoke with warmth and love, who served, who quietly prayed in the background for the success of a conference in his hotel. I saw Jesus in that bellman, and there was no "only" about him.

Who will be the kings of the New Earth? I think that bellman will be one of them. And I'll be honored to carry his bags.

FINAL THOUGHTS ON
SPURGEON AND HEAVEN

❀

Though Spurgeon was often ill throughout his life, he was a difficult man to keep down. In addition to founding and directing sixty-five ministries and speaking up to ten times a week, he was prolific in his correspondence. He typically wrote five hundred letters each week, with a pen that had to be dipped in ink every few seconds. And he often did so while suffering from painful arthritis.

David Livingstone, the pioneer medical missionary to Africa, once asked Spurgeon how he could accomplish all he did. Considering how many people asked Livingstone the same question, it's particularly remarkable that he would ask it of Spurgeon. On Livingstone's death in 1873, a worn copy of one of Spurgeon's printed sermons, "Accidents, Not Punishments," was found among Livingstone's few possessions. At the top of the first page Livingstone had written, "Very Good," and initialed it "D.L." The missionary had carried it with him throughout his travels in Africa.

Spurgeon gave the following advice to young pastors not long before his death. In his shoes, I might have recommended a more balanced approach to ministry. I include it, though, because its heart, urgency, and eternal focus are commendable, even if some of the practical wisdom is subject to debate.

> If I have any message to give from my own bed of sickness it would be this: if you do not wish to be full of regrets when you are obliged to lie still, work while you can. If you desire to make a sickbed as soft as it can be, do not stuff it with the mournful reflection that you wasted time while you were in health and strength. People said to me years ago, "You will break your constitution down with preaching ten times a week," and the like. Well, if I have done so, I am glad of it. I would do the same again. If I had fifty constitutions I would rejoice to break them down in the service of the Lord Jesus Christ.
>
> You young men who are strong, overcome the wicked one and fight for the Lord while you can. You will never regret having done all that lies in you for our blessed Lord and Master. Crowd as much as you can into every day, and postpone no work till tomorrow. "Whatever your hand finds to do, do it with your might" (Ecclesiastes 9:10).

Spurgeon found that his great suffering drew him closer to God. In an address to ministers and students he says, "I daresay the greatest earthly blessing that God can give to any of us is health, *with the exception of sickness.* If some men whom I know of could only be favored with a month of rheumatism, it would, by God's grace, mellow them marvelously."

He also writes, "I am afraid that all the grace I have got of my comfortable and easy times and happy hours might almost lie on a penny. But the good I have received from my sorrows and pains and griefs is altogether incalculable. . . . Affliction is the best bit of furniture in my house. It is the best book in a minister's library."[62]

Spurgeon died in 1892 at age fifty-seven, in the south of France, where he often wintered because of his poor health. His secretary, J. W. Harrald, immediately telegraphed a message to the Metropolitan Tabernacle in London. It read, "Our beloved pastor entered Heaven, 11:15 Sunday night."

Four funeral services for Spurgeon were held to accommodate the crowds. Sixty thousand mourners came to view his body at the Metropolitan Tabernacle, and several hundred thousand people lined the streets for the five miles from the church to his burial place at Norwood Cemetery.[63]

Pastor Archibald Brown, a friend of Spurgeon's, conducted his graveside service. It's more than a tribute to Spurgeon; it's also a fitting picture of what believers can anticipate as they look toward Heaven. (To give you a feel for the way Brown, like Spurgeon, spoke in his day, I've decided not to contemporize his speech.)

> Beloved president, faithful pastor, prince of preachers, brother beloved, dear Spurgeon—we bid thee not "Farewell" but only for a little while "Good night."
>
> Thou shalt rise soon at the first dawn of the resurrection day of the redeemed. Yet is the good night not ours to bid, but thine; it is we who linger in the darkness; thou art in God's holy light. Our night shall soon be passed, and with it all our weeping. Then, with thine, our songs shall greet the morning of a day that knows no cloud nor close; for there is no night there.
>
> Hard worker in the field, thy toil is ended. Straight has been the furrow thou hast plowed. No looking back has marred thy course. Harvests have followed thy patient sowing, and Heaven is already rich with thine ingathered

sheaves and shall still be enriched through the years yet lying in eternity.

Champion of God, thy battle, long and nobly fought, is over; thy sword, which clave to thy hand, has dropped at last: a palm branch takes it place. No longer does the helmet press thy brow, oft weary with its surging thoughts of battle; a victor's wreath from the great Commander's hand has already proved thy full reward.

Here, for a little while, shall rest thy precious dust. Then shall thy well-beloved come, and at his voice thou shalt spring from thy couch of earth, fashioned like unto his body, into glory. Then spirit, soul, and body shall magnify the Lord's redemption. Until then, beloved, sleep. We praise God for thee, and by the blood of the everlasting covenant, hope and expect to praise God with thee. Amen.

This year I turn fifty-seven, the age Charles Spurgeon was when he died. Whether I have thirty years or thirty days left in this life, I am profoundly grateful for how God has spoken to me through Spurgeon. Every time I read his sermons, whether on Heaven or anything else, my heart is drawn toward my Savior and my King. I think of Spurgeon fondly, as a friend and mentor. I think he could appreciate this, as he had similar thoughts toward various Christians from previous generations, including John Bunyan.

I look forward to meeting Spurgeon in Heaven and thanking him face-to-face for his investment in the study of God's Word and the careful communication of God's truths. I also look forward to meeting every reader of this book who knows Jesus. And above all, I look forward to meeting and beholding the glorified God-man: my Savior, my King, and my dearest friend.

Think of all that awaits us because of what our Jesus has done for us. Together with all God's people, we'll have the privilege of forever celebrating the riches of God's grace and kindness to us in Christ Jesus in that new world of endless adventures. To God alone be glory!

> I shall rise from the dead. . . . I shall see the Son of God, the Sun of Glory, and shine myself as that sun shines. I shall be united to the Ancient of Days, to God himself, who had no morning, never began. . . . No man ever saw God and lived. And yet, I shall not live till I see God; and when I have seen him, I shall never die.[64]
>
> — JOHN DONNE

NOTES

1. I've drawn information on Spurgeon from a variety of sources but should give particular recognition to Arnold Dallimore's *Spurgeon: A New Biography* (Edinburgh: Banner of Truth, 1986).

2. Dallimore, *Spurgeon*, 39.

3. C. J. Mahaney, "Loving the Church," audiotape of message at Covenant Life Church, Gaithersburg, MD, n.d.

4. Jonathan Edwards, *The Sermons of Jonathan Edwards: A Reader*, ed. Wilson H. Kimnach, Kenneth P. Minkema, and Douglas A. Sweeney (New Haven, CT: Yale University Press, 1999), 74–75.

5. Augustine, *The City of God*, 22, 30, and *Confessions* 1, 1, quoted in John E. Rotelle, *Augustine Day by Day* (New York: Catholic Book Publishing, 1986).

6. Jonathan Edwards, "The Christian Pilgrim," sermon preached in 1733, quoted in Alister E. McGrath, *A Brief History of Heaven* (Malden, MA: Blackwell, 2003), 115.

7. Charles Spurgeon, *Lectures to My Students* (Grand Rapids, MI: Zondervan, 1954), 160.

8. *Time* (March 31, 1997): 55, quoted in Paul Marshall with Lela Gilbert, *Heaven Is Not My Home: Learning to Live in God's Creation* (Nashville: Word, 1998), 234.

9. R. A. Torrey, *Heaven or Hell* (New Kensington, PA: Whitaker House, 1985), 68.

10. Anthony A. Hoekema, "Heaven: Not Just an Eternal Day Off," *Christianity Today* (June 6, 2003), http://www.christianitytoday.com/ct/2003/122/54.0.html.

11. See http://www.spurgeon.org/catechis.htm for the complete text of Spurgeon's "A Puritan Catechism."

12. Variously attributed to Henry Scott Holland and Henry Van Dyke; source uncertain.

13. Jonathan Edwards, *Heaven: A World of Love* (Amityville, NY: Calvary Press, 1999), 18.

14. W. G. T. Shedd, *The Doctrine of Endless Punishment* (Edinburgh: Banner of Truth, 1986), 153.

15. J. I. Packer, "Hell's Final Enigma," *Christianity Today* (April 22, 2002): 84.

16. Erroll Hulse and David Kingdon, eds., *A Marvelous Ministry: How the All-Round Ministry of Charles Haddon Spurgeon Speaks to Us Today* (Ligonier, PA: Soli Deo Gloria Publications, 1993), 39.

17. Amy Carmichael, *Thou Givest . . . They Gather*, quoted in *Images of Heaven: Reflections on Glory*, compiled by Lil Copan and Anna Trimiew (Wheaton, IL: Harold Shaw, 1996), 111.

18. W. Graham Scroggie, *What about Heaven?* (London: Christian Literature Crusade, 1940), 93.

19. Augustine, quoted in Colleen McDannell and Bernhard Lang, *Heaven: A History* (New York: Vintage Books, 1988), 58.

20. Augustine, *On the Christian Doctrine* (New York: Prentice Hall, 1958), 1:32–33.

21. Richard Baxter, *Saints' Everlasting Rest* (Hagerstown, MD: Christian Heritage, 2000).

22. Richard Mouw, *When the Kings Come Marching In* (Grand Rapids, MI: Eerdmans, 1983), 47.

23. Bruce Milne, *The Message of Heaven and Hell* (Downers Grove, IL: InterVarsity, 2002), 321.

24. Sam Storms, "Joy's Eternal Increase," an unpublished manuscript on Jonathan Edwards's view of Heaven.

25. Augustine, *The City of God*, quoted in Alister E. McGrath, *A Brief History of Heaven* (Malden, MA: Blackwell, 2003), 182–83.

26. Albert M. Wolters, *Creation Regained: Biblical Basics for a Reformational Worldview* (Grand Rapids, MI: Eerdmans, 1985), 62.

27. Ibid., 58.

28. John Milton, *Paradise Lost* (New York: Random House, 2008), book 5, lines 574–76.

29. C. S. Lewis, *Letters to Malcolm: Chiefly on Prayer* (Boston: Houghton Mifflin Harcourt, 2002), 132.

30. I develop this idea in my book *The Treasure Principle* (Colorado Springs, CO: Multnomah, 2001).

31. Walton J. Brown, *Home at Last* (Washington, DC: Review and Herald, 1983), 192.

32. Steven J. Lawson, *Heaven Help Us!* (Colorado Springs, CO: NavPress, 1995), 108.

33. "Westminster Shorter Catechism with Proof Texts," Center for Reformed Theology and Apologetics, http://www.reformed.org/documents/index.html?mainframe= http://www.reformed.org/documents/WSC_frames.html&wsc_text=WSC.html.

34. Wolters, *Creation Regained*, 58–59.

35. Milne, *The Message of Heaven and Hell*, 194.

36. C. S. Lewis, *The Problem of Pain* (New York: Macmillan, 1962), 115.

37. Donald Bloesch, *Theological Notebook* (Colorado Springs, CO: Helmers and Howard, 1989), 183.

38. W. Graham Scroggie, *What about Heaven?* (London: Christian Literature Crusade, 1940), 93–95.

39. Alister E. McGrath, *A Brief History of Heaven*, 5.

40. Samuel Rutherford, quoted in Charles H. Spurgeon, *Morning and Evening*, January 17, morning reading.

41. Martin Luther, quoted in James M. Campbell, *Heaven Opened: A Book of Comfort and Hope* (New York: Revell, 1924), 148.

42. John Piper, *Desiring God: Meditations of a Christian Hedonist* (Sisters, OR: Multnomah, 1996), 50.

43. Augustine, *On the Christian Doctrine*, 1:32–35.

44. J. B. Phillips, *Letters to Young Churches: A Translation of the New Testament Epistles* (London: G. Bles, 1947), 66.

45. Milne, *The Message of Heaven and Hell*, 257.

46. Calvin Miller, *The Divine Symphony* (Minneapolis: Bethany, 2000), 139.

47. Mark Twain, quoted in Charles Ferguson Ball, *Heaven* (Wheaton, IL: Victor, 1980), 19.

48. Dorothy Sayers, *A Matter of Eternity*, ed. Rosamond Kent Sprague (Grand Rapids, MI: Eerdmans, 1973), 86.

49. Lewis, *The Problem of Pain*, 118.

50. K. Connie Kang, "Next Stop, the Pearly Gates . . . or Hell?" *Los Angeles Times*, October 24, 2003.

51. C. S. Lewis, *The Screwtape Letters* (New York: HarperCollins, 2001), 61.

52. Dante Alighieri, *Inferno*, canto 3, line 9.

53. Randy Alcorn, *Lord Foulgrin's Letters* (Sisters, OR: Multnomah, 1999).

54. Paul Helm, *The Last Things* (Carlisle, PA: Banner of Truth, 1989), 92.

55. Randy Alcorn, *Deadline* (Colorado Springs, CO: Multnomah, 1994), 341.

56. D. A. Carson, *How Long, O Lord?* (Grand Rapids, MI: Baker Academic, 2006), 92.

57. Edwards, *Heaven: A World of Love*, 16.

58. Ruthanna C. Metzgar, from her story "It's Not in the Book!" copyright © 1998

by Ruthanna C. Metzgar. Used by permission. For the full story in Ruthanna's own words, see Eternal Perspective Ministries, http://www.epm.org/articles/metzgar.html.

59. Cornelis P. Venema, *The Promise of the Future* (Trowbridge, UK: Banner of Truth, 2000), 478.

60. Wolters, *Creation Regained*, 11.

61. Colleen McDannell and Bernhard Lang, *Heaven: A History* (New Haven, CT: Yale University Press, 2001), 52.

62. Darrel W. Amundsen, "The Anguish and Agonies of Charles Spurgeon," *Christian History* 29, vol. X, no. 1 (1991): 25.

63. Charles Spurgeon and Tom Carter, *2,200 Quotations: From the Writings of Charles H. Spurgeon* (Grand Rapids, MI: Baker, 1995), 2.

64. Henry Alford, *The Works of John Donne, with a Memoir of His Life*, vol. 5 (London: John W. Parker, 1839), 93.

RESOURCES

Spurgeon Resources

For an up-to-date list of recommended books about Spurgeon, and for a complete list of Spurgeon's own writings, see www.epm.org/spurgeon.

Online Resources

For resources related to Spurgeon from Logos Bible Software, including the complete Spurgeon sermon collection, see www.logos.com/epm.

ABOUT THE AUTHORS

❋

Charles Haddon Spurgeon (June 19, 1834–January 31, 1892) preached to approximately 10 million people in his lifetime, often speaking ten times a week at various locations, including congregations his own church had planted. His 3,561 sermons are currently bound in sixty-three volumes and total about 20 million words. In addition to his sermons, Spurgeon wrote many books, including a four-part autobiography; a massive, seven-volume series on Psalms called *The Treasury of David*; books on prayer and other single topics; and the classic devotionals *Morning by Morning* and *Evening by Evening* (best known in their combined form, *Morning and Evening*).

Over the span of six years more than 6 million copies of Spurgeon's books were sold. It's possible that even today no author—Christian or otherwise—has as much material in print as Charles Haddon Spurgeon.

His preaching and writing affected his world far and wide while he lived, and they continue to do so today. His sermons have been printed in Chinese, Japanese, Russian, Arabic, and many other languages. Today, some 120 years after his death, Spurgeon's works are still read and studied and preached on by Christians of various backgrounds and denominations.

Randy Alcorn is the founder of Eternal Perspective Ministries (EPM). Prior to starting EPM, he served as a pastor for fourteen years. He has spoken around the world and has taught on the adjunct faculties of Multnomah Bible College and Western Seminary in Portland, Oregon.

Randy is the best-selling author of more than thirty-five books (with 4 million copies in print), including the novels *Deadline*, *Dominion*, *Deception*, *Lord Foulgrin's Letters*, and *Safely Home*. His nonfiction works include *Heaven*; *If God Is Good*; *Managing God's Money*; *Money, Possessions, and Eternity*; *The Treasure Principle*; *The Grace and Truth Paradox*; and *The Law of Rewards*. Randy has written for many magazines and produces the popular periodical *Eternal Perspectives*. He has been a guest on more than 650 radio and television programs, including Focus on the Family, The Bible Answer Man, FamilyLife Today, Revive Our Hearts, Truths That Transform, and Faith Under Fire.

The father of two married daughters, Randy lives in Gresham, Oregon, with his wife and best friend, Nanci. They are the proud grandparents of several grandchildren.

You may contact Eternal Perspective Ministries through their website at www.epm.org; by mail at 39085 Pioneer Blvd., Suite 206, Sandy, OR 97055; or by phone at 503-668-5200.

Visit Randy Alcorn's blog at www.epm.org/blog. You can also connect with Randy at facebook.com/randyalcorn and at twitter.com/randyalcorn.

OTHER BOOKS BY RANDY ALCORN

FICTION

Deadline
Dominion
Deception
Edge of Eternity
Lord Foulgrin's Letters
The Ishbane Conspiracy
Safely Home

NONFICTION

Heaven
Touchpoints: Heaven
50 Days of Heaven
In Light of Eternity
Managing God's Money
Money, Possessions, and Eternity
The Law of Rewards
ProLife Answers to ProChoice Arguments
Sexual Temptation booklet
The Goodness of God
The Grace and Truth Paradox
The Purity Principle
The Treasure Principle
Why ProLife?
If God Is Good
The Promise of Heaven

KIDS

Heaven for Kids
Wait until Then
Tell Me about Heaven